icing details and vivid portraits of the titans who drove New
30s, *Gotham Rising* is a delightful caper through one of the
amic eras. Jules Stewart deftly weaves history with heroes and
ascinating tales of La Guardia, FDR and Robert Moses, as well
ho built the Empire State Building and Rockefeller Center.'

ERIC SCHMITT
Pulitzer Prize-winning *New York Times* correspondent

that the decade following the Wall Street Crash should be the
ade the city what it is today. The book is a terrific read, bursting
s with beguiling stories and extraordinary facts. If you want to
New York became New York, this is the book for you. An inspir-
rossing work which has so much to tell us about what is still the
y on earth, at the same accounting for so much about its present
any ways, this is America in essence – told from the right time
ht place.'

PAUL STRATHERN
author of *The Medici*

JULES STEWART is a journalist,
York where his career took him fr
His books include *Madrid: The H*
Kabul; *On Afghanistan's Plains: The*
by I.B.Tauris); *Crimson Snow: Britai*
Border: The Story of the North-West
and the Mapping of the Himalaya and
to Al Qaeda. He lives in London.

'Filled with en
York in the 19
city's most dyn
villains, with f
as the men wl

'How ironic
one which r
at the seam
know how
ing and eng
greatest cit
state. In r
and the ri

'From its opening irreverent quotations from
Jules Stewart's *Gotham Rising: New York in*
through a remarkable decade that in many v
great American metropolis. So often it seen
shores to see New York in all its glory, and
and contrasts that New Yorkers take for grant
religious Jewish Sabbath observance around th
clubhouse. As Stewart's eye sweeps across the p
his attention is caught equally by the glories of bi
of organized crime providing the jazz clubs' bootle
Opera and the Stork Club and the striking taxi-c
their patrons; high society at the Waldorf-Astori
the Great Depression. The Harlem Renaissance, G
Tammany Hall politics, the Empire State Building,
the larger-than-life figures directing so much of th
story, well worth telling. And, oh yes, it all really ha

A

author of *New York Art Deco: A Guide to Goth*

GOTHAM RISING

NEW YORK IN THE 1930s

JULES STEWART

I.B.TAURIS

LONDON · NEW YORK

Published in 2016 by
I.B.Tauris & Co. Ltd
London • New York
www.ibtauris.com

ISBN: 978 1 78453 529 2
eISBN: 978 1 78672 043 6
ePDF: 978 1 78673 043 5

A full CIP record for this book is available from the British Library
A full CIP record is available from the Library of Congress

Library of Congress Catalog Card Number: available

Endpapers: A view of Times Square at the intersection of Broadway and 7th Avenue, New York City, New York, 1937. (Photo by P.L. Sperr/Getty Images)

Text design and typesetting by Tetragon, London
Printed and bound in Sweden by ScandBook AB

CONTENTS

LIST OF ILLUSTRATIONS

1. Protesters outside the Bank of United States during the Depression (Library of Congress / Public Domain).
2. A street band in Yorkville, Upper Manhattan (Library of Congress / Public Domain).
3. Federal Hall in Wall Street (Public Domain).
4. Fiorello La Guardia and Robert Moses (photo by Bob Mortimer/NY Daily News Archive via Getty Images).
5. Newspaper columnist Walter Winchell and W. C. Fields (Public Domain).
6. Police at the scene of a gangland murder (US National Records and Archives Administration / Public Domain).
7. Boxer Jack Dempsey celebrates the end of Prohibition in 1933 (Bettmann/Getty Images).
8. Duke Ellington in his dressing room at the New York Paramount Theater, a top venue for swing music (William P. Gottlieb/Ira and Leonore S. Gershwin Fund Collection, Music Division, Library of Congress).

9. The view of the Chrysler Building from the Empire State Building (Library of Congress / Public Domain).

10. The Waldorf-Astoria (courtesy of the Waldorf Astoria Hotel).

11. 'Lunch break' on the Waldorf-Astoria (courtesy of the Waldorf Astoria Hotel).

12. Construction workers on the Waldorf-Astoria (courtesy of the Waldorf Astoria Hotel).

13. Jewish merchants on the Lower East Side (Library of Congress / Public Domain).

14. A Bowery restaurant (Berenice Abbott / New York Public Library / Public Domain).

15. The 21 Club (courtesy of the 21 Club, New York / Belmond (UK)).

16. The jockeys of the 21 Club (courtesy of the 21 Club, New York / Belmond (UK)).

17. Nightclub map of Harlem by Elmer Simms Campbell (copyright holder unknown).

18. Jitterbug dancers (Library of Congress / Public Domain).

19. Grand Central Terminal (Royal Geographic Society).

20. The Third Avenue 'El' (Library of Congress / Public Domain).

21. New York tenements, 1934, by Marjorie Content (courtesy of Yale University).

22. Manhattan in 1931 (Public Domain).

23. Refugee children and the Statue of Liberty (courtesy of the United States Holocaust Memorial Museum).

New York is an ugly city, a dirty city. Its climate is a scandal, its politics are used to frighten children, its traffic is madness, its competition is murderous. But there is one thing about it – once you have lived in New York and it has become your home, no place else is good enough.

JOHN STEINBECK
'Making of a New Yorker' (1953)

Before them was spread out the ragged panorama of south Manhattan, the wonder island of the West. A narrow hump of rock sheltered from the Atlantic by the broad shoulder of Brooklyn [...] on which the indomitable cussedness of Man had elected to build a city.

LESLIE CHARTERIS
The Saint in New York (1935)

The residents of Manhattan are to a large extent strangers who have pulled up stakes somewhere and come to town, seeking sanctuary or fulfillment or some greater or lesser grail.

E. B. WHITE
Here Is New York (1949)

FOREWORD

When I moved to Manhattan in 1989 at the age of 24, I lived in the East Village in a six-storey walk-up right next door to the New York City headquarters of the Hell's Angels – the notorious motorcycle club. One Saturday, I went out into the Lower East Side to get lunch. As I was walking along Houston Street I passed a nondescript two-storey building – which I must have passed a hundred times before – and a man dressed in black with a long grey beard approached me.

'Excuse me,' he said in an accent with hints of Eastern Europe. 'Are you the sort of person who when you meet a person who needs help, that you will help this person?'

That's a hell of a question, I thought to myself. But don't we all like to imagine that we're the kind of people who might help a stranger in need? So, I told him: 'Sure.'

'Good, good,' he replied. 'Come with me.'

The old man ushered me into this nondescript building and down a narrow staircase leading to the basement. Now, this must have been before I saw *The Silence of the Lambs*, because I don't know what I was thinking; but I dutifully followed him and there in the basement were 50 men, women and children gathered around two long tables laid out with food – in the dark.

What I had stumbled upon was the Sabbath meal of an Orthodox Jewish congregation. The Orthodox Jews have a strict prohibition against performing work on the Sabbath, and this prohibition extends to turning on and off electrical devices. Their practice is to switch on their lights on Friday afternoon and then leave them on for Saturday. Someone had obviously forgotten to do so, and the congregation now found themselves gathered for their weekly meal without the benefit of God's first gift.

In the Orthodox tradition there is also a strict prohibition against asking someone else to work on your behalf on the Sabbath – as that is seen as cheating. So, the old gentleman began speaking to me in a terrifically roundabout way:

'As you go about the room, you may see strings hanging from the ceiling, and if you are curious as to the purpose of these strings, then you should explore your curiosity…'

At this point, young men were leaping off benches:

'Wait!'

'Stop!'

'What is he doing?'

But the old man gave me a smile and waved his hands at the room. 'Go, go,' he encouraged. 'Go with God!'

Such is the wisdom of the elderly.

At the time, what struck me most about this incident was the realisation that two such alien groups could be living peacefully in such close proximity. Over on 3rd Street were the Hell's Angels with their leather jackets, Harley-Davidsons and reputations for barroom brawling and drug running. While here, just around the corner, was this devout gathering of Orthodox Jews. If you criss-crossed the country, I don't think you could find two subsets of America that were further apart. These two groups differ radically in terms of their food, their fashion, their world views… In fact, the only thing they have in common is the beards.

But that, of course, is one of the splendours of New York City: that groups so disparate can coexist side by side, nodding to each other with rough familiarity when they pass in the street, while accepting with a shrug all the wide-eyed new arrivals to their neighbourhood. And this has been an essential quality of the city for well over 100 years.

In the late 1930s, the Works Progress Administration (WPA), in conjunction with the Federal Art Project and the Federal Writers' Project, hired a cadre of unemployed writers, artists and historians to create a travel guide for New York City. Published in 1939, this 650-page work – illustrated with photographs, paintings, drawings and woodcuts – provides a wonderful window on a moment in the life of the metropolis.

Although the Hell's Angels had yet to arrive in New York, the same proximity of the disparate clearly existed. At the opening of the guide, for instance, is a list of major annual events in the city that a visitor might be interested in attending. Naturally, the list includes the city's Easter and Thanksgiving Day parades, as well as the annual visit of the Ringling Brothers and Barnum & Bailey Circus. (When I arrived in the city there was a still a sizeable contingent of New Yorkers who would gather on Second Avenue at midnight in order to watch the circus's elephants emerge from the Midtown Tunnel on their annual walk to Madison Square Garden.) But in addition to these well-known events, the list includes the Chinese New Year celebration in Chinatown, the Feast of San Gennaro in Little Italy and the St Patrick's Day Parade all over town; it includes celebrations of the Rumanian and Hungarian independence days as well as the Danish Constitution Day and the Swedish Festival of Folk Dances. Which is to say, New York in the 1930s already offered a mosaic of the *world's* festivities.

Similarly, on the guide's relatively short list of recommended nightclubs – in addition to the Stork and Kit Kat clubs – can be found the El Morocco, Casa Mañana, Café Latino, Casino Russe, Versailles and Mon Paris, each offering food and a floor show in the international style suggested by their names.

What is important to understand is that these international festivals and nightclubs were not whimsical cosmopolitan inventions or tourist attractions. They were very much a part of the authentic fabric of the city. For by 1939,

New York was already the world's most populous Italian city outside Italy; the world's third-largest Irish city; one of the world's largest Jewish communities; and so on. That's what happens when you marry a hint of a better life with open immigration policies.

By the 1930s New York had already served for half a century as the gateway into America for the world's tired, its poor and its huddled masses. In 1907 alone, Ellis Island welcomed 1.3 million immigrants – at a rate of about 3,500 per day. Certainly many of the new arrivals then headed north to Boston, west to Chicago or south to Atlanta; but a significant number went no further than Brooklyn, Queens or the Lower East Side. Seeking out the neighbourhoods where their countrymen dwelled, where the language and food were familiar, these new arrivals unpacked and planted their flags in the pavement not simply as Americans, but as New Yorkers.

For over 100 years, New York has been known as a 'melting pot', reflecting its absorption of the world's ethnicities. But over this same time frame, New York has also been a melting pot of the passions.

From early on, New York City has been the epicentre of many aspects of American culture and commerce. It has long been a – if not *the* – capital of food, fashion and finance; of architecture and advertising; of painting, theatre and broadcasting. When you take a single city and make it the national capital of such a wide array of human endeavours, a side effect is that every year thousands of young people with completely different backgrounds, sensibilities and talents flock there to pursue their individual dreams. From ballerinas to bakers to bankers, they arrive, share apartments and intermingle in bars and restaurants, acting as catalysts to the city's vibrant chemistry.

The social complexity of New York City has been enriched further by the depths of the two rivers that shape its boroughs. Unlike the rivers that grace many European capitals, the Hudson River is so deep that it can easily accommodate battleships, ocean liners and freighters. In the 1930s, these would sail straight up to the docks that lined the West Side of Manhattan and unload their respective 'cargos' – within walking distance of the Empire State Building.

As a result, New York is one of those cities that was simultaneously a cultural and financial hub (like Paris and London), and also a roughshod port city in the manner of Liverpool and Marseilles. As the 1939 guide tells us, 'out of an early morning fog come brooding, ghostly calls' signalling the arrival of 'coffee from Brazil, rubber from Sumatra, bananas from Costa Rica […] wine from Capri, olive oil from Spain'. While at day's end, the attentive Manhattanite could hear the opposing blast that signalled the departure of ships bearing American 'wheat for Bordeaux, Kansas City hides for Brazil, Virginia tobacco, Massachusetts shoes, Chicago canned meats, [and] lumber from the Pacific Coast'.

As a transportation hub where raw materials and finished goods easily crossed paths, it was natural for Manhattan to house manufacturing plants with their own dedicated railway lines. The High Line – that raised railroad for freight, which is now both a park and an international tourist phenomenon – was opened in 1934 to service the movement of goods along the West Side.

And just as the ballerina and banker are likely to have very different personalities, I think we can assert without prejudice or fear of contradiction that the temperaments of those who worked on the West Side docks and rail yards differed significantly from those who sat in the boxes of the Metropolitan Opera… And since Manhattan is only ten miles long and two miles wide, the rough-and-tumble have no choice but to rub elbows with the refined.

In recognition of this paradox, here is how the WPA guide describes Times Square in the 1930s:

> It is the district of glorified dancing girls and millionaire playboys and, on a different plane, of dime-a-dance hostesses and pleasure-seeking clerks. Here, too, in a permanent moralizing tableau, appear the extremes of success and failure characteristic of Broadway's spectacular professions: gangsters and racketeers, panhandlers and derelicts, youthful stage stars and aging burlesque comedians, world heavyweight champions and once-acclaimed beggars.[1]

It speaks volumes about New York City and how it perceives itself that the description above was written to *entice* the prospective traveller. How many cities in the world have attempted to boost tourism with the promise of 'gangsters and racketeers, panhandlers and derelicts'?

If for no other reason than the sheer number of people passing through, New York has long been a place where there is no resident aristocracy or firmly established society. The immigrants arriving from across the globe, the young and ambitious arriving from across America, the debutantes and longshoremen, all have a rightful claim upon the city; all can take pride in having shaped it in some material way; and all can look to it for the possible satisfaction of their dreams.

The 1930s in New York, as in America, were defined by the Depression; it was a decade perfectly bracketed by the economic downturn that began with the Stock Market Crash in 1929, and the economic recovery fuelled by the march to war in 1939.

From a distance of three-quarters of a century, we can all visualise what New York was like in this decade. Beginning with the loss of fortunes great and small and the leaping of stockbrokers from windows to the street below, there followed the runs on the banks, massive unemployment, breadlines, civil unrest, the rise of the labour movement. And, in fact, all of this is perfectly accurate; but it hardly defines Depression-era New York.

For the 1930s were also the decade of the glamorous movie musical and the madcap comedy – both of which sprang from the stages of New York. Of the ten films that Fred Astaire and Ginger Rogers starred in together, nine were made in the 1930s – including *The Gay Divorcee*, *Top Hat* and *Swing Time* – in which the two stars sang and danced to the sophisticated songs of Cole Porter, Jerome Kern et al. The Marx Brothers made over 15 movies, but the ones that matter – *Monkey Business*, *Horse Feathers*, *Duck Soup*, *A Night at the Opera*, *A Day at the Races* – were all products of the 1930s. While patently different in style, the Astaire–Rogers and Marx Brothers movies shared many elements, including glamorous settings, youthful pranksterism, happy accidents, instances of love at first sight and rags-to-riches outcomes.

This was also the era of swing music. Jazz had been building as a cultural force in a variety of forms throughout the 1920s, but in the 1930s it swept the nation in the form of the big-band sound. Orchestras led by the likes of Count Basie, Duke Ellington, Benny Goodman and Fletcher Henderson, many of which were based in New York, became renowned as their music was broadcast live from hotel ballrooms and large-scale dance halls. Having seen Duke Ellington at the Cotton Club, one could shoot across town to see Count Basie's orchestra perform at the Woodside Hotel or Roseland, and then head back uptown to the Savoy Ballroom, where there would be two orchestras set up on opposing stages so that there would never be a break in the dancing. (At its peak, the Savoy would host 700,000 people in a single year.) And when one got home, one could turn on the wireless to listen to Benny Goodman's band broadcasting live from NBC Studios – until 3.30 a.m., so that the west coast could tune in to the fun.

What the big-band sound brought to jazz was a large orchestra and a musical style that not only accommodated but encouraged dancing, shouting and drinking. As an art form, swing was naturally gregarious and perfectly designed for late-night expressions of joy and abandon. (How different from bebop, the reigning jazz of a decade later, in which four or five musicians would perform on small stages in basement cafes playing music of moody introspection...)

If one had to choose an anthem for the swing style, it might as well be 'Sing, sing, sing'. Written by Louis Prima in 1935 and made immortal by Benny Goodman, the song is an unapologetic hellraiser. Opening with the sound of native tom-toms, it draws on the flutes of Arabian snake charmers, the sirens of police cars, the midnight mewing of alley cats. In sequences of cascading call and response, different segments of the horn section grow louder and louder as if they are drawing closer and closer, gaining speed, with every intention of running us over. Where most swing songs were around three minutes long (so they could fit on one side of a standard 78 rpm record), the irrepressible 'Sing, sing, sing' ran well over eight minutes. From anywhere in the middle of a three-minute song, you can sense its beginning and end. But in the middle of 'Sing, sing, sing', you can't see where you've come from or where you're going; all you know is where you *are*.

If the Benny Goodman Orchestra could bring down the house playing this song in the middle of the Depression, this was not a matter of Nero fiddling while Rome burned. On the contrary, where Nero was playing a requiem for the end of an age, 'Sing, sing, sing' was a defiant and exuberant pronouncement that we weren't done yet.

Last but not least, the 1930s were the decade of Rockefeller Center. The building of this extraordinary complex in the heart of Manhattan was launched in 1932, three years after the Stock Market Crash, and took the rest of the Depression to complete.

After the Roaring Twenties, with soaring stocks and profligate ways, one might have imagined the Depression would serve to chasten New York – prompting an era of conservatism and humility. But there is nothing conservative or humble about Rockefeller Center. Covering 12 acres of land with more than ten separate skyscrapers – including the 850-foot Radio Corporation of America (RCA) Building, then the largest office tower in the world in terms of square footage – the development was a record for a project undertaken by private enterprise.

Architecturally, the buildings in the complex share a single style, one pronounced by vertical lines in glass and steel running straight up from the ground to the sky with only limited adornment. Looking up at the buildings from the pavements of Fifth or Sixth Avenue one experiences a variation of vertigo – from the sense that one is about to fall upwards.

Complementing the unabashed confidence of the architectural style are all the various art forms strategically incorporated into the grand scheme. Scattered through the complex are murals intended to represent 'man's intellectual mastery of the material universe' and sculpted panels with titles like 'Genius receiving the light of the sun' and 'Spirit of progress'. But perhaps the single most unapologetically audacious of them all is Paul Manship's golden sculpture of Prometheus that floats over the ice rink at the base of the RCA Building. What could better adorn this structural statement of ascendancy than a celebration of him who stole fire from the Gods on mankind's behalf? Or, to put it another way: *Hubris be damned.* For here in 1930s New York was a populace that intended to continue striving no matter where the Dow Jones Industrial Average finished the day; and they were quite willing to overreach, to stumble, and to falter along the path of their ambitions. Here then is wilful optimism on a majestic scale. No wonder they put the restaurant with the rotating dance floor on the sixty-fifth floor and named it the Rainbow Room.

If you found an anthropologist from outer space and gave him three arte-facts – the movie *Top Hat*, a recording of Benny Goodman playing 'Sing, sing, sing' and a model of the RCA Building – and then asked him to describe the environment from which they sprang, there is no way he would come up with the Depression. For these three items are unambiguously upbeat.

Popular wisdom tells us that the success of the Marx Brothers and Astaire–Rogers movies during the Depression simply reflected America's need for escape. But I find this explanation woefully inadequate. For one thing, trying times do not intrinsically lead to escapism. In the 1970s, an era of economic and political turmoil when a crime-ridden New York City teetered on the edge of bankruptcy, audiences flocked to movies with dark overtones, shocking violence, political corruption and morally ambiguous outcomes. In the wake of 9/11 and the 2008 global financial crisis, we have seen a surge in dystopian movies for the young and old alike, each attempting to imagine a bleaker future than the last. But even if you insist that the success of Fred Astaire and the Marx Brothers stems from the desire to escape, how do you explain Rockefeller Center?

Rather than escapism, I believe that what the glamorous musical, swing music and Rockefeller Center all reflect is a native spirit so irrepressible that even a Depression couldn't squelch it.

I didn't know I was moving to New York City until the day I did it. It was a morning in June. Having just finished with an obligation in New Haven, Connecticut, I called a childhood friend in the East Village to catch up. When I told him I had $5,000 and nowhere to go, he said that was an amazing coincidence because he was living in an illegal sublet and couldn't make the rent. Eight hours later, I was unpacking my bags in the six-storey walk-up next door to the Hell's Angels.

But in retrospect, perhaps I should have known that New York City was where I would end up. After all, four of my heroes had written with great enthusiasm about what they saw when standing on the exact same spot: at the top of the Brooklyn Bridge looking towards Manhattan.

In the mid-1960s, Jack Kerouac wrote an ecstatic blues about standing there. Thirty years before, in 1935, Le Corbusier, the great French architect, wrote about it. Ten years before that, the Spanish poet Pablo Neruda wrote about it. And in that same year of 1925, Vladimir Mayakovsky, the poet laureate of the Russian Revolution, came all the way from Moscow and wrote about it too.

Here's what Le Corbusier had to say:

> The sky before you bristles with the skyscrapers of Wall Street; they are rose-colored, gay, in the maritime sky. They are shaggy, crowned with gold or debatable architectural ornament [...] There should be sensations of contriteness, of troubled judgment and taste, reservations, doubt, cacophony. But no! There is a dominating force: unity; a subjugating element: magnitude.[2]

And here's Mayakovsky:

As a crazed believer
                    enters
                              a church
[...]
so I,
     in graying evening
                         haze,
humbly set foot
               on Brooklyn Bridge.
As a conqueror presses
                       into a city
                                   all shattered
[...]

so, drunk with glory,

          eager to live,

I clamber,

     in pride,

         upon Brooklyn Bridge.[3]

To some degree, it seems extraordinary that four restless members of the rolling international avant-garde – who not only shaped their art forms, but their eras – had come from four different countries over a span of 40 years to stand on the same spot and rhapsodise about what they saw.

But I can understand why. For from wherever and whenever they came, what lay before them when they stood on the top of the Brooklyn Bridge was New York City – that great melting pot not just of ethnicities and religions and social classes, but of the creative, the courageous and the corrupt; of the four cardinal virtues and the seven deadly sins; and of all the human passions.

AMOR TOWLES
(bestselling author of the novels
A Gentleman in Moscow and *Rules of Civility*)
New York City, 2016

ACKNOWLEDGEMENTS

F irst and foremost, I am grateful to Rita Jakubowski, who opened all the doors, portals and gateways to her astonishing knowledge of New York City's history and culture, as well as her contacts, for all of which I cannot thank her enough. Helen Crisp, as always, gave unsparingly of her busy time to cast her eye over the manuscript and come up with timely suggestions for improving the narrative. The friendly staff at the New York Public Library, the New-York Historical Society and the Center for Jewish History, and the knowledgeable Laura Gottesman at the Library of Congress were helpful in walking this world-class technophobe through their electronic treasure chests of research material. Suzanne Wasserman of the Gotham Center for New York City History proved to be a gold mine of information about the Lower East Side and its immigrant history. In London, I am indebted to the German Historical Institute, to the Wiener Library for the Study of the Holocaust and, of course, to every researcher's best friend, the British Library. David Nathan, research archivist at the National Jazz Archive (www.nationaljazzarchive.co.uk), made available much useful research material at the library, an unsung facility tucked away in an unlikely corner of London's Far East. Thanks for the tenth time round to my agent Duncan McAra, who on the day of our last meeting endured a two-hour wait in an

Edinburgh pub, to greet me with a smile and a drink in hand after my delayed flight and a meandering drive around the Scottish countryside, courtesy of the British Army (that is another story). Joanna Godfrey, my editor at I.B.Tauris, has from the start been an enthusiastic supporter of this project and has put nearly as much work into the book as I have. As always, at our meetings she was prepared to listen patiently to the rants of a highly stressed author, pencil and notebook in hand, in the manner of Dr Freud – not an unreasonable analogy. Every author needs a diligent copy-editor and once again it has been a pleasure to have my manuscript placed under the scrutiny of Alex Middleton. Thanks are also due to Alex Billington at Tetragon for his helpful role in the production process. The delightful cultural historian and tour guide Sibyl McCormac Groff (www.nychristmas.com), known as 'the Spirited New Yorker', was invaluable in unravelling the complexities of Rockefeller Center. She is also wonderful company over a drink (or two) at the complex's Brasserie Ruhlmann, in itself an art deco gem. Avery Fletcher, marketing manager of the 21 Club, not only gave me a full briefing on New York's most celebrated speakeasy, but also revealed the basement entrance to the club's secret boozing venue of the Prohibition years. The Waldorf-Astoria's archivist Deidre Dinnigan and her predecessor Erin Allsop steered me in the direction of historical documents on the hotel and generously allowed me to make use of images from their photo archive. Much appreciation is due to Anthony W. Robins (www.anthonywrobins.com), architectural historian, lecturer, tour leader, author and art deco authority par excellence, for sharing his knowledge with me. Stephen H. Van Dyk, head of the Smithsonian Libraries Art Department and vice president of the New York Art Deco Society, was instrumental in shedding light on multifarious aspects of New York in the 1930s, from architecture and design to the importance of new technology. I am grateful for the guidance of jazz trumpeter and guitarist of note Randy Sandke. Jack Stine, president emeritus of the New Jersey Jazz Society, generously shared his memories of the New York jazz scene, which stretch back to the 1930s. Many thanks to the outstanding jazz clarinettist, saxophonist and bandleader Dan Levinson, whose familiarity with the New York jazz scene proved invaluable and whose hospitality was delightful. Do not omit to check Dan's website (www.danlevinson.com) when you are in

New York, for you may be fortunate enough to coincide with one of his shows. Thanks are also owed to Brian Caplen for kindly offering to cast his expert eye over my jazz section, and to Quentin Bryar, saxophonist extraordinaire, for pointing me in the direction of useful sources. No reference library of New York in the Depression years would be complete without Kenneth T. Jackson's *The Encyclopedia of New York*, Daniel Okrent's *Great Fortune: The Epic of Rockefeller Center*, Donald L. Miller's *Supreme City: How Jazz Age Manhattan Gave Birth to Modern America*, *The WPA Guide to New York City*, compiled by the Federal Writers' Project, and Robert Caro's *The Power Broker: Robert Moses and the Fall of New York*, the classic narrative of the Robert Moses years. For a dazzling account of Manhattan and its glamorous 1930s high life, nothing can hold a candle to Amor Towles's novel *Rules of Civility*.

INTRODUCTION

I magine taking a stroll up midtown Manhattan on a summer evening in 1931. Swankily attired women are to be admired along the street, in long skirts and backless evening frocks. This is a time when hemlines have dropped with a bang to supplant the bare-leg flapper style of the Roaring Twenties. Most certainly some of the ladies are out to show off the daring new fad for leisurewear, lampooned in the *New York Times* fashion pages as 'formal pyjamas for street wear'. A few women might be strolling along on their own, proudly taking advantage of America's new age of gender equality: after all, it is now more than a decade since they earned the right to vote. But more than likely they are accompanied by debonair young men in loose-fitting jackets or striped summer blazers and billowing 'Oxford bags'. There is no disguising the craze to emulate the dapper and elegant Duke and Duchess of Windsor, those two fashion icons of the 1930s, who bestow their glamour on the salons of the newly opened Waldorf-Astoria Hotel, the Stork Club and other gathering spots of the Manhattan smart set.

With two years to go before the repeal of Prohibition, many of these couples are no doubt heading to one of New York's speakeasies, which number in the thousands. The classiest of these clandestine gin palaces is the 21 Club in 52nd Street, whose cellar is cleverly concealed in a bar well stocked with imported wines and spirits. The 21 Club counts among its distinguished clientele the cream of New York society, including its flamboyant mayor, 'Gentleman' Jimmy Walker.

The most classily turned-out men are identifiable by their broad-shouldered, double-breasted suits and wide-brimmed soft-felt hats. These are the bootleggers, most of them Italian mobsters who keep the speak-easies supplied with booze, smuggled in from Canada and Europe. This is a time of widespread Mafia violence, when it is not uncommon to find bullet-riddled bodies in the streets in the wake of a gangland feud between whiskey barons.

The more adventurous Manhattanites setting out for a night on the town are travelling to 125th Street, in the heart of Harlem, to listen to Duke Ellington at the Cotton Club, where the jazz legend's orchestra plays as the house band. Others head for Broadway's famed 'Great White Way', to take in one of the popular musicals of the day. Topping the reviews are George and Ira Gershwin's *Of Thee I Sing* and Cole Porter's *The New Yorkers*, the latter a Prohibition satire that takes no prisoners, be they socialites or bootleggers.

Only a few months earlier, in April, the Empire State Building was completed, eclipsing its rival the Chrysler Building as the world's tallest skyscraper. Both these art deco masterpieces light up Manhattan's night sky with an almost mystical radiance that is visible from Central Park (to the north) all the way to the Bowery (two miles south).

Now imagine that, for whatever reason, perhaps out of simple curiosity to explore another corner of the city, you execute a volte-face and direct your feet to the murky side of the street. You pass Union Square, bounded north and south by 17th and 14th streets, east and west by Park Avenue South and Union Square West. A great tumult has erupted on the north corner, where speakers are haranguing the crowd from makeshift soapboxes. Without warning, baton-swinging mounted police have lost patience with the Communist Party USA (CPUSA) rally that has blocked traffic with its noisy call to join the class struggle and overthrow the capitalist system.

You pick up the pace, heading to the darkened recesses of the Bowery. Here you are greeted by an entirely different spectacle, of thousands of the homeless and the hungry, clustered in the streets, with nowhere to spend the night and with no idea where their next meal is coming from. Unshaven men of all ages, their eyes blank, indifferent to the clatter of the Third Avenue elevated subway rumbling overhead. The streets are lined with derelict tenements and boarded-up shops, whose doorways shelter the destitute from the elements. Knots of men crowd together around makeshift bonfires – when the winter comes they will hold their caps over the flames just long enough to absorb the heat and then replace them on their heads. They will perform this ritual hour after hour.

Such is the pulse of New York City in 1931: blithe and vibrant for the privileged, who still savour the good life of the Roaring Twenties; a wretched slide into ruination for the first wave to be crushed under the heel of the Great Depression. Over the course of the next decade, New York will confront the most challenging time in its history. These are some of the city's most exhilarating and creative years, which witness the rise of the great skyscrapers and Rockefeller Center, the opening of world-class museums, the flourishing of the Harlem Renaissance in literature, an injection of new life into culture and the arts by refugees from Europe's totalitarian regimes, and the building of a vast network of roads, bridges and tunnels – all set against record unemployment, breadlines, soup kitchens, street riots and Mafia lawlessness. New York stands on the brink in the 1930s, but finds its way back.

Now you are navigating the crowded streets of Times Square and Broadway – the Theater District – where the lurid colours and ear-splitting sounds merge into a science-fiction assault on the senses. Streams of yellow cabs grind their way angrily up the broad avenue; flashing neon advertisements promise whiter teeth and a brighter smile, the juiciest double cheeseburgers at the lowest prices in town, or eternal salvation only two blocks away at the Congregation of the Great Redeemer. And all this razzmatazz against a dark Manhattan sky streaked orange and green, an unreal spectacle, the likes of which can only be seen in regions where the aurora borealis is visible. The roar and honking of traffic, the crowds pressing forward as if in flight from an oncoming cataclysm, the shrieks of the street vendors hawking watermelons, hot dogs, cigarettes, all in a riot of languages. The quality of apocalyptic foreboding is captured in Irish writer Joseph O'Neill's dark novel *Netherland*:

'Sometimes, to walk in shaded parts of Manhattan is to be inserted into a Magritte: the street is night while the sky is day.'[1]

The Manhattanite on a night stroll through some of these tumultuous parts of the city treads a world in which nothing lies outside the realm of plausibility. The unexpected is deemed unremarkable; events out of the blue are met with indifference. This air of cool nonchalance was put to the test on 30 October 1938, when much of the nation, New York no exception, listened to a newsflash about an invasion by Martians. That night, the actor and director Orson Welles broadcast a dramatisation of H. G. Wells's 1897 science-fiction fantasy *The War of the Worlds* in the form of a series of 'live' news bulletins. Many of those who tuned in late were led to believe that the Earth was under alien attack. A New York theatre manager reported a mass exodus of customers, while in one area of Harlem people rushed into police stations saying they had packed their household goods and had come for evacuation instructions. One man insisted he had heard President Roosevelt's voice on the radio advising all people to leave the cities. The switchboard of the *New York Times* was overwhelmed by panic-stricken callers. As far away as Indiana a woman ran into a church screaming, 'New York has been destroyed! It's the end of the world.' More sensible voices would have reassured panic-stricken citizens that if there was one city capable of shrugging off an attack by Martians, that would be New York.

The nocturnal spectacle of New York engenders at once wonder and a sense of menace. The traffic fumes, the angry tumult of car horns, the dazzling lights, the otherworldly colours, the crush of the multitude – this is the poetry of raw energy, of a people who have cast off the strictures of the society that they, or their forebears, discarded on arriving at Ellis Island, and who passionately embrace the no-holds-barred way of life of the New World: 'New York City, the incomparable, the brilliant star, city of cities, the forty-ninth state, a law unto itself, the Cyclopean paradox, the inferno with no out-of-bounds, the supreme expression of both the miseries and the splendours of contemporary civilisation.'[2] One would be hard-pressed to hear words such as these from the lips of a Londoner, for instance – a veritable gush of rapture, verging on frenzy, of enthusiasm for a city.

THE WHY AND THE WHEREFORE

The idea of writing a history of New York in the 1930s came to me over breakfast one morning in 2014, when I was glancing through Robert Greenberger and Matthew K. Manning's *The Batman Vault*, an anthology of collectible reproductions about Gotham's hero. The book had been a birthday present from someone well acquainted with my addiction to the exploits of the Dark Knight. This is an understandable passion, it must be stressed, for I was born in Manhattan's (now defunct) Gotham Hospital and spent my adolescence under the spell of superhero comics and radio programmes featuring crime-fighters like The Shadow and Dick Tracy. It occurred to me that day that Batman's debut was in 1939, making this his seventy-fifth birthday. No sooner was the first issue of the comic released than the 'Caped Crusader' rapidly rose to stardom and became part of the cultural fabric of New York – referred to in the strips as Gotham[3] – a city whose glamour, energy, cultural awakening and soaring landmarks were rooted in that era.

A torrent of recollections came gushing out that day, thoughts that for more years than I care to remember had lain dormant in some remote compartment of my mind. These memories taken together, I was convinced that I must write this book. Moreover, I say unabashedly that I saw myself as uniquely suited for the task. I spent some time rooting through a cabinet, where I found a dusty 45-rpm record that I had made in 1952, when I was ten years old, on a visit with my father to the Empire State Building's observation deck. Starting from there, my excited memory fast-forwarded to my Wednesday-night pilgrimages to Birdland in the 1960s, when the club was located in Broadway and 52nd Street, and where for a $1.50 entry ticket jazz fans could sit enthralled by late-night jam sessions by Art Blakey, Charlie Parker and other immortals.[4] I also recalled having seen a stand-up song-and-comedy routine by Sammy Davis Jr at the Stork Club in 1957, and attending the premiere of *West Side Story* at the Winter Garden Theatre that same year. My Manhattanite credentials were sealed by the many glorious nights spent in long-vanished Greenwich Village cafes like the Fat Black Pussycat and Café Figaro, and the less glorious months of getting to know New York at its worst as the driver of one of the city's famous yellow cabs.

Having taken the decision to delve into the history of New York in the Depression years, I did not have to do a great deal of library work to realise that the city as we know it today came of age precisely in the period leading up to the Second World War. The great decade of the 1930s was the successor to the razzle-dazzle years of the Roaring Twenties. These were the years that bequeathed to the world a pantheon of eminent New Yorkers, each of whom symbolised a part of the city's cultural and social identity: Humphrey Bogart, Lauren Bacall, Barbara Hutton, Walter Winchell, Eugene O'Neill, George and Ira Gershwin, James Cagney, Danny Kaye and Fiorello La Guardia, to name but a few of Gotham's best-known celebrities.

The 1930s was also the decade in which the New York skyline acquired its present splendour: the Chrysler Building, the Empire State Building, Rockefeller Center, the Waldorf-Astoria. This was also the era that brought New York intellectual life to the boil, with the ongoing expression of the Harlem Renaissance of the previous decade, and the arrival of eminent academics, writers, thinkers and artists, many of them European Jews on the run from Nazi persecution.

This book sets out to be the story of the decade in which New York rose to become the cultural, artistic and financial powerhouse of the United States. And it could not have happened at a more unlikely time in the city's history.

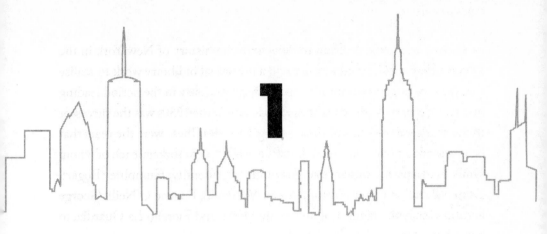

BROTHER, CAN YOU SPARE A DIME?

By the beginning of the 1930s all hopes had finally been dashed of an early recovery from the worst financial collapse in American history. The system was shutting down and taking with it people's dreams and savings. The brightly lit department stores along Fifth Avenue proclaimed the city's wealth amid glowing neon adverts and honking traffic, while one third of New Yorkers lived in squalid and cramped tenements. At the same time, hundreds of millions were being spent on skyscrapers in a frenzied race to erect the world's tallest buildings; another $350 million was sunk into the sprawling Rockefeller Center complex, already under construction; Broadway theatres and cinemas were packing in the audiences, and New York City teetered on the verge of bankruptcy. These were at once the most opulent and most desperate of Gotham's days.

How did this come about?

In the beginning was Manhattan, whose name is thought to be derived from the Munsee word *manahactanienk*, meaning 'the place of general inebriation'. Numerous scholars have sought to explain the origin of the name, but this is arguably the most compelling.[1] This 22.6-square mile island was inhabited by several tribes before the arrival of Dutch settlers in 1624. It is generally accepted that in 1609 the English navigator Henry Hudson, seeking a western sea lane to China on behalf of the Dutch East India Company, became the first European to explore the bay area around lower Manhattan. However, this is not entirely accurate, for earlier records show that more than a decade before Hudson's exploration a handful of Dutch seafarers in the employ of a 'Greenland Company' took shelter from winter storms in the island's coves.[2] Going back ever further, one can cite the Italian father-and-son team of explorers John and Sebastian Cabot, who arrived at New York in 1497 but decided not to stay. The urban legend has it that John turned to his son Sebastian with the comment, 'This is a fine place to visit, but I wouldn't want to live here.' The remark has been repeated throughout the centuries.

The first Dutch settlers fortified the southern tip of Manhattan, where it abuts Upper New York Bay. Two years after the colonists' arrival, the Dutch governor, Peter Minuit, purchased the island of Manhattan from its original inhabitants for beads and trinkets worth $24 in today's money. Shrewd entre-preneurs, those Dutch, for no one can deny that they negotiated a favourable deal. Today $24 is what one would pay for a glass of Duc de Romet sparkling wine at the Waldorf-Astoria's Peacock Alley bar.[3]

It would require an energetic stretch of the imagination to envisage the landscape of Lower Manhattan nearly four centuries ago, in the days of the original Dutch trading settlement. Consider Battery Park, the 25-acre site where the new arrivals from the Netherlands erected their first outpost. During the Dutch occupation, this spot, which today witnesses a ceaseless stream of cars roaring out of the exit of the Brooklyn–Battery Tunnel, past Sicilian American sculptor Arturo Di Modica's bronze *Charging Bull*, and then debouching into the snarl of downtown traffic was, in the words of one nineteenth-century historian, a place of 'wood-crowned hills and beautiful grassy valleys, including a chain of swamps and marshes and a deep pond'.[4] The once-bucolic Lower Manhattan waterfront that so impressed the early settlers is now clogged with noisy crowds of day-trippers, devouring hot dogs and ice creams as they join the long queues for the ferry journey to the Statue of Liberty and Ellis Island. It is a short walk northwards from Battery Park to the bustle of Wall Street, the site of the world's largest stock exchange.[5] This colonnaded neoclassical structure stands on the spot where in the seventeenth century Dutch traders exchanged their baubles for the Native Americans' beaver pelts, between rivers 'as yet unstirred by the keels of ships'.[6] What had been a network of rural trails cutting through fields 'grassy and rich in wild fruits and flowers',[7] four centuries later has become a grid of concrete pavements, emblazoned with blobs of discarded chewing gum and brass plaques commemorating ticker-tape parades. This was where 'grapes and strawberries grew in abundance in the fields, and nuts of various kinds were plentiful in the forests, which were also filled with abundance of game'.[8]

In the fateful year of 1664, New Amsterdam, as the Dutch settlement had come to be known, was rechristened New York in honour of the Duke of York, later James II of England. This came about shortly after a heavily armed naval squadron sailed into the harbour demanding the settlement's surrender in the name of the English Crown.

At the dawn of the age of mercantilism, the Netherlands was England's chief rival for dominion of the seas. It was obvious, the merchants of London and other English trading cities reasoned, that this New World enclave with access to the great expanse of a largely unexplored continent to the west could not remain a Dutch monopoly. Therefore, in March 1664, Charles II set the stage for two years of warfare with the Dutch by granting his younger brother James the deed of ownership to a tract of land stretching from Maine to Delaware Bay.[9] The icing on this cake of wilderness was the trading post of New Amsterdam, whose 'Narrows', an inaccurately named expanse of water that was in fact a mile across, were the port of entry for the majority of goods landing in the territory.

Instead of the spirited resistance that the Dutch governor, the one-legged Peter Stuyvesant, expected from his countrymen, nearly 100 of the settlement's leading gentry, gazing apprehensively at the English cannons aimed squarely at their town, called on the governor to throw in the towel. Three days later an outraged Stuyvesant signed the surrender document and, without a shot being fired, New Amsterdam became New York.

The Dutch troops marched out of Fort Amsterdam and along the wharf to board a ship waiting in the harbour. The three-master would transport them across the Atlantic, leaving behind a civilian population that overwhelmingly expressed little enthusiasm for returning to the Netherlands. From that day New York was England's to have, but not to hold, at least not for long. Less than a decade after Stuyvesant's surrender, in July 1673, Dutch warships were sighted in the harbour off Staten Island. When they let loose a cannonade on the garrison the astonished English, finding themselves under bombardment from the sea while fighting a rearguard action against a spontaneous insurgency by Dutch residents, handed over the settlement to the attackers. For the next 15 months the colony reverted to Dutch rule, this time under the name New Orange, in tribute to the royal house of Orange-Nassau. But then, in November 1674, a treaty was agreed between the rival colonists, under which New York reverted to English sovereignty. Manhattan was once again an enclave of the English Crown, and it was to remain so for more than a century, until 1783, when General George Washington's Continental Army pushed the redcoats off the island.

That was when New York became an American city and, what is more, it was designated the national capital and seat of Congress. That lasted until 1790 when, to the regret of most of New York's citizenry, Washington moved the capital temporarily to Philadelphia, pending completion the following year of the federal city in the District of Columbia. Abigail Adams, wife of John Adams, who served as the second US president, echoed the sadness many felt at leaving behind the animated life of Manhattan: 'When all is done,' she lamented, 'it will not be Broadway.'[10] In the earliest days of European occupation, Broadway came to an end just north of Wall Street, vanishing into a tangle of forest tracks. By the eighteenth century, it stood as the gateway to New York, running 15 miles north–south through Manhattan and the Bronx, starting from where Battery Park stands today, and where in 1760 the British naval captain Archibald Kennedy built a Palladian mansion house in which Mrs Adams would have delighted in *thés dansants* and gala dinner parties.

In the nineteenth century, New York, and in particular Manhattan, expanded at an astonishing pace. The influx of tens of thousands of émigrés provided the labour needed for what had become the nation's manufacturing centre, rivalling in output the industrial cities of the Old World. Manhattan steadily grew to become the throbbing heart of the grandly named 'Empire State'.[11] Like all hubs of empire, Manhattan sought to expand its dominion beyond its natural frontiers, which are formed by rivers to the east, south and west, as well as by a land border to the north, the Bronx, which reached across miles of rich farmland.

An abundant supply of manual labour, mostly from the community of Irish immigrants who fled the devastation of the potato famine in the 1840s, as well as of educated talent from German-speaking Europe and, in an ironic twist of history, Great Britain, provided Manhattan with the human capital the settlement needed to create the new empire's working and cultured classes. Around the middle of the nineteenth century, more than half of the island's residents were foreign-born, the vast majority having entered the country through New York Harbor.[12] By the end of the Civil War in 1865, New York's population had grown to half a million, and there was a great diversity of expertise among those who had braved the transatlantic crossing from the Old World. The city's streets, offices and shops bustled with nearly 10,000 tailors, 855 piano makers, more than 1,200 lawyers, nearly 1,000 jewellers, similar numbers of barbers and engineers, 1,500 teachers and 2,200 printers. There were also 33,000 carpenters, labourers, masons and stonecutters, who developed skyscraper skills in Manhattan and erected the New York World and Park Row buildings, which in the 1890s ranked as the tallest in the world.

Manhattan's municipal authorities, along with the state legislature, had for some time cast a covetous eye at the up-and-coming settlements across the surrounding waterways, as well as the land-connected district called the Bronx, the latter having the added appeal of being the only part of New York (apart from a tiny sliver of Manhattan) with direct access to the North American mainland.[13] These outlying territories were explored and colonised from the early sixteenth century to the founding of New Amsterdam in 1625. The Florentine seafarer Giovanni da Verrazzano, whose name was given to the suspension bridge that connects Staten Island with Brooklyn, sailed past these two future boroughs on his exploration of New York Bay in 1524. The first sightings of the Bronx and Queens were made by Henry Hudson on his early seventeenth-century voyage. It was not until 1898, however, at the outbreak of the Spanish–American War, that all four boroughs were consolidated, along with Manhattan, into what bore the title 'the City of Greater New York'.[14]

Each of the boroughs that were annexed into Greater New York boasted characteristics that in some respect distinguished it from the others and held a special appeal to its settlers. The rich soil and dense woodlands of Queens, the largest of the boroughs, were a source of grain, livestock and timber for the rapidly expanding building trade. Staten Island enjoyed a strategic position at the entrance to Manhattan's harbour and dockyards, and became a focal point for industrial growth after the Civil War. The Bronx was a magnet for German settlers in the mid-nineteenth century. These were for the most part people with entrepreneurial ambitions who set up small businesses as well as great ironworks, which were to play an important role as munitions suppliers during the Civil War. One of the most celebrated New Yorkers with origins in the Bronx is none other than Batman, born of the sketching pencil of Bob Kane, the son of German Jewish immigrants who settled in a depressed neighbourhood of the borough.[15] Bruce Wayne, the millionaire playboy who becomes the invincible 'Caped Crusader' by night, embodied the fantasies of countless poor New York youths in the Depression.[16]

The borough of Brooklyn was the city's prize catch, with its miles of dry dock and freight terminals lining the shore facing the East River and New York Bay: 'Manufacturers found the waterfront of Brooklyn ideal for the region's heavy and bulky industries, including grain storage, sugar refining and glass manufacturing.'[17] Even today, over a century later, Brooklyn's 2.8 million residents outnumber by 700,000 the population of Manhattan, while the other three outlying boroughs are regarded by many as junior partners.

The official celebration to mark the founding of Greater New York brought thousands of people onto the streets of Manhattan, in the spirit of boisterous pageantry so beloved by the city's inhabitants. This event, on New Year's Eve 1897, was commemorated with a hundred-gun salute, fired in a driving snowstorm that failed to chill the revellers' determination to throw a party. On that night a new metropolis had come into being, one of 3 million inhabitants, a city larger in area than Paris and not far behind the sprawl of London. Gotham had taken its first bold step into the twentieth century.

In 30 years' time the city's population had grown to 8 million. New York had now overtaken London as the world's largest metropolis. It was also the most cosmopolitan of all the great urban centres, with a quarter of its citizens having been born abroad. By the late 1920s, New York was the nation's undisputed centre of banking, commerce and most of the arts. It was also the nation's largest industrial centre, home to 30,000 factories. By the end of the Roaring Twenties, the city accounted for a tenth of America's commercial output – the city's growth seemed unstoppable. Until, that is, 29 October 1929.

FROM BEST TIMES TO BUST

No one was prepared to believe it could happen, not in those halcyon days of bouncing flappers, popping champagne corks and soaring stock prices. So when on the eve of the 1930s, the founder and chairman of the International Acceptance Bank of New York, Paul Warburg, argued that if the present orgy of 'unrestrained speculation' were not brought promptly to a halt there would ultimately be a disastrous collapse, his words were hooted down by a multitude of bankers and stockbrokers, and dismissed as wet-blanket pessimism by a clutch of toadying financial journalists.[18] 'The United States may reasonably be said to be immune from economic and social disturbance,' was the reassuring pronouncement from Dr Max Winkler, lecturer in international finance at the School of Business of the College of the City of New York. Winkler never doubted that economic recovery was just around the corner and would be 'more pronounced than the period of crisis'.[19] This, after all, was the brief interval between two world wars, when people were desperate to banish from their minds the horror of the 37 million left dead and injured across the globe in the Great War. But in a few years' time, to everyone's disbelief, the dark clouds of armed conflict would be building over Europe for the second time in a generation.

These were days of perpetual gaiety, and there was good cause to celebrate the country's wave of prosperity, or so it would seem. The poor and the jobless of Europe might be suckered in by the Soviet revolution, which had consolidated its conquest of Russia and held out the promise of liberation for the ground-down working classes. But in America there was little doubt in anyone's mind that capitalism was the way forward, the only system capable of satisfying people's eagerness to make a fast buck. The 1920s was a period of unprecedented growth in US industry, a decade in which output nearly doubled compared with the pre-war years. The automobile, that most conspicuous symbol of consumer affluence, was hailed by everybody as the success story of free enterprise. In the three years prior to the 1929 Crash, the number of vehicles on the roads of America rose to 5.3 million, an increase of a million in that period alone, and a figure that was not to be surpassed for another quarter of a century. Nearly 80 per cent of the world's stock of automobiles was now owned by the American middle class. This blinkered confidence in everlasting good times was not without its ironies. In September 1929, scarcely a month before the Stock Market Crash, contracts were being signed, amid great celebration, to erect several of the buildings that now delineate the New York skyline, including that supreme monument to Mammon, the Empire State Building.

We take for granted that the Great Crash was the result of economic failings inherent in a culture of rampant speculation and easy credit, which was available to all punters seeking to try their hand at investing in stocks on margin. There is no more persuasive debunking of this misconception than that put forward by John Kenneth Galbraith, whose classic account of the market meltdown pins the blame on a single word: mood. By late 1928 the mood in Wall Street, one that was shared by small investors and large institutions alike, had begun to shift from fervent optimism to a wild escape into fantasy. The following year saw months of roller-coaster rises and falls in the market, every successive drop followed by an even more spectacular upswing, but leaving a deeper chasm after each rebound. Finally, on 28 October 1929, the writing leaped off the wall: the market took a headlong plunge, only this time there was no rally. The next morning's trading session brought 'the most devastating day in the history of the New York stock market, and it may have been the most devastating day in the history of markets.'[20] The impact of what Galbraith calls 'mood', if so anodyne a word can do justice to the ensuing decade of national and global financial calamity, had swiftly begun to tip the country into the Great Depression.

Yet even at this stage the Establishment refused to take on board what lay in store for the country. With Manhattan recovering from its traditional all-night New Year's Eve celebrations, the *New York Times* waxed dismissive of the reality staring the markets in the face:

> The afternoon hours were given over in Wall Street to hilarious celebrations, there was no slackening in the pace of the trading on the Exchange and in the brokerage offices, and final quotations were at the best of the day in most stocks [...] Professional Wall Street is moderately bullish on the immediate outlook for the stock market in 1930.[21]

Paul Warburg's warning of the approaching disaster had suddenly become a prophecy fulfilled. The speed with which the market headed due south took the country by complete surprise. Within four months of the Great Crash, thousands of the unemployed were marching in the streets of America's largest cities to protest against factory closures. In the depths of a New York winter, passers-by looked on in shock as every morning some 2,000 of the jobless stood shivering in breadlines along the Bowery. This mile-long street in Lower Manhattan, which once served as the main highway to Boston, became the squalid abode of the homeless and the hungry. After the Crash, the 'huddled masses' of Emma Lazarus's poem, engraved on a plaque at the base of the Statue of Liberty, had reverted to being the 'wretched refuse of the teeming shore' whence they had arrived filled with hope, and who now spent their days and nights wandering the Bowery in search of shelter. The 1930 tune 'Brother, Can You Spare a Dime?', crooned by radio and film stars like Rudy Vallée and Bing Crosby, became the anthem of an army of down-and-outs.

In an astonishingly short period of time, the New York of unbridled merrymaking, ruled over by Mayor Jimmy Walker, also known as 'Beau James', had been transformed into a fearful and hungry place. The Roaring Twenties had vanished in a puff of smoke, and now the city and the rest of the country had fallen into the depths of the Great Depression. One December night in 1932, Gan Kolski, a jobless 33-year-old Polish immigrant, an artist whose haunting wood engravings seemed to foreshadow the impending collapse of the American economy, leaped from the George Washington Bridge into the icy waters of the Hudson River. Kolski left behind a note that summed up the thoughts of millions of victims of the Crash: 'To All: If you cannot hear the cry of starving millions, listen to the dead, brothers. Your economic system is dead.'[22]

The banking system took its worst ever hammering in the fallout from the market implosion. Hundreds of thousands lost their savings in the failure of the New York-based Bank of United States. In December 1930, great crowds of panicked investors gathered outside a Bronx branch of the bank to withdraw their savings. A near riot broke out, igniting a stampede on deposits that sent the bank's shares, which through the year had been worth nearly $100, plummeting overnight from $11.50 to $3.00. Mounted police had to be called in to control the crowds and within days the institution was placed in the hands of the superintendent of banks. More than 600 banks across the country shut their doors in the turbulent months of November and December 1930. Deposits at the Bank of United States accounted for a third of the $550 million lost in those two months alone. In the days that followed scores of wage earners, who had been reduced to a life of homelessness, were found dead on park benches and in the darkened recesses of Grand Central Terminal. Some had lost the battle against exposure and the biting winds of a Manhattan winter. Others had died of hunger, in the heart of what had been held up as America's most dynamic city.

On the face of it, the mayoral election that took place in November 1929 (the mayor takes office on 1 January of the following year), with the city still reeling from the stock market disaster, seemed to substantiate the theory that voters are loath to change horses in times of severe economic crisis. Mayor Walker embodied in his sybaritic lifestyle the very essence of the jazz age. As befitted a man who symbolised the 1920s, Walker began his career as a songwriter for Tin Pan Alley, only to be pushed into the law and then politics by a father who had other ambitions for his son.[23] Walker emerged into the political limelight with the backing of a clutch of corrupt politicians who ran the so-called Tammany Hall machine, thrashing the lacklustre incumbent mayor John F. Hylan for the Democratic nomination in the upcoming 1926 election.[24] Tammany was a familiar name to every New Yorker, and, unsurprisingly, the machine even found its way into popular fiction of the 1930s:

'Up at the top of this city,' he said slowly, 'there's a political organisation called Tammany Hall. They're the boys who fill all the public offices, and before you were born they'd made electioneering into such an exact science that they just don't even think about it anymore. They turn out their voters like an army parade, their hired hoodlums guard the polls, and their employees count the votes.'[25]

In the nearly seven years in which he served as mayor, from January 1926 to September 1932, New Yorkers turned a blind eye to Walker's incorrigible boozing and notorious philandering. Such was the spell that Beau James had cast over his constituents that, in the fateful year of 1929, this dapper son of Irish-immigrant parents effortlessly saw off Republican candidate Fiorello La Guardia, his firebrand Italian Jewish neighbour from Greenwich Village.

La Guardia lost his bid to become mayor first and foremost because New York had almost from time immemorial been held securely in the grip of the Tammany bosses who controlled City Hall, an apparatus so powerful that even New York State governor Franklin D. Roosevelt backed away from taking it on. Democrat voters outnumbered Republicans two to one in New York, and Walker enjoyed the enthusiastic support of a sympathetic, even sycophantic press. William Randolph Hearst, whose newspapers had an audience of 20 million, was one of the powerful media moguls who gave his backing to Walker's campaign.

For La Guardia it was more than a loss. It was a humiliation. He failed to carry a single assembly district, and he accounted for only 26 per cent of the total vote, the lowest figure for any mayoral candidate since the creation of Greater New York in 1898.[26]

Few would have laid odds on La Guardia returning with a vengeance to serve three successive terms as mayor. But by the time the 'Little Flower' (the literal translation of La Guardia's Italian first name) became the city's ninety-ninth mayor in 1934, the New York Establishment had had its fill of

Walker's excesses: his undisguised affair with the chorus girl Betty Compton, a star of the lavish theatrical revue the Ziegfeld Follies; his luxurious sojourns in Europe; his nightly debaucheries at the Casino nightclub of Central Park or the hidden drinking hole of the 21 Club.

Hearsay has it that Polly Adler was among Jimmy Walker's stable of mistresses, but it is an established fact that the mayor was a regular visitor to the secret passages and stairwells of her West 75th Street brothel. Adler, the daughter of a Russian Jew, emigrated to New York in 1914, at the age of 14, where she toiled in sweatshops and dreamed of finding a husband. Her dreams ended in rape and abortion, leading her into the underworld as a brothel-keeper, under the protection of notorious New York mobsters Dutch Schultz and Charles 'Lucky' Luciano. She was soon lining up dates for men in a tiny two-room Riverside Drive apartment, where her clientele included the writers of the Algonquin Round Table (the equivalent of London's Bloomsbury Group), as well as Broadway stars, business moguls and politicians, including Walker. Adler provided a touch of sparkle to the gloom of the Depression. In 1935, she pleaded guilty to charges of possessing 'a motion-picture machine with objectionable pictures' and was sentenced to 30 days' scrubbing prison floors. At the trial, Justice Charles Pope Caldwell said he would like to see 'at least part' of the pictures at her next arraignment. The crowds turned out in droves at the courthouse to watch Polly being escorted to jail in a mink coat.

Inveterate charmer as he might have been, Walker's flamboyant lifestyle could not stand up to the censure hurled at him by eminences like the Catholic archbishop of New York, Patrick Joseph Hayes, the state governor, Franklin D. Roosevelt or – eventually – the New York judiciary. A legislative committee of enquiry spent 14 months digging into Walker's multifarious activities and finally brought him before a judge on charges of corruption within his administration. Ten thousand people sought to gain entrance to the courthouse on the first day of the proceedings, and the few hundred who were admitted greeted the mayor with a roar of cheers, repeatedly shouting their approval of their dapper hero Beau James's facetious retorts to Justice Samuel Seabury's interrogation. When all is said and done, Walker enjoyed enormous popularity among his constituents, who revered him as the man who supported the adoption of an extensive public transportation system, unified the public hospitals and created the Department of Sanitation. But Seabury unleashed a barrage of incriminating questions: where had Walker obtained the money to fund his luxury holidays? What could the mayor tell the court about his speculative stock market dealings, specifically his investment in oil stocks, which was set up by a broker, J. A. Sisto, who was interested in obtaining certain municipal legislation for the benefit of his client, a taxicab company? How had Walker and his wife come to receive $26,000 in bonds from J. A. Sisto & Co., a major investor in the taxi industry? This same Sisto had lobbied hard to be granted ownership of a single fleet of cabs, which would amount to snatching monopoly control of the city's taxi industry. In return for Walker's support, Sisto had passed on to the mayor a lucrative block of oil shares.

When in the summer of 1932 it was revealed beyond any reasonable doubt that Walker had pocketed kickbacks in exchange for municipal contracts, Roosevelt decided to take action by having the discredited official removed from public office. But to save himself this disgrace, Walker abruptly resigned from office. He sailed away, in the style to which he was accustomed, to the less embarrassing soil of Europe, his Ziegfeld Follies sweetheart in tow. He came back to New York in 1940, when a forgiving La Guardia made him a municipal arbiter for the garment industry. At the time of his death six years later, Walker had returned to his musical roots as chairman of Majestic Records.

Shortly after Walker's resignation, in December 1932 Tammany Hall called a special election in which their stop-gap candidate, John Patrick O'Brien, who was not a native New Yorker, thrashed acting mayor Joseph V. McKee at the polls. Given the unique circumstances of this poll and occurring in the wake of the Walker scandal, O'Brien's inauguration ceremony was a muted affair, one at which the Tammany bosses thought it tactful to keep a low profile. It soon became patently obvious that an O'Brien administration would lack the sparkle that had characterised the years of his flamboyant predecessor. When asked at a news conference who would be the new police commissioner, O'Brien told the reporters, 'I don't know, they haven't told me yet.' It came as no surprise that the full election held in November 1933 later turned out to be a walkover for the feisty and self-assured La Guardia.

O'Brien's defeat notwithstanding, Tammany was far from a spent force in New York politics. The machine had historically claimed the allegiance of the city's strong Irish community, and through it that of the police force, whose ranks by the mid-nineteenth century were more or less one-third Irish. The ability of Tammany to rely on police non-interference, if not outright complicity, opened the gates to a jamboree of unfettered City Hall gangsterism. Tammany chicanery ensured that invoices for City Hall purchases, from office furniture to window cleaning, were inflated to tens and often hundreds of times their true cost. More than half these payments ended up in the bosses' pockets.

For nearly two centuries, from 1789 to 1967, New York politics and business remained in the clutches of Tammany sachems, a few of them colourful rascals like the bloated and bearded William Magear 'Boss' Tweed and the amusingly nicknamed 'Honest' John Kelly, who earned his ironic sobriquet for having built an opaque and efficient system of graft. City Hall appointments were the undisputed preserve of racketeers drawing public salaries. One of Tweed's more arresting statements was: 'There never was a time when you couldn't buy the Board of Aldermen.'[27] Tweed, using his law practice as an extortion vehicle, siphoned an estimated $30 to $200 million from the city coffers. In his supreme arrogance, the Tammany boss would tolerate no criticism. In 1869 he fulminated over a cartoon in *Harper's Weekly* lampooning himself and his associates. He thundered that he had no interest in press reports, for, in his words, his constituents 'didn't know how to read', but they could all too easily identify him in a caricature.

Tweed's career came to a sticky end in 1873, when he was handed a 12-year prison sentence on 204 counts of fraud. But the machine soldiered on, fiddling the books and dispersing patronage for almost another century. It was not until the 1960s that its crumbling vestiges were swept away by Mayor Robert F. Wagner Jr, who wrested control of the Democratic Party from the Tammany bosses.

THE LITTLE FLOWER AND GOLIATH

T he first politician to launch a resolute offensive against Tammany Hall was gearing up to become one of the bosses' bitterest enemies. Fiorello La Guardia stepped into office as New York City's chief executive in 1934, in an election in which 2 million people cast their votes, a record turnout for the city. La Guardia was determined to break the power of 'that formidable organisation of old-line Democrats under the leadership of a series of astute Irishmen'.[1] His opponent was none other than the Goliath of New York, the omnipotent Tammany machine that treated City Hall as its personal fiefdom.

Never before had a mayor of New York, or quite possibly of any city, been called upon from day one to confront such a multitude of crises. La Guardia was charged with setting the city on its feet. His immediate tasks were to repair and expand the city's crumbling infrastructure, create jobs, provide shelter for the tens of thousands of homeless victims of the Depression and keep the lid on social unrest in Harlem and other deprived areas. What he encountered when he took office in January 1934 amounted to far more than a full-time job: it was a crusade. But the mayor waded into the rats' nest of organised crime with gusto, fortified by an iron will to rid the city of its mobsters. In the coming clash, the Mafia giants seriously misjudged the resolve of their Little Flower adversary.

The Great Depression and the resultant flood of corporate failures had engendered an unprecedented level of unemployment and homelessness. Organised crime was digging its tentacles into almost all sectors of business life. City Hall was riddled with corruption and teetered on the verge of insolvency. And all this was occurring during New York's coldest winter on record. La Guardia's resources for combating this host of tribulations were limited to an unshakeable belief in the virtue of his cause and an ability to face down the challenges. Having the president of the United States as a close personal ally was another helpful factor.

La Guardia, a Republican by party allegiance, had come into office on the 'Fusion Party' ticket, a combination of New York Democrats disenchanted with Tammany Hall and its shenanigans, disaffected Republicans and a number of reform groups.[2] It was this broad-based appeal, which won the backing of several influential newspapers, as well as the huge pool of the city's poorest voters, that secured La Guardia a majority in each of the five boroughs and catapulted him into office.

On the morning of 1 January 1934 La Guardia took the oath of office at City Hall, having made the journey downtown from his modest four-room tenement in the Potomac Park Apartments block in East Harlem. It was not until 1942 that the Board of Estimate decided that La Guardia needed to reside in accommodation in keeping with his exalted office.[3] They designated the historic Gracie Mansion, located on a promontory in 88th Street, overlooking the East River, as the official residence of the mayor and his successors.[4]

La Guardia became mayor of New York at a time when the city was in the clutches of an unparalleled cold snap that, within a few weeks of his taking office, saw temperatures plunge to a record low of −15° Fahrenheit. On 9 February, six people died of exposure, dozens passed out from carbon monoxide poisoning while trying to thaw automobile radiators in closed garages, and hundreds of schoolchildren, along with 40 policemen, were treated for frostbitten hands, noses and ears. It was, if one may be forgiven the pun, a bitter reminder of the crisis whose shadow hung over the city La Guardia had been called upon to govern.

New York was three years into the Great Depression, a calamity that La Guardia, in contrast to many of his fellow politicians, had foreseen and warned of during his term as a Republican congressman. Throughout his time in Washington, the future mayor's ear was attuned to the pleas that poured in daily from his New York constituents. The Little Flower's ability to listen to people and respond in Yiddish, Italian or another of several languages – he had worked as an interpreter at Ellis Island early in his career – helped endear him to his supporters.

The market collapse was beginning to strangle economic life in the city in a way never before witnessed in New York. People were being made destitute in their tens of thousands, unable to pay their rent or cover basic necessities such as medical care. In the year following the Crash, unemployment began to take its toll. The national jobless rate more than doubled from 4.2 to 8.7 per cent between 1928 and 1930. Two years later it peaked at an all-time high of 23.6 per cent. In New York, many of the city's almost 200,000 jobless stood in breadlines to collect food handouts and spent their nights dossing in alleys and on park benches. Others tried to eke out a meagre income by selling apples in the streets, as depicted in some of the most emotive photographs of New York in the Depression years. The streets of Gotham were filled with these vendors, who had eagerly accepted an offer by the International Apple Shippers' Association to sell their surplus produce on credit to the jobless at five cents each.

La Guardia faced a mammoth task in dealing with the hardships of the Depression. Chief among these was the acute personal suffering brought on by the collapse of economic life. Two years after the Crash, hundreds of New York's factories had shut their doors and a third of the city's manufacturing capacity had been lost and, along with that, many thousands of jobs. More than a million and a half New Yorkers were drawing emergency relief and a quarter of the population lacked any regular source of income.

Many of the homeless sought warmth in the Municipal Lodging House in East 25th Street, which at the beginning of the Depression provided shelter for 3,300 men, and later women, who fought every night to claim a sleeping space. In November 1930 alone, 43,280 men found shelter in what was basically a replica of a medieval almshouse. Within a year the figure had more than doubled to 111,223 vagrants. By 1932, two adjacent piers needed to be renovated to raise the shelter's total capacity to 4,500 beds. One outcome of this situation, according to social workers, was that people put on the street could sink into despair in a few short days.

A first-hand account of the full horror of these insalubrious billets comes from the pen of the 1930s novelist Albert Halper:

> Broken men were snoring in the 15–20–30¢ flop-houses. Each man had a tiny booth, sprawled on a hard iron cot, and if he wasn't drunk spent most of the night scratching himself until he drew blood. All the mattresses were old, discolored, spattered with years of tobacco stain, nasal excretion and vomit. Bedbugs, like systematic squads of Marines, scoured each hairy leg and chest.[5]

Some of the destitute resorted to extreme measures to keep body and soul together. In one incident, several homeless men were arrested when the police discovered them living in a tunnel under the Central Park Reservoir. This subterranean abode became an instant headline-grabber, which the papers dubbed the 'Little Casino', a mocking reference to former mayor Jimmy Walker's Central Park gin palace.

The impact of the Depression on the city's youth was particularly catastrophic. Some 5,000 boys between the ages of 16 and 21 were found to be adrift in the streets, while 10 per cent of those in this age group were homeless. This army of the disillusioned, the bewildered and the vulnerable posed a real menace to law and order in the city. Racketeers preyed on many young men, who were lured into robbery and other criminal activities. The police already found themselves up against a well-entrenched syndicate of professional mobsters scheming to reap the rewards of Prohibition, and a widespread contempt for the law that it had encouraged. Much of this Mafia activity took place with the connivance of Tammany which, along with tackling the economic hardship and destitution of the Depression, was one of La Guardia's targets. Taking on the corrupt City Hall machine was never going to be an easy task. Tammany was a wounded beast but still a dangerous one, with the capacity to claw at the entrails of its enemies.

Clearly La Guardia could not shoulder this multiplicity of challenges on his own. In his pre-congressional days the future mayor had joined a New York law firm as a specialist in immigration cases. His secretary was the glamorous New York-born Marie Fisher, who later served as one of La Guardia's few trusted political aides. Fisher also worked alongside him when he served as president of the New York Board of Aldermen. In 1929, during his tenure in Congress, she became his second wife, following the death from tuberculosis in 1921 of his first, Thea Amerigotti, at the age of 26.

FRIENDS IN HIGH PLACES

Among those the mayor could count as his invaluable confidants and supporters of his anti-Tammany campaign were Roy Howard, the liberal publisher of the *New York World-Telegram*, and most notably Charles Burlingham, a fighter for civil reform and one of the few advisers whose criticism the mercurial La Guardia was prepared to consider, if not always accept.

However, the city was only spared all-out, protracted devastation at this time of desperate economic straits thanks to the unique working relationship forged between La Guardia and the most improbable of allies: Franklin D. Roosevelt. Today hundreds of people driving to LaGuardia Airport in Queens will travel northbound along the FDR Drive to the 59th Street Bridge exit, turning east onto Northern Boulevard to follow the Brooklyn–Queens Expressway to the waterfront airport on the northern edge of the borough.[6] Some might carry on along the FDR Drive to the Triborough Bridge, continuing eastbound along Astoria Boulevard's colourless suburban sprawl to link up with Grand Central Terminal.

The FDR Drive–LaGuardia Airport connection symbolises a partnership forged in the 1930s between two public figures of contrasting social circumstances and political loyalties. Fiorello La Guardia was the product of a classic first-generation New York upbringing. He was born in 1882 in Sullivan Street, Lower Manhattan, a few minutes' walk from New York University, where he was to take his law degree. La Guardia's ethnic background crossed a number of religious and geographical lines. His parents were Irene Coen and Achille La Guardia, respectively an Austrian Jew of Sephardic origin and a Sicilian Catholic employed as a US Army bandmaster.

Coming from lowly origins and with his enormous popular appeal, La Guardia later rose to stand as a hero of the demoralised New York masses. But strike out 'lowly' and replace it with 'patrician', and a similar statement can be made about Franklin D. Roosevelt. The thirty-second US president and architect of the New Deal was an American aristocrat, a New Yorker who could trace his roots to the mid-seventeenth century, when his ancestor Claes Martenszen van Rosenvelt landed at the Dutch colony of New Amsterdam.

La Guardia and Roosevelt were both born in 1882 and died within two years of one another. In childhood, their school lives ran roughly in tandem, but this is where their paths began to diverge. La Guardia received his primary education in the state school system and later attended New York University, a highly rated academic institution but one lacking the veneer of gentility associated with the Ivy League. Roosevelt was born in a stately home in the leafy New York State town of Hyde Park, where he was brought up by governesses. The future president was packed off to the fashionable Groton School in Massachusetts and, as befitted a young man of his class, he followed the well-trodden path from this upmarket institution to the venerable halls of Harvard University. Where La Guardia was bumptious in nature and tiny in stature, and spoke in a squeaky, heavily New York-accented voice, Roosevelt cut a ducal figure, complete with cape, and was a polished orator, well known for his paternal 'fireside chats' to the nation, transmitted by radio during the Depression years.

These disparities of upbringing and character in no way detract from the remarkable similarities in Roosevelt and La Guardia's early careers. Shortly after an initial chance encounter during the First World War, when Roosevelt was serving as assistant secretary of the navy and La Guardia as commander of a bomber squadron on the Italian–Austrian front, the two men's lives moved on to political triumph, followed by personal tragedy. They both entered the political arena in 1910 and, exactly seven years later, Roosevelt took up office in the New York State Senate and La Guardia was elected to the US Congress. Disaster struck in 1921, when La Guardia's daughter Fioretta died of spinal meningitis and his first wife Thea was carried off by tuberculosis. In that same year Roosevelt contracted polio, which left him paralysed below the waist. The parallels between the lives of Roosevelt and La Guardia, despite the great chasm that separated their social status, must stand as evidence that their coming together and cooperation were a case of political destiny.

Their separate paths to prominence diverged in dramatic fashion, once again in the same year, when in 1932 Roosevelt crushed the incumbent Herbert Hoover in the presidential election and La Guardia lost his congressional seat to the Democratic challenger James J. Lanzetta. On 3 March 1933, La Guardia and his wife Marie boarded the sleek National Limited Pullman service at Washington's Union Station for the journey back to New York. The following day, Roosevelt took up residence in the White House. For Roosevelt the polished statesman, this was the final rung on the political ladder: 'As for La Guardia the defeated congressman, he could hardly have realized at the time that within less than a year, a remarkable close working relationship would be forged between New York's City Hall and the White House.'[7]

La Guardia the Republican and Roosevelt the Democrat stood on opposite sides of the party divide, yet what bound the two men together had nothing to do with party politics. They shared a sincere compassion for the widespread suffering of the American people and the conviction that it was the government's duty to do something about it. For Roosevelt as well as for La Guardia, this was a matter of social responsibility, not an act of charity. This philosophy was given substance shortly after Roosevelt's electoral victory. It came in the form of the New Deal, the package of reform and aid measures that became crucial in pulling New York and the rest of the country back from the brink of total collapse.[8] It may have seemed illogical for Roosevelt to choose the Republican mayor of Gotham as a close collaborator in this venture. But disregarding their opposing political allegiances, it required the levelling process of the Depression to bring together two outstanding leaders, albeit from different parties, who had New York's best interests at heart.

The New Deal was a sweeping, ongoing body of legislation enacted by the federal government, starting in 1933. Immediately after Roosevelt's inauguration, Congress went into special session to approve a series of measures designed to combat the Depression and bring about a long-term transformation of the country's economic and social institutions. This included relief for hard-hit farmers, tighter regulations for banks (which many condemned as the prime culprits behind the economic collapse) and the roll-out of major public works projects. Several institutions that are still functioning today, like the Securities and Exchange Commission (SEC) and the Federal Deposit Insurance Corporation (FDIC), were created as part of the New Deal reform programme.

The mayor and the president worked in close harmony on the course of action necessary to restore to health the country's largest city, which appropriately received a greater share of federal funding than any other. One of the programme's chief architects was Harry Hopkins, a Roosevelt confidant who in his youth had experienced first-hand the plight of New York's poorest, when he took a job as a social worker in a Lower East Side ghetto. Hopkins headed the Works Progress Administration (WPA), which in the Depression became the country's largest employer, and he was all along one of La Guardia's most enthusiastic supporters. One of Hopkins's early efforts was to expand New York's employment programme, the Temporary Emergency Relief Administration (TERA), which granted funds to place low- or unskilled workers in government jobs. In New York City, tens of thousands were able to find employment through this scheme.

La Guardia's political credo was in many ways a precursor of the New Deal. As early as the 1920s he had fought for the recognition of trade unionism. This brought him into direct confrontation with political and business circles whose hostility towards the Left reflected a widespread fear of the Communist revolution in Russia. His decade-long battle to prevent the courts issuing anti-union injunctions set a precedent under which the New Deal was to encourage workers to sign up as union members. The future mayor was also ahead of his time in proposing an initiative for job creation through government-funded infrastructure projects such as bridge and road building, housing and other public-sector undertakings.

These included the $40 million North Beach Airport, which in 1953 would be renamed in honour of La Guardia, the person who had almost single-handedly seen the project through to completion. The mayor was outraged by the extraordinary fact that New York lacked an international airport of its own. Before the former Curtiss Flying School in Queens was rebuilt as North Beach, visitors to the city were obliged, to the mayor's chagrin, to fly to Newark in neighbouring New Jersey. He once refused to disembark in Newark, complaining that his ticket read New York and not New Jersey. The pilot had no choice but to restart his engines and fly his grumpy passenger to Floyd Bennett Field in Brooklyn. Upon landing, La Guardia vowed he would see to it New York got the airport it deserved.

True to his word, on 15 October 1939, only two years after the ground-breaking ceremony, 325,000 people flocked to attend the North Beach inauguration. The now-replaced Floyd Bennett Field went out in a blaze of dubious glory, leaving for posterity one of the most astonishing anecdotes in the history of US aviation. Three months before work began on the new airport, the celebrated aviator Douglas Corrigan took off at dawn from Floyd Bennett Field in his second-hand Curtiss Robin OX-5 monoplane on what was scheduled to be a non-stop flight to Long Beach, California. More than 28 hours later Corrigan spotted an airfield in a break in the clouds and set his aircraft down. He said to the men who came out to the runway to meet him: 'Just got in from New York. Where am I?' To the immense delight of the ground crew, Corrigan was informed that he had landed at Baldonnel Aerodrome in Ireland. The aviator was taking no chances on his return trip, packing himself and his aircraft onto the steamship *Manhattan* for the crossing to New York. In spite of his colossal navigational 'error' – many believe that he had in fact deliberately set out on a transatlantic crossing, having been denied permission to do so – Corrigan was given a ticker-tape parade up Broadway and, from that day, 'Wrong Way Corrigan' entered New York jargon for someone who has lost his bearings.[9]

North Beach was the first US airport of the Depression years to have been built with federal government funds. On the opening day, as a jubilant La Guardia stepped up to the podium to address the crowd, 150 military aircraft flew overhead to the great enchantment of the spectators, many of whom were to make the airport a weekend family outing just to catch a glimpse of planes taking off and landing. There was even a crowd of onlookers in attendance at one minute past midnight on 2 December 1939, to witness the first scheduled arrival, a TWA twin-engine DC-2 from Chicago. It was an event to gladden La Guardia's heart, as this was the same route he had flown in 1934 when, after landing at Newark, he vowed to provide New York with an airport befitting a great city. It cost ten cents to enter the viewing area and this was soon bringing in hundreds of thousands of dollars a year in revenue.

The inauguration of New York's first airport ushered in an opportunity to partake in the allure of air travel in the 1930s. A few days after North Beach opened for business, 5,000 young women rushed to fill 20 vacancies as American Airlines flight attendants. The applicants needed to be single and possess nursing qualifications to do a job 'women consider glamorous and exciting', according to an airline recruiting brochure. With capacity at North Beach filling up like a hole in the sand, a few years later work began on a new airport at the 5,000-acre Idlewild Beach Golf Course, also in Queens, a site that in 1963 changed its name from Idlewild to John F. Kennedy International Airport – JFK for short.

La Guardia had finally achieved his objective of putting New York on the US aviation map, while at the same time focusing his efforts on other urgent matters, like restoring the city to economic health and getting people into employment. But during this period he also had to face down the threat of social turmoil and Mafia lawlessness.

TROUBLE IN THE STREETS

L a Guardia was a lifelong and unabashed proponent of the welfare-state system, as well as an implacable adversary of privilege, his intimate friendship with the aristocratic Roosevelt notwithstanding. His 'leftist' orientation had earned La Guardia more than a few enemies within the Republican Party. Roosevelt's welfare measures came into force at a moment of despair in New York's history. Contrary to received wisdom, however, tales of numberless stockbrokers and ruined investors hurling themselves from Wall Street windows do not stand up to scrutiny. The suicide rate for New York in 1929 actually showed a slight decline from the previous year. While not resorting to the ultimate extreme, many New Yorkers did succumb to chronic depression and other manifestations of mental illness. The number of people suffering from these ailments, whom hospital records of the day categorised in not very politically correct terms as 'insane', increased from 439.2 per 100,000 in 1929 to 472.3 in 1933 and continued to rise until the end of the decade.

Despondency and mental breakdown are not the only consequences of a severe economic collapse such as the one that ravaged New York City in the 1930s. The longer people are deprived of the essentials of a decent existence – jobs, food, education and shelter – the greater the likelihood of civil strife surfacing in the streets. La Guardia recognised this home truth in the early 1920s when he remarked in a radio broadcast that 'a well-fed, well-housed, well-schooled people' make up the bedrock of freedom and social stability. In addition to struggling to restore the economy to health, therefore, the Depression mayor faced the challenge of growing social unrest. Much of this was promoted by the Communist Party USA (CPUSA) and other leftist groups. But organised extremism was not confined to the Left. The rise of Nazism galvanised many adherents among Americans of German descent and their sympathisers, who in 1936 founded the 'German American Bund'. They staged rallies that more often than not turned into street battles with leftist groups. This problem of civil strife had been plaguing New York before La Guardia took office, and it now became a priority, with Harlem coming to the boil.

The press was quick to label the protestors Communist subversives, and there is no lack of evidence that the CPUSA was indeed behind much of the agitation. But in the 1930s, largely due to stories emerging from the Soviet Union about the true nature of the Stalinist regime, the CPUSA was rapidly becoming a spent force. By 1932 national membership had dwindled to 6,000, a quarter of its pre-Crash strength. That did not stop a respected newspaper of record like the *New York Times* headlining its front-page story covering a day of clashes with '3 red hunger riots stir only the police'. In the same article, the paper acknowledged that people had taken to the streets of Brooklyn not to call for the overthrow of the government, but to demand free food, electricity, gas and shelter for the jobless. The protests, like many others that followed, were put down with brute force: 'In Brooklyn the mounted police rode into the crowd, while a small contingent of patrolmen and detectives beat back men and women with fists and blackjacks.'[1]

The wave of social unrest spread beyond a demand for decent living conditions. The frustrations that went with the prevailing mood of hopelessness meant that disputes, which in better times might have been fought in the law courts, more often than not degenerated into pitched street battles. These conflicts erupted in some of the most unexpected sectors. The first few years of the Depression saw tens of thousands of people thrown out of jobs, and nowhere was the crisis more acute than among unskilled workers.

New York's black community suffered most, with some 40 per cent of males unemployed and seeking benefits. One avenue of employment open to those with a working knowledge of the city streets was driving a cab, or 'hacking'. By 1931, over 73,000 men held hack licences. This allowed them to compete for jobs behind the wheels of the city's 21,000 licensed cabs. The scramble for work was so severe that fleet owners took advantage of the situation to dictate terms of employment, which to say the least were not to the cabbies' liking. Once tempers reached boiling point, drivers went on the offensive and a wave of scuffles, which frequently turned into free-for-all melees, engulfed the streets of Gotham.

This is how the *New York Times* reported several days of clashes between police and New York's taxi drivers, beginning on 5 February 1934: 'Wholesale violence marked the strike of taxicab drivers [...] when thousands of strikers paraded noisily in Manhattan, the Bronx and Brooklyn, dragging passengers from cabs driven by non-strikers, damaging the machines and giving the police lively tussles.'[2] This particular brawl left Times Square strewn with doors wrenched from their hinges, mufflers, headlights and any other car parts the rioters were capable of ripping off strike-breakers' cabs. The violence had erupted over working conditions and was directed against large fleet owners, who vehemently opposed union membership for their drivers. In all, more than 4,500 cabbies immediately went on the rampage, exhorted by the likes of union organiser Joseph Gilbert to 'go out and wreck' any taxi spotted touting for business.

New Yorkers found themselves searching in vain for cabs when the number of strikers swelled to 12,000, while licensed cabbies prowled the streets in search of scabs. The drivers did not let themselves be intimidated by the police: one striker recalled how cabbies slashed the tyres of police cars and tossed marbles under the hoofs of police horses, which were having a difficult enough time staying upright on the icy streets.[3] It was at this point that La Guardia decided to intervene. The mayor conjured up a deal that offered an olive branch, consisting of a compromise on pay and work hours that was accepted by fleet owners and drivers. So ended the three-day strike, which cost the city $300,000 and sparked a flurry of protests by commuters who missed their trains and sailings, as well as pregnant women, who were unable to reach hospital in time to give birth.

The issue of law and order was not contemplated in New Deal legislation. But there was growing evidence that labour and market reforms could not take effect in time to extinguish the smouldering volcano of unrest that was building in New York's most deprived communities. By the mid-1930s the city's black population stood at roughly 350,000: about 5 per cent of Gotham's 7 million inhabitants. The majority were poor, uneducated and unskilled, virtual refugees escaping violent persecution in the cities and farming country of the south. They fled in their thousands to cities north of the Mason–Dixon Line, notably New York, most of them settling in the neighbourhood of Harlem in northern Manhattan, which was to become the focus of some of the most alarming social disorder of 1930s America.

HARLEM ON MY MIND

The earliest records of European contact with the upper reaches of Manhattan date from Henry Hudson's 1609 voyage, which took him up the river that today bears his name. It was not a happy time for the English navigator. He had so far failed to find the elusive North-West Passage to China, which had after all been the objective of his journey. What he did encounter were Native Americans, who were not at all pleased by the sight of white interlopers, and who showed little fear at their first taste of musket fire. Several bloody skirmishes and a dozen or so dead Europeans and Native Americans later, Hudson turned the prow of his ship, *Half Moon*, to the south, never again to return to the hostile shores of what would later be called Harlem.

Three decades after Hudson's hapless encounter with the Native American warriors of Harlem, the Danish-born Jochem Pietersen Kuyter became the first European to establish a permanent settlement there. Shortly after disembarking on the shores of Upper Manhattan in 1639, Kuyter acquired from the Dutch the flatlands on which Harlem now stands. He built a farmhouse about eight miles north of City Hall, only to see it burned to the ground by rampaging Native Americans five years later.

From that time onwards things went from bad to worse for Kuyter. In 1647 he was banished from New York for three years and ordered to pay a hefty fine after an altercation with Willem Kieft, the Dutch colony's director general. The somewhat bizarre charge brought against Kuyter was of 'having threatened Kieft with his finger'. Once back in the Netherlands Kuyter successfully petitioned the Dutch courts to revoke the sentence, whereupon he returned to Harlem. The New Amsterdam authorities, however, were not finished with Kuyter: he was obliged by Kieft's successor, Peter Stuyvesant, to cede three-quarters of his landholding, after which, in 1654, the unfortunate Kuyter was ambushed and murdered by Native Americans.

The move to settle the northern end of Manhattan began in earnest in 1668, when the Dutch Council of New Amsterdam took the decision to establish a new village or hamlet near the lands of the deceased Kuyter. The first mention of black settlers in Harlem appeared in a Dutch Council decree mentioning 'Negroes', who were enlisted to assist families choosing to resettle in the north of the island with the transport of their wagons. Shortly thereafter, the village was given the name New Harlem, after the ancient Dutch trading town of Haarlem.

As more colonists from New Amsterdam ventured north to clear the woodlands, along with their Native American inhabitants, Harlem came into vogue among the good Dutch burghers. According to a nineteenth-century account of life in the Dutch colonies, on one wintry occasion, when snow covered the fields of Manhattan, some ladies turned out at noon 'in linsey-woolsey cardinals, with hoods of immense size'. Their sleigh was driven by a black servant, known as Caesar, who doubled as a fiddler, to the accompaniment of sleigh bells. He drove them up to Harlem for a cup of tea and a dance. The partying continued until eight in the evening, when they hastened back home: 'for to be out after nine, on common occasions, was considered a certain sign of bad morals.'[4]

By the time of the 1929 Crash, Harlem could claim to have the largest African American community of any city in the country. The mass movement of people known as the Great Migration had begun roughly in 1915, with an exodus of some 500,000 black people from the rural south.[5] The uprooting of such an immense segment of the population had a dramatic impact on New York's demographics: between 1910 and 1920 the city's black population soared by 66 per cent, and with more than 300,000 new arrivals, African Americans outnumbered by 20 times any other of New York's ethnic minorities. Most of those who came up from the Deep South, refugees in the truest sense of the word, settled in Central Harlem, where a black community was already established. The result was that in the course of a quarter of a century the social profile of the uptown Manhattan neighbourhood had reinvented itself.

African Americans were not the only people vying for living space in Harlem's crowded streets. Another group of early arrivals from Europe, the Irish, had been established in Harlem for the better part of 80 years, roughly since the potato famine of the 1840s. East Harlem had long been home to a sizeable Jewish community as well, which counted among its residents future celebrities like the Marx Brothers, Milton Berle, Arthur Miller and George and Ira Gershwin. By the 1920s, however, Jewish Harlem was becoming a relic of history, as newly acquired affluence led many Jews to abandon their tenement flats, cramped and squalid rooms lacking proper plumbing, ventilation or heating. These prosperous Jewish professionals and entrepreneurs set their sights on statelier parts of the city, such as the Upper West Side and Washington Heights.

The combination of a massive increase in the African American population, the steady deterioration of housing conditions and the continuing high rents charged for now inferior accommodation quickly convinced Harlem's remaining upwardly mobile Jews that uptown's 'Jewish era' had come to an end.[6] The emigration took place on an unprecedented scale. In its heyday, Harlem boasted the world's third-largest Jewish community, after the Lower East Side and Warsaw. Before the 1920s, this corner of Manhattan was home to almost 200,000 Jews: by 1940 all but some 5,000 had packed up and left. In the heterogeneous yet clannish city that is New York, the Jews viewed with uneasiness the influx of immigrants from alien cultures, people who professed different faiths and adhered to foreign traditions. It was the arrival en masse of Irish Catholics, who began to settle in Harlem in the late nineteenth century, followed at the turn of the century by the first wave of Italian immigrants, that began to dislodge Judaism as Harlem's prevalent religion. The influx of African Americans from the south was the final factor that persuaded most of the Jews to seek new homes in other neighbourhoods. The tenements that had served as home for generations of Jews were gradually taken over by black families, whose numbers increased by almost 120 per cent in the 1920s. By the beginning of that decade, 70 per cent of Manhattan's black community already resided above 118th Street.

The departure of the Jews did not signal the demise of Harlem as a multi-ethnic neighbourhood. The black community remained the largest in Harlem, rising from around 10 per cent of the population in 1910 to 89 per cent by the end of the 1930s. However, the Italians and Irish were still established segments of Harlem's citizenry, and by that date together numbered more than 150,000 residents. Most of the Italians had emigrated from Sicily, along with a sprinkling from other Italian regions. Their community became known as Italian Harlem, until they too eventually departed what was becoming an overwhelmingly black neighbourhood. From the start of the twentieth century and accelerating thereafter, most of them moved downtown, to an area that developed into Little Italy, an enclave adjoining Chinatown, the Bowery and the Lower East Side.

Many of the Irish left Harlem to set up communities downtown in Hell's Kitchen; others found work in the Brooklyn dockyards, while Irish neighbourhoods also began to spring up in Queens. After the First World War, part of former Italian Harlem was gradually taken over by a wave of Latinos, the vast majority of them Puerto Ricans, who had begun to secure a foothold in the district. The transition from their Caribbean-island home to the socially unwelcoming environment of Harlem could hardly be described as seamless. Unskilled and poorly educated for the most part, the Puerto Ricans found themselves scavenging for the same menial jobs sought by poor African Americans and even some of the poorer Jews. In July 1926 this led to an outbreak of rioting by Puerto Rican youths. The protests turned violent when many took to the streets armed with sticks, while others clambered onto rooftops to hurl bottles at their perceived enemies, including non-Puerto Rican Latinos. It was a foretaste of worse to come.

THE GHETTO BOILS OVER

Harlem's social and economic way of life went into a tailspin in the Depression years. Slumlords ruthlessly exploited the scramble for limited living space by pushing up rents to levels unknown even in some of the well-heeled neighbourhoods of Manhattan. They also divided up properties into ever smaller units and generally allowed large areas of Harlem to fester and decay until they could be classified as slums. In the early 1930s more than half of Harlem's population lived in apartments that cost between $40 and $100 a month. In other sections of the city similar apartments were let for $30 to $50 a month. 'Bunching up', as it was called, meant that several families were forced to live under one roof. Even at the higher end of the black community's social scale, modern cooperatives and private residences that were home to professionals and entertainers commanded higher rents than in fashionable Park Avenue. Harlem was the abode of celebrities like the heavyweight champion boxer Harry Wills, the actor Bill Robinson and blues vocalist Ethel Waters.

By the mid-1930s a palpable swell of exasperation filled the air of Harlem and the outrage was in no way lacking in justification. Most of the anger was voiced by the immigrants, or their children, who had fled racial discrimination, which often took the form of brutal persecution, below the Mason–Dixon Line during the Great Migration that began in 1915. More than a decade had passed since their move to the north, and in supposedly tolerant New York City they still found themselves living as victims of prejudice, albeit of the economic rather than the lynch-mob variety:

> The average [black] Harlemite made under $18 per sixty-six-hour week, compared to whites, who were paid about $23 for a sixty-hour week for similar work during the early years of the Depression. For women, things were even more bleak, with domestic servants making $15 per week and laundresses making less than half of that, while whites in those positions brought home nearly twice as much.[7]

By 1933, fully half of Harlem's working-age black population was jobless, while people shivered idly in their dilapidated and unheated tenements. It was common for several families to share a single bathroom; infant malnourishment was rampant and health care so deficient that the number of black people with respiratory infections or lung diseases was more than twice the city average.

The newly elected La Guardia was sitting on a powder keg, which even before he took office in 1934 had threatened an impending explosion. On a sultry July afternoon in 1930, several hundred angry Harlem residents had gathered outside a dry cleaner's shop in Lenox Avenue, near 130th Street. The police emergency squad was called out to disperse the crowds when it became apparent that they intended to storm the shop. The source of the trouble was a minor altercation between the shop's white proprietor and a black female customer. The woman claimed that a ribbon had gone missing from a hat she had brought in to be cleaned. The argument turned into a heated exchange of insults and, at one point, the shop owner pushed the woman out the door. Word of this 'attack' quickly got round the streets of Harlem. In short order, what had started as a trivial confrontation brought a multitude of enraged people out of their tenements, seeking revenge for the alleged assault by a white man on one of their women.

The following year, in July 1931, in the midst of another of New York's sweltering summers, Harlemite tempers flared anew. The centre of Harlem found itself engulfed in race riots, this time with tragic consequences. A mob about 1,000 strong took to the streets with knives and pistols. The brawl erupted over alleged insults and attacks on black women by local Filipinos. The Filipinos countered with identical charges against black people. An emergency police squad and 100 patrolmen from every nearby precinct had to be rushed to the scene of the violent free-for-all, which turned an area from 110th Street to 117th Street into a battleground, with one man shot dead and several others left with stab wounds.

One of Harlem's most turbulent explosions of outrage, a day that for the people of this community came to symbolise protest over social injustice, took place on 19 March 1935. The event that sparked a full-blown race riot in central Harlem echoed in its unlikelihood, if not in the enormity of its consequences, the firing of a pistol in Sarajevo in 1914. That afternoon a 16-year-old boy of Puerto Rican descent, Lino Rivera, walked into the S. H. Kress & Co. 'five-and-dime' store in 125th Street and filched a 10-cent penknife from a display case.[8] The young, mustachioed have-a-go shoplifter explained in a police interview, 'I wanted the knife, so I took it.'[9] He claimed the person who caught him had threatened to drag him down to the cellar for a thrashing.

The incident would scarcely have merited a police call-out had it not been for the scuffle that ensued between Rivera and the two shop assistants who caught him in the act. Rivera went into a fury and sank his teeth into the employees' hands. Within minutes frenzied rumours began racing through a large crowd assembled outside the shop. Though Rivera was not himself African American, black Harlemites saw him as a fellow victim of the white Establishment. Some of the bystanders claimed Rivera had been savagely beaten by the white shop assistants, though the charge was never substantiated. As if confirmation were needed, one had only to look at the ambulance that pulled up in front of the shop – no matter that it had been called out to attend to the two workers' badly scratched and bitten hands. As bad luck would have it, at that moment a hearse was spotted parked nearby. Somebody in the crowd cried out that the boy had been murdered by the police. The mood swiftly turned ugly, as people shouted abuse at the white owner and employees. The premises were ransacked and looted for the better part of an hour, until the police managed to clear the crowd from the street.

The police had their hands full that afternoon and it took several hours of baton-swinging to break up the angry mob. The rioters were eventually dispersed, but only after a pitched battle, and that was not the end of it. By evening the rioters had regrouped in force under cover of darkness, first to take revenge on the Kress store by smashing up the shopfront, then, for good measure, to smash the windows of more than 200 other retail outlets. Next came a looting spree across 125th Street. The Merchants Association of Harlem telegraphed the state governor, Herbert H. Lehman, to request 'military assistance'. Few took notice when La Guardia ordered photographs to be distributed of a hale and hearty Lino Rivera, smiling sheepishly outside his mother's flat and flanked by Lieutenant Samuel Jesse Battle, New York's first black police officer.

The 1935 riot was not the most destructive upheaval Harlem was to experience in the 1930s. Nevertheless, it took 500 police to restore some semblance of order to the streets. The mayhem left three black protestors dead and more than 200 people in hospital with gunshot and knife wounds. It marked the beginning of La Guardia's awakening to the volatile social conditions in Harlem. The mayor lost no time in instructing New York county district attorney William Dodge to investigate the circumstances of the riot. It was not the most felicitous of appointments. Dodge was a crony of James Joseph Hines, one of the most powerful of Tammany Hall bosses. Hines's name was later brought into disgrace when he was accused of being involved in illegal gambling, specifically the illicit lottery known as the 'numbers game' or the 'policy racket', in connivance with Dutch Schultz, a notorious New York mobster of the 1930s. The specific charge against Hines was that he attempted to put pressure on magistrates, notably Dodge, to take a soft approach on policy-racket prosecutions. Hines was quoted in his own trial as stating that Dodge was 'my man'.

Dodge's first public statement to the press on the day he was put in charge of the investigation could not be considered a paradigm of tact. His remarks showed a woeful lack of understanding of Harlem's predicament: 'My purpose is to let the Communists know that they cannot come into this country and upset our laws. From my information Communists distributed literature and took an active part in the riot.'[10] CPUSA agitators may well have been behind some of the violence, on the principle that any trouble they could stir up for the authorities was a blow struck in the name of working-class liberation. A case in point was the Young Communist League, which put out an inflammatory and wholly fictitious statement alleging Rivera's 'brutal beating' by the shop workers. But as Harlem's black residents perceived it, they had taken to the streets seeking social justice, not the overthrow of the state. Black leaders themselves played down the involvement of political radicals in the clashes. Some witnesses claimed that the Communists stepped in to exploit the pandemonium once the rioting began. The *New York Times* wrote: 'All seemed to agree, however, that the basic cause is economic maladjustment, segregating and discriminating against Negroes in the matter of employment.'[11]

Sensing Dodge's lack of suitability, La Guardia also set up a committee of prominent New Yorkers to investigate the causes of the riot. The team was composed of six black and five white members. They elected as chairman Charles H. Roberts, a dentist who in 1919 had been the first black alderman of New York. However, the committee's most forceful spokesman was the celebrated journalist and civil rights campaigner Oswald Garrison Villard, whose analysis of the riot amounted to a clear repudiation of William Dodge's benighted humbug: 'The committee is already agreed that the disturbances were merely symbols and symptoms, that the public health, safety and welfare in colored Harlem have long been jeopardized by economic and social conditions, which the Depression has intensified.'[12]

HAVES AND HAVE NOTS

Those living in the ghettos of Harlem, the wind-battered alleyways of the Bowery, the squalid tenements of the Lower East Side or wherever the destitute of New York struggled against their lot, were each day confronted with exasperating sights of opulence. Even as Wall Street crumbled to pieces, the homeless languishing on Manhattan's park benches gazed with bewilderment at the steady rise of the Chrysler Building, the 77-storey art deco masterpiece that, on completion in 1930, became the world's tallest skyscraper – until it was surpassed only 11 months later by the Empire State Building, the 102-storey colossus that held the world title until the 1970s when it, too, was overtaken by the New York City World Trade Center. There was no need to venture far from the tenements and shanties to run smack into the ghost of the Roaring Twenties, flourishing and vibrant as ever, totally heedless of the economic and social debacle that had now locked its grip on New York, plunging the city into financial default.

The Stork Club, which operated initially as a speakeasy after its opening in 1929, was located in West 58th Street until its move seven city blocks downtown to 51st Street in 1931. In September 1930, during its speakeasy days, it was described by the *New York Daily Mirror* gossip columnist Walter Winchell as 'New York's New Yorkiest place'. The club subsequently moved again to East 53rd Street in 1934, where it remained until its closure in 1965. Its owner, the former bootlegger Sherman Billingsley, ruled over his well-heeled customers like an absolute monarch.[13] A thumbs-up behind a table was a signal to his bouncers that the offending guests were to leave and be banished from the club. Stardom was not a consideration: comedians Jackie Gleason and Milton Berle, and even a Hollywood giant like Humphrey Bogart, were summarily escorted to the door. On the other hand, glitterati regulars like Ernest Hemingway, Orson Welles and, it goes without saying, the Duke and Duchess of Windsor, remained forever in Billingsley's good books.

Directly west of Billingsley's exclusive watering hole, under the elevated railway that regularly bombarded pedestrians with the deafening roar of trains and a hail of cinders, stood Radio City Music Hall.[14] The trains passing overhead along Sixth Avenue caused buildings to tremble, but it was not the railway that shook the country's largest entertainment palace, but rather the high-class acts in a hall seating 6,000 spectators, who had retreated momentarily from the Depression to luxuriate in top-quality variety shows and gasp in admiration at the sumptuous art deco foyer.

The impoverished of Manhattan could only gaze in wonder at the bejewelled ladies in ermine coats accompanied by cigar-smoking men in dinner jackets emerging from the Waldorf-Astoria. Another art deco landmark, the 47-storey, 1,410-room hotel, the tallest in the world, opened its doors in Park Avenue in 1931, in sheer defiance of the Depression.[15] The hotel's Peacock Alley bar was famed among Manhattan's smart set for serving hand-crafted cocktails to iconic celebrities like Clark Gable, Joan Crawford and the dance duo Fred Astaire and Ginger Rogers. This grandest of New York hotels quickly gained worldwide recognition, and several of the foreign dignitaries to make the Waldorf-Astoria their New York abode included Winston Churchill and the king and queen of Siam. In spite of everything, a life of merriment carried on in the soaring towers of the Waldorf-Astoria, in the skyscrapers and in Manhattan's cocktail lounges, from the Stork Club in midtown to the Cotton Club in the very heart of Harlem.

There existed, in tandem with both the high life of dry martinis at the Stork Club and the precarious existence of those forced to sleep on park benches, another echelon of New York society, one that was fierce but unseen by most. The Waldorf-Astoria counted among its less illustrious customers Benjamin 'Bugsy' Siegel, one of the city's most charismatic gangsters and an uncontrollable killer, who kept an apartment in the Waldorf Towers, the hotel's most exclusive and costliest suites. Likewise Charles 'Lucky' Luciano, the scar-faced mobster credited with having split New York into five Mafia families. Frank Costello, dubbed the 'Prime Minister of the Underworld', regularly turned up to have his hair cut and nails trimmed at the hotel's barbershop.

These villains were the successors to a family of well-established New York racketeers. So efficiently organised was the mob, in fact, that as early as the turn of the twentieth century it had fixed the rates for a list of criminal activities, from $1 for a slash on the cheek with a knife, to up to $100 for a murder.[16] The mobsters were out in force in the 1930s, more often than not in violent style. This was a fight to the death for domination of the rackets, and supreme among these was the trade in illegal alcohol.

The bootleggers contemplated with alarm the public's growing demand for an end to the all but unenforceable ban on alcohol consumption. In 1932, more than 100,000 New Yorkers partook in Jimmy Walker's 'We Want Beer' parade through the streets of midtown Manhattan. Less than a year later, comedian Jimmy Durante presented the first glass of legal beer to prizefighter Jack Dempsey at the Paradise Restaurant on Broadway and 48th Street. Speakeasies began to come in from the cold and traditional landmark establishments once more welcomed their thirsty customers. Sherman Billingsley, the ink scarcely dry on his alcohol licence, reopened the Stork Club, the star of New York nightclubs, on East 53rd Street, having previously relocated to 51st Street after the original 58th Street premises were raided by federal agents in 1931. The repeal of Prohibition came with the ratification of the Twenty-First Amendment to the Constitution in 1933, and, when the illegal liquor business dried up, a Mafia war broke out for control of New York's gambling casinos, the speakeasies' cash-cow replacement.

It was La Guardia's astonishing victory in the 1937 mayoral election, his second, that equipped him, morally and politically, with the resources needed to lock horns with some of the nastiest criminals in the United States. He scored a crushing defeat over his Tammany-backed rival Jeremiah T. Mahoney, securing more than 1.3 million votes, the largest electoral win in any mayoral contest in the city's history. The day the results were announced, the *New York Times* sounded the death knell for the corrupt Tammany bosses who controlled City Hall: 'Doom of Tammany is seen in defeat' ran the headline. 'Tammany Hall, symbol of the political machine since the days of [William Magear] Tweed, suffered its most serious defeat at the polls yesterday. It was a blow from which the organisation may never recover.'[17]

La Guardia had scored more than a decisive electoral win. His victory was proof that he had the people of New York behind him, in particular those suffering most from the Depression, who now saw City Hall as a friend and source of aid, instead of a breeding ground for corrupt politicians. The people's mayor was as good as his word. A woman whose husband's employer was in arrears with his wages wrote to La Guardia complaining that her grocer had refused her credit. The mayor promptly dispatched a food parcel to her door. A blind down-and-out struck by a car was promised a job at City Hall and paid two weeks' salary in advance while waiting to be released from hospital. These were the gestures that endeared La Guardia to his electorate in a way that no other mayor had achieved in the past. Now the Little Flower rolled up his sleeves and squared up for his battle with organised crime. He went in swinging his not inconsiderable fists, but he had his work cut out for him.

'**I CAN'T FIGGER WHAT DIS CITY IS COMIN' TO**'

Atlantic City in the 1920s was a bustling town to which well-heeled New Yorkers would flock on weekends, to take the sea air and glide along the Boardwalk seated in the resort's carriages on wheels. In the evening, after dinner, many visitors would retire to the back rooms of nightclubs and restaurants to partake in the city's star after-hours attraction: an abundance of alcohol, served freely and at a safe distance from the meddlesome killjoys of New York's law-enforcement agencies. The resort city's officials turned a blind eye to the bootlegged whiskey and gin served in their establishments. After all, if a Coke was all they could offer the day-trippers, visitors could easily satisfy their thirst closer to home at Coney Island, or take their chances in one of New York's frequently raided speakeasies.

On a balmy afternoon in May 1929 a group of men, some expensively suited and booted, others in seaside attire that might generously be described as flamboyant, met for the start of a three-day conference at one of Atlantic City's seafront Italian restaurants. They, too, were enjoying the benefits of the city's permissive drinking policy. Indeed, to their minds they had every right to do so, for these were the Mafia bosses who supplied Atlantic City (and speakeasies across the United States) with illicit alcohol. Assembled in a banqueting hall of well-stocked tables that day was one of the most fearsome collections of rogues one could envisage.

The delegates' tempers were frayed due to a social gaffe on the part of the conference organiser and host, the Atlantic City political boss and racketeer Enoch 'Nucky' Johnson. The mobsters had been booked into the stylish Breakers Hotel, a sedate, Gothic pile on the Boardwalk whose house policy excluded non-WASP (White Anglo-Saxon Protestant) guests. The coarse, thuggish assortment of Italian and Jewish gangsters who turned up at reception clearly did not match that description. They were informed that there had been a booking error and that, unfortunately, no rooms were available. The hotel had no idea who they were, but luckily for them the gangsters, who had to keep their identities secret, had little choice but to accept the indignity of seeing their bags carried out the front door.[1] Al Capone, the gangland equivalent of visiting royalty, came close to blows with Johnson over this affront. A nasty scene was averted when the men were bundled into limousines and whisked off to the Ritz, where a still-fuming Capone proceeded to vent his rage on the lobby decor, hurling at least one of the wall paintings at Johnson.

The guest list included more than 40 delegates from 11 states. Brooklyn-born Capone's resemblance to a kindly Italian neighbourhood grocer belied a ferocious character, one that, at the age of 26, had elevated him to the role of Chicago's undisputed crime boss. Capone had inherited the job from Johnny 'the Fox' Torrio, hailed by federal agents as the country's most prominent gangster, second to none in the gainful pursuit of gambling, prostitution and bootlegging. Also present in the conference room was the droopy-eyed, scar-faced mobster Charles 'Lucky' Luciano, who wielded such extraordinary power that he was able to partition New York's gangland territory between five powerful Cosa Nostra families.[2] Torrio's specialities were many and varied, but Luciano could claim an even broader portfolio of activities, from drugs, extortion and loan-sharking to the iron-fisted control of Manhattan's docks.

Frank 'the Prime Minister' Costello was also in attendance. He rolled up in Atlantic City in his habitual dapper attire, as befitted the chieftain of a vast gambling empire. Costello was much admired by his fellow gangsters, and was one of the few to ply his trade without feeling obliged to pack a gun. Then there was Albert 'Mad Hatter' Anastasia, who had earned his nickname through his control of 'Murder, Inc.', as the Mafia's enforcement arm was dubbed by the press. He was also affectionately known to his colleagues as 'the Lord High Executioner'.

One of Murder, Inc.'s most ruthless executive directors was Louis 'Lepke' Buchalter, a Jewish American criminal who ran a gang that gained notoriety as the terror of numerous New York industries. Lepke was convicted of participating in more than 80 murders before his life was ended in Sing Sing prison's electric chair in 1944. He had once arranged to meet Max Rubin, one of his enemies, who also happened to be a co-religionist, under a shop awning in the Bronx during a thunderstorm. 'You're 48?' Lepke rubbed in as the two men shook hands. 'That's a ripe old age.' Without exchanging another word, he pulled out a revolver and shot Rubin dead.

No Mafia jamboree of so high a calibre would have been complete without the presence of Dutch Schultz, who like Lepke was a member of the Jewish American mobster clan. It was, in fact, a hit squad from the Murder, Inc. syndicate that six years later gunned down Schultz in the gents' washroom of his New Jersey chophouse headquarters.

The 1929 Mafia summit had been convened in an atmosphere of professional grudges and festering wounds. Two years prior to the Atlantic City meeting, New York had been shocked by a particularly vicious bloodbath between rival mob factions fighting for dominance of the bootlegging racket. In October 1927 Jacob 'Little Augie' Orgen, the racketeer son of an Orthodox Jewish family, was gunned down while walking the streets of the Lower East Side with Jack 'Legs' Diamond, his Irish American bodyguard. Diamond took two bullets below the heart, but survived, prompting one of his enemies to remark, 'Ain't there nobody can shoot this guy so he don't bounce back?' Orgen's error of judgement had been to embark on a career change in 1925, shifting from the organised-labour racket in the illegal alcohol trade. He failed to take into account the displeasure this would cause the successors of the syndicate set up by Nathan 'Kid Dropper' Kaplan, who had been murdered in the street by one of Orgen's gunmen in a gangland feud.

The Mafia bosses had been summoned to Atlantic City to agree a master plan for integrating the country's warring Italian and Jewish factions into a national confederation of criminals. Johnny Torrio, at 47 a relatively elder statesman as well as an innate survivor, put before the meeting the strategy for such an organisation, which the press dubbed the 'National Crime Syndicate'.[3] There was a certain urgency about agreeing a ceasefire, in view of the lingering image in everyone's minds of the St Valentine's Day Massacre that had taken place three months before the meeting, in which seven members of mobster George 'Bugs' Moran's gang, sworn enemies of Al Capone, were lined up against a garage wall and blown to shreds by Thompson sub-machine guns. As if to drive home the point, only a few days before the conference kicked off, three of Capone's henchmen were machine-gunned in a retaliatory killing.

When the Mafia summit broke up on 16 May 1929, an air of buoyancy prevailed among the homeward-bound delegates. The seaside get-together was hailed a success, inasmuch as turf lines and business interests had been amicably demarcated apparently to the satisfaction of all. This was no mean achievement, considering the personalities involved and the financial stakes, especially those of the New York faction, which had sent the most numerous delegation and which counted among its representatives the likes of Lucky Luciano, Dutch Schultz, Johnny Torrio and several other of the criminal underworld's most feared characters. However, two of New York's top crime bosses had been absent from the Atlantic City conference: Joe Masseria and Salvatore Maranzano had more pressing business affairs on their plates.

THE BUSINESS OF CRIME

Organised gangsterism had been an ingrained feature of New York life since the early nineteenth century. Bands of thugs, murderers and thieves, in the early days made up largely of Irish and Italian immigrants, operated out of the ramshackle tenements of Lower Manhattan. Feuds raged on an almost daily basis between the all-powerful Bowery Boys and its rival gangs, who inhabited the Five Points, a crime-infested slum bounded on the east and west by the Bowery and Centre Street respectively, with Park Row and Canal Street as its southern and northern borders. As was frequently the case in the shifting fortunes of New York neighbourhoods, the Five Points had started life in the early nineteenth century as a respectable community. Around 1820 the drained swamp on which it had been built began to refill, giving off a foul stench as the land gradually subsided and taking with it buildings whose tenants swiftly fled to more salubrious quarters.

By the time a cholera epidemic struck the neighbourhood in 1832, the Five Points had surpassed Victorian London's notorious East End in filthy living conditions and rampant criminality. At least, that was how Charles Dickens judged it when he visited the neighbourhood in 1842:

> What place is this, to which the squalid street conducts us? A kind of square of leprous houses, some of which are attainable only by crazy wooden stairs without. What lies beyond this tottering flight of steps, that creak beneath our tread! A miserable room, lighted by one dim candle, and destitute of all comfort, save that which may be hidden in a wretched bed.[4]

Dickens's fellow Englishman, the Reverend Fred Bell, who became known as 'the singing preacher', turned up in New York some years later on an evangelical mission. In Baxter Street, the main road that formed the notorious Five Points intersection, Bell came across 'certain sorts of human vermin that infest its dark places, who live by preying on human prosperity, womanly virtue and human souls'.[5] Bell, a native of Yorkshire, had set sail for America in 1871 to preach the gospel, with £10 in his pocket, 'the price of two fat pigs' in his home town of Rotherham. On coming into contact with his 'parishioners' in the dosshouse where he was to sing his sermon, Bell exclaimed, 'Oh, the dark, shameful things that night frowns sadly upon, and the dark places of the day hide from human eyes. Oh, the sad muffled groans smothered by rough hands, and dark noisome dens under the sidewalks.'[6] A far cry indeed from the regenerated Five Points, which is now home to neat, tree-lined streets and three parks to which parents take their children to play. The neighbourhood, now called Civic Center, encompasses New York City Hall and New York Police Department (NYPD) headquarters, along with a cluster of government offices and courthouses.

By the turn of the twentieth century, taking 1912 as an average year, mobster violence was wreaking widespread havoc in some of the less gentrified parts of the city. That year found Johnny Torrio on the rampage, while other mobsters like Joe Baker and Joe Morello were slugging it out for control of the Upper East Side. In a single day, five men were gunned down in a pitched battle at 114th Street and Third Avenue. Police officers with the courage to venture onto this gangland turf did so at great peril to life and limb. Those who went to investigate a crime scene and emerged unscathed came away with gruesome tales of bloodied, bullet-riddled bodies in the streets, vendetta victims of stabbings and, for the fortunate few, severe truncheon beatings. By the latter part of 1913, New York was infested with more gangs than at any other time in the city's history.[7]

In January 1920 Congress enacted Prohibition, the Eighteenth Amendment to the Constitution, which outlawed the production, sale, transportation and import of alcoholic beverages in the United States.[8] None of the advocates of this quixotic piece of legislation, from the crusading Protestant zealots of Congress to militants of the Women's Christian Temperance Union, could have foreseen that the Mafia would come to commemorate 20 January 1920 as a day of great jubilation. Prohibition was for some a triumph of Christian morality and for others an assault by religious fanatics on a cherished pursuit of pleasure. For the mob it was a godsend.

It was around the same time that the street gangs of New York, which had thrived in the years prior to and immediately following the First World War, began to disintegrate, along with the diminishing power of their Tammany Hall mentors. This was largely a result of an energetic crackdown by the NYPD and federal law-enforcement agencies. New Yorkers on their way to work began to rejoice in the hope of picking up their morning papers without having to recoil from screaming headlines, accompanied by unabashedly graphic images of the latest gangland murders. The general sentiment of repulsion at the crime wave was summed up in vernacular New Yorkese by a cabbie taking Leslie Charteris's fictional anti-hero the Saint to Grand Central Terminal: 'I can't figger what dis city is comin' to.'[9]

Alas, the worst days of Mafia criminality were yet to come. The mob grew into a more 'businesslike' and well-oiled machine. Years of violence lay ahead, for bootlegging was a deadly enterprise and the fragile truce that had been thrashed out by the mobsters in attendance at the Atlantic City conference proved to be a chimera. As far as the Mafia was concerned, Prohibition represented a challenge, one that the gangsters with admirable skill turned into a multi-billion-dollar cash cow. The statistics speak for themselves: in less than a decade from the advent of Prohibition, the number of speakeasies in New York had soared from 5,000 to 30,000, which was twice the number of legal bars in existence before the law came into effect. Thousands of these illicit saloons were owned by mobsters, and all of them were supplied by the Mafia. This was big business on a scale that rivalled, or even exceeded, the annual turnover of some of America's top corporations in the 1930s. In New York, the so-called 'Broadway Mob', a clique ruled by four gangsters – Lucky Luciano, Frank Costello, Joe Adonis and Bugsy Siegel – was taking in about $12 million a year from booze.[10] In a perverse way, this particular gang was helping to relieve New York's chronic unemployment problem: they had more than 100 people on the payroll, each earning ten times the average shop assistant's weekly wage.

LET THE GOOD TIMES (QUIETLY) ROLL

The name 'speakeasy' in itself explains the nature of these establishments. One needed to speak in a hushed voice to avoid alerting the police to illegal drinking and gambling activities therein, or risk a party-spoiling raid. The speakeasies of New York often became headline-grabbers, on several occasions for reasons that had nothing to do with the illegal sale of alcoholic drinks. For instance, in the early 1930s a dispute between the owner and a patron in a saloon in East 48th Street led to a murder trial (which netted the killer a mere seven-year prison sentence), while in another bar a woman brought a $30,000 suit against the proprietor for serving drinks to an intoxicated customer, who then proceeded to beat her husband, leaving him unable to provide family support.

The 21 Club in West 52nd Street was the most celebrated of New York's speakeasies. The club's original incarnation was the Red Head, which opened in the East Village in 1922, under the stewardship of Jack Kreindler and Charlie Berns. The owners' affability made them popular hosts, so that this thinly disguised 'tea room' became an instant success. The two cousins moved their operation to larger premises in the heart of Greenwich Village, just off Washington Square. But the bar, then called the Frontón Club, stood directly above a new and noisy subway line that was under construction. So once again the speakeasy was on the move, this time to 49th Street, where unfortunately John D. Rockefeller Jr was shortly to purchase the land to build Rockefeller Center. Jack and Charlie were fed up with running a nomadic speakeasy and feared that their customers, who included F. Scott Fitzgerald, H. L. Mencken, Will Rogers and Mayor Jimmy Walker, would also grow weary of criss-crossing Manhattan to keep up with their favourite boozing hole. So they finally acquired a building and the land it stood on at 21 West 52nd Street and, on New Year's Day 1930, began welcoming guests to 'Jack and Charlie's 21', as it was called. It later changed its name to '21 Club', under which it still operates today.

The two owners had devised an elaborate network for illicitly importing the finest spirits from Canada and Europe. The 21 Club attracted patrons from all walks of life, including the world of journalism – reporters were of course as happy as other patrons to partake in a good drinking session. There was only one nasty brush with the press, and that was in 1930, when the house blacklisted *New York Daily Mirror* gossip columnist Walter Winchell for leaking stories about 21 Club's clandestine activities. To get his revenge, Winchell printed a column that questioned why the club had never been raided, a none-too-subtle tip-off to federal agents.

The next day a squad of federal tax agents pulled up outside the door and briefly arrested Jack and Charlie, who were well connected to the Walker administration and hence got off with a slap on the wrist. But they took drastic measures to deal with a repeat visit by the feds by hiring the architect Frank Buchanan, a Prohibition specialist, to design a system of collapsible shelves which, at a signal from the doorman, sprang open to drop the bottles lined up on the bar down a three-storey chute. The precious though incriminating merchandise was shattered on specially installed metal bars and washed into the city's sewer system.

The club's *pièce de résistance* in this cat-and-mouse game was a basement wine cellar, which failed to appear on the feds' floor plans, even though they came with matches for detecting air currents. The management had cleverly camouflaged the access point to the cellar: a row of brick archways used for hanging dried meats and cheeses. The first archway on the left had a small hole with an 18-inch metal meat skewer hanging next to it. When the skewer was inserted into the hole, and twisted sharply to the left, the lock on the two-and-a-half-ton cellar door sprang open to reveal a room filled with up to two thousand cases of wines and spirits.

One of the most colourful incidents in the cellar took place in 1932, when Jimmy Walker was entertaining one of his girlfriends at a table tucked away in the corner snug. The feds chose that night to stage a raid, never suspecting that the mayor was wining and dining beneath their feet. The upshot was that Walker, who was stuck for five hours in the basement, was so outraged that he telephoned the police and instructed them to come at once to ticket the feds' cars.

Prohibition was doomed to fail: the writing was on the wall as soon as Franklin D. Roosevelt won the 1932 presidential election and, a year later, when La Guardia became mayor. Indeed, Roosevelt had swept into office partly on his promise to put an end to Prohibition. As a first step in that direction, on 22 March 1933, a fortnight after taking up residence in the White House, he signed into law the Cullen–Harrison Act, which legalised the sale of low-alcohol beer. As for La Guardia, his stand on Prohibition was well known on Capitol Hill even when he was serving as a congressman in the 1920s. In 1924, in a move that smacked of outright political cynicism, he was appointed to the Committee on Alcoholic Liquor Traffic. As the board's only anti-Prohibition member, it was a foregone conclusion that La Guardia's lobbying would be ignored.

The government's attempt to ban alcohol consumption opened the floodgates to a tsunami of profit. While it lasted, Prohibition proved to be a bonanza for bootleggers involved in illegal importing of alcohol and the equally unlawful and sometimes lethal production of beer and spirits in clandestine breweries and distilleries. The typical cost of a homemade cask of beer in the 1920s was $5, but by the time it was unloaded at a speakeasy the price had gone up at least sevenfold, with the added bonus that one would not have to deal with the taxman. Furthermore, while the going was good, and with enough money sloshing around to satisfy everyone's greed, the mobsters' feral behaviour was kept more or less in check. But things began to turn messy with the repeal of Prohibition in 1933, and, in short order, the Atlantic City agreements were consigned to the dustbin.

The Mafia needed to find fresh sources of income. Before Prohibition, organised crime made its money from general racketeering, wherever a successful business could be infiltrated and taken over, and now extortion was the name of the game once again – only this time it was deployed on a far larger scale. The vast sums the gangsters had pocketed from bootlegging had but fuelled their lust for lucre. Now Gotham's Mafia kingpins began to diversify their protection-racket interests, branching out into businesses like bakeries, restaurants, laundries and limousine services, as well as into the garment industry and the Fulton Fish Market. The powerful gangs waged an unremitting battle to corner ever greater market shares of their new ventures. More than 1,000 had met a violent end in the bootlegging wars of the Prohibition years. More blood was to flow in the battles to come for control of these new businesses.[11]

SENDING THE BOYS AROUND

When Prohibition was approaching its inevitable demise, the dilemma presented itself of who was to exercise supreme command over the New York underworld. In 1930, the curtain went up on one of the most savage acts in New York's Mafia drama. This was the 'Castellammarese War', which was fought between two rival Mafia factions, controlled respectively by Joe 'the Boss' Masseria and Salvatore Maranzano, the latter of whom was born in the ancient Sicilian fishing town of Castellammare del Golfo, the birthplace of a generation of notorious crime bosses. The opening salvo in what was to become a year and a half of tit-for-tat assassinations was the murder of Gaetano 'Tommy' Reina in February 1930. Reina operated under the command of Masseria, who ordered him to be put out of the way ('Remove the stone from my shoe' was Masseria's coded order to eliminate an opponent) for suspected acts of treachery – Reina had begun to support Maranzano. As Reina left his aunt's home in the Bronx one evening after their traditional weekly dinner, he was approached by Masseria's hit man Vito Genovese, who stepped out of the shadows and blew Reina's head off with a shotgun.

New York's Castellammarese War spiralled into a murderous free-for-all, a campaign waged with barbaric savagery between two gangland factions fighting to capture a slice of the rackets. Joe Masseria was a puny and pudgy killer from the Genovese crime family, whose eyes reflected a take-no-prisoners instinct for survival. He had gunned his way to the top of the rackets in Manhattan, the Bronx and Brooklyn, successfully dodging in his ascent to chiefdom the bullets of several would-be assassins. From his base in East Harlem, Masseria held sway over what he fully believed to be his undisputed fiefdoms. That was, however, until he came up against a formidable threat in the person of Salvatore Maranzano. Maranzano had left his crime-ridden homeland of Sicily for the United States in 1925, anxious to put some distance between himself and the anti-Mafia campaign spearheaded by Italian dictator Benito Mussolini. When his ship docked in New York Harbor, Maranzano slipped ashore as an illegal immigrant, carrying in his suitcase a sizeable fortune in cash, which he had amassed during his racketeering days in Sicily.

Maranzano had nursed a natural hatred of Masseria even before the two men laid eyes on one another. He was repelled by what he had been told of Masseria's uncouth appearance and boorish lack of sophistication. Maranzano, on the other hand, cut a debonair figure, with his handsomely chiselled face and smartly tailored double-breasted suits. He also fancied himself something of a classical scholar, for in his youth he had trained for the priesthood and later came to look upon Julius Caesar as his role model for expanding the bootlegging empire he was to set up in New York.

It was not long before Maranzano began denouncing his arch-rival Masseria as 'the poisonous snake of our family', a man without honour, as the term is understood in Mafia circles, and one who he believed was bent on wiping out the sons of Castellammare. Maranzano now became a protagonist in what was to turn into an 18-month-long bloodletting. Maranzano's rage was fuelled by the shooting in July 1930 of his henchman Vito Bonventre, a key operator in the Castellammarese bootlegging ring. This affront to the Maranzano mob would not be allowed to go unavenged. A month later the axe fell on of one of Masseria's bodyguards, Giuseppe 'Clutch Hand' Morello, whose nickname referred to his one-fingered, claw-like right hand. On a steaming-hot afternoon in East Harlem, two of Maranzano's executioners forced their way into Morello's office, guns blazing. One of the gunmen recalled how their victim ran about crazily in a futile attempt to flee, even as the bullets were pumped into his body.

Maranzano raised the stakes a few weeks later by putting out an order for the assassination of Joseph Pinzolo, the late Gaetano Reina's replacement in the Masseria hierarchy and a man reputed to be even more slovenly in appearance and habits than his boss. Several former Masseria loyalists who were unhappy over Reina's murder lured Pinzolo into a trap: he was shot to pieces in an office in Broadway belonging to the Lucchese family faction, who did not disguise their personal distaste for Masseria and went over en masse to the Maranzano camp.

By this time, Masseria and Maranzano had begun to square off for the final confrontation. They knew that sooner or later, only one of them could hold sway as New York's crime boss, and that the victor could not be proclaimed while both of them continued to draw breath. In November 1930, Maranzano once more turned up the heat by hiring three killers to set an ambush for Masseria. A few days later, two of Masseria's men were torn apart by shotgun blasts as they left a meeting with their boss. The choice target, however, again proved himself an innate survivor. He managed to hide behind locked doors in his office until the wail of police sirens frightened off his would-be assassins. From that time onwards neither of the Mafia chieftains ventured out unless surrounded by a phalanx of heavily armed bodyguards. When they did so, passers-by looked on in fearful silence as convoys of black, bullet-proof limousines cruised the tenement-lined streets of East Harlem.

No one was taking any chances.

Masseria had crowned himself *capo di tutti capi*, or 'boss of bosses', the first criminal to claim the title in the history of America's Mafia families. Maranzano's intention was to see his enemy stripped of that crown, which he believed should rightfully be sitting on his own head. To his old-school way of thinking there was only one foolproof method of achieving a dethronement. The major player in this final, or, to be more accurate, penultimate act, was Lucky Luciano. Maranzano and Luciano held a secret meeting in Brooklyn in April 1931 to agree the details of their plan of action, Maranzano unsuspecting that his associate was at the same time quietly hatching other ideas.

On 15 April Luciano and Masseria were enjoying a meal in one of the mob's favourite Italian restaurants, Nuova Villa Tammaro in Coney Island. On his way to lunch, Masseria had parked his steel-armoured car, with plate glass an inch thick, at a nearby garage. The two Mafia chiefs were finishing up a postprandial game of cards, in the company of three of Luciano's gangland associates, when, at a few minutes past two o'clock, Luciano excused himself to go to the bathroom. The moment the bathroom door shut the three gunmen at the table – Vito Genovese, Albert Anastasia and Joe Adonis – put four bullets in Masseria's back and one in his head. For the first and last time, Masseria had failed to see it coming.

The former boss of bosses was found lying face up in a pool of blood, clutching the ace of diamonds. Whether or not the card was placed in his hand as an ominous warning to Masseria's friends remains a matter of speculation. When the police arrived on the scene they found Mrs Tammaro leaning over the body and Luciano, who had by now emerged from the bathroom, explaining that he had just finished drying his hands and came out to see what was causing all the commotion. Luciano had shown himself to be an astute card player, and he had yet another trick up his sleeve.

The crown of *capo di tutti capi* now passed to the modishly pomaded head of Salvatore Maranzano. With a touch of Shakespearean melancholy, a multitudinous celebration banquet was convened in early August 1931 in the same Coney Island restaurant, Nuova Villa Tammaro, where the new monarch's predecessor had met his untimely fate. Five thousand Italian Americans, accompanied by a sizeable contingent of hit men, bootleggers and assorted racketeers, journeyed in relays to the Brooklyn waterfront leisure spot over a three-day period. The guests sat down to a lavish if unimaginative set menu of antipasti, spaghetti, scaloppine, artichokes, roast chicken, salad, fruit, coffee and sweets. The official beverage was mineral water, a euphemism for bootlegged wine, beer and spirits.

The event had ostensibly been sponsored by the 'Maritime Society of Sciacca' (a town in Sicily) to raise donations for its annual August street festival. The organisers chalked up a record sale of 5,000 tickets for the festivities. However, police estimated the number of guests at more than 20,000, and they did not seem entirely convinced that the object was solely to gather donations for the religious feast day. The police were taking no chances, the memory still fresh of what had transpired in the Nuova Villa Tammaro at another get-together of Italian Americans, less than four months prior to the bacchanalia now in progress. On the first day of banqueting, a squad of detectives stormed the restaurant and ordered everyone to line up against the walls. A body search yielded five loaded pistols, a negligible haul considering the numbers and profiles of those in attendance. Moreover, their owners were found to be in possession of legitimate firearms permits, and hence no action could be taken. A police guard was put on the door to keep a watchful eye on activities. This included detectives from New York's gun squad, a unit that had been set up in response to the recent spate of gangland killings.

The NYPD's suspicions were well founded for, under cover of staging a charity fundraiser, hundreds of guests from the criminal underworld had come to Coney Island to pay homage to New York's new boss of bosses. During those heady three days of feasting, Maranzano seemed to have truly crowned himself the ruling monarch. Every afternoon a fresh contingent of mobsters arrived at the restaurant bearing tribute in the form of envelopes stuffed with cash, which they placed on a tray before their anointed capo.

Lower Manhattan's Little Italy of the 1930s was a warren of tenements, rusted fire escapes and narrow, cobbled streets that echoed with the cries of pushcart vendors, not unlike the working-class neighbourhoods of some of the cities in the old country. Maranzano did not deem it a worthy base of operations for a man of his station. The self-appointed boss of bosses therefore relocated his headquarters to a luxurious suite of offices, occupying a floor of the midtown New York Central Building under the name of the 'Eagle Building Corporation'. Had Maranzano taken a watchful look about from his ninth-floor eyrie, he might have caught sight of the pockmarked, brooding face of Lucky Luciano, reflecting on a piece of news passed on to him by a former Maranzano lieutenant: the boss of bosses had contracted the cold-blooded Irish killer Vincent 'Mad Dog' Coll to take out Luciano in a machine-gun attack. Luciano reasoned that betrayal added to ingratitude was a rather shabby way of repaying a friend for having put his arch-enemy Masseria out of the way. For his part, Maranzano feared that the ruthless Luciano had come to represent a threat to his authority, and he was right. The received wisdom in some Mafia circles is that Luciano had planned all along to purge the two chieftains, who were frustrating his plans to reorganise the Cosa Nostra.

The young Sicilian Luciano was well versed in procedures for dealing with traitors. On 10 September 1931, four men brandishing pistols stormed into the anteroom of Maranzano's Park Avenue offices, ordering seven men and the secretary, Frances Samuels, to line up facing the wall. One of the gunmen kept watch on the terrified men and woman, while the other three kicked open the door to Maranzano's private chambers. There was an angry exchange of insults, followed by the sound of blows and, finally, a volley of shots.

The four gunmen dashed out of the suite and the seven clients, who had been waiting to see Maranzano, lost no time in making a break for the street. Samuels stood trembling at her desk for a moment and then rushed into her boss's office. She found Maranzano slumped in a chair, his body riddled with bullets and punctured with stab wounds.

Lucky Luciano was 34 years old, with another three decades of life before him, when he was proclaimed the supreme Mafia boss of New York and, for that matter, of the United States. Disposing of Masseria and Maranzano had effectively ended the rule of what Luciano and his associates disparagingly referred to as the 'Mustache Pete' faction, a reference to the older generation of Sicilian gangsters. Eschewing the title *capo di tutti capi*, which he considered too divisive and likely to provoke rivalries among the Mafia families, Luciano devised a scheme to be spearheaded by the next generation, the so-called 'Young Turks', who would run the rackets in a more efficient and businesslike manner.

A FAMILY AFFAIR

The entire panoply of New York's unlawful activities fell into the hands of the Commission, as it came to be known, a power-sharing arrangement of mobsters with Luciano at the summit. This was in reality a national syndicate made up of seven factions: New York City's 'Five Families' – 'Given Gotham's importance, each of the five bosses of the New York families received a seat'[12] – plus two others. It would have been inconceivable to deny Al Capone a place at the table, so he was appointed representative for Chicago, while Stefano 'the Undertaker' Magaddino, the longest-serving boss in the history of the American Mafia, was made a member for Buffalo, New York.[13] The core New York City group was in the hands of Luciano himself (head of the Genovese family), Tom Gagliano (head of the Lucchese family) and Giuseppe Profaci (head of the Colombo family), with Joseph Bonanno (head of the Bonanno family) and Vincent Mangano (head of the Gambino family) representing the Brooklyn section. Their average age was 37, all were Sicilian-born and, as this was a family enterprise, they shared power over every facet of New York's criminal life, from bootlegging and prostitution to drugs, gambling and labour-union racketeering.

Throughout his long career, Luciano had conducted his criminal activities in a supremely astute fashion. His nickname, 'Lucky', reflected an ability to overcome all challenges, as well as to dispose of all challengers to his multiple and varied business interests. Then, suddenly, his luck ran out, or so it would seem. After years of investigation and an all-night jury session, at 5.25 a.m. on 7 June 1936, Luciano was convicted, along with eight co-defendants, on 62 counts of forced prostitution. This was, in fact, one of his minor rackets. The special prosecutor Thomas E. Dewey, presiding at the trial, handed him a 30- to 50-year sentence, a record for such an offence.[14] This was for Luciano particularly vexing: after all, had he not the previous year ordered the execution of Dutch Schultz, the mobster who had proposed having Dewey murdered? Luciano had vetoed the latter operation, which he feared would have triggered an all-out police crackdown on Mafia operations. Schultz threatened to go ahead with his plan, unheeding of Luciano's objections, and he suffered the ultimate penalty for defying orders.[15]

Luciano spent several years at the Clinton Correctional Facility in Dannemora, known as the 'Siberia' of New York's jails, tucked away in a small town 320 miles north of New York City.[16] A few influential friends later arranged for their boss to be transferred to more congenial facilities in open-prison-type accommodation. Even at this distance from his centre of operations and behind bars, and years later in his Italian exile, Luciano managed to keep his businesses running on an even keel. No one dared challenge Luciano's power over the New York syndicate.

After Dewey granted him parole and had him deported to Italy in 1946, Luciano slipped away and flew to Cuba to attend a summit of US Mafia bosses. Dewey's decision was granted after taking into account Luciano's 'wartime services' to the country. The story goes that Luciano's mobsters had, in 1942, sabotaged the French liner SS *Normandie*, at that time the world's largest vessel, which had been seized by US authorities at New York Harbor two days after war broke out in Europe in September 1939. According to this interpretation of events, this act of arson was designed to look like 'enemy' sabotage, and carried out precisely in order to secure Luciano's release from prison, in a diabolically contrived deal whereby the mob offered in exchange a guarantee that it would use its power over the local longshoremen's union to ensure that New York's docks remained safe from enemy interference for the duration of the war.

Luciano continued to exercise uncontested and, when deemed necessary, bloody authority over the mob. While attending the Havana conference, he ordered the assassination of Bugsy Siegel, a Jewish American gangster who had reputedly been one of the hit men in the Masseria and Maranzano killings. The mob suspected Siegel of pilfering funds from the Mafia coffers and squandering them on a gimmicky and money-losing hotel venture in Las Vegas.

Luciano spent his declining years in sybaritic comfort at a villa in Naples. From time to time, he cheerfully granted interviews to the press, in which he always eschewed the 'gangster' label, a slur he blamed on Dewey. Luciano collapsed and died of a heart attack in 1962, at the age of 64, while waiting to board a flight at Naples airport, destination unknown.

Organised crime continued to prosper in post-Prohibition New York, only some lateral thinking was required to ensure the Mafia had an enhanced income from the rackets. It could still rely on its cornerstone businesses: illegal gambling in its various guises, prostitution, drugs, money laundering and illegal-immigrant trafficking, to name some of its more lucrative activities. But as they built up their range of interests in the 1930s, especially after the repeal of Prohibition in December 1933, the mobsters sought to expand their power base in the organised-labour movement.

The mob held an iron grip on the union of dock workers that was active on the Manhattan and Brooklyn waterfronts, the International Longshoremen's Association (ILA). Elected union leaders were powerless to make a move without the Mafia's consent. Bribes and illegal payments exchanged hands on a regular basis between corrupt union leaders and shipping companies, and a cut would be forthcoming as a matter of course on the value of all cargo loaded or unloaded across New York Harbor. The mobsters also kept a stranglehold on the construction and garbage-removal industries. With regard to the latter, each borough was answerable to one of the Five Families, a structure that survived and continued to prosper well after Luciano disappeared from the scene. The modus operandi was to send the workers out on strike for higher pay, and then pressurise political bosses to give in to their demands, which translated into higher fees collected from the unions.

The 'numbers game' was one of the most widespread rackets of its day. The game put down roots in Harlem, though some of the bosses were of Italian or Jewish origin. It was a form of lottery in which punters placed small bets amounting to a handful of change on three numbers of their choosing, with the chance of a pay-off of 600 to one. In the 1930s, the winning numbers were drawn from the New York Clearing House; later they came from the New York Stock Exchange. When the racket was uncovered by the police and Wall Street officials, the winning numbers were shifted to horse-racing results.

The numbers game was one of the few gambling operations that was not controlled exclusively by Italian or Jewish gangsters. The Harlem numbers kingpin was Casper Holstein, a native of the West Indies and a colourful character who kept the authorities at bay by treading a narrow and shadowy ridge between legitimate and criminal business activities. He was considered the founding father of the numbers racket in Harlem. In this sense his legacy lives on, for the racket remains a popular form of gambling in many communities across the United States. There was, to be sure, a Mafia-operated Italian lottery as well, run by the Morello family capo Joseph 'Bananas' Bonanno, who ruthlessly expanded the business to encompass his entire Brooklyn turf.

It was Samuel Seabury, the presiding magistrate at the Jimmy Walker investigation, who identified New York's huge garment industry as another of the city's most deeply penetrated Mafia operations, along with businesses like the Fulton Fish Market and the docks. In his days of grandeur before being sent to the electric chair at Sing Sing prison, Louis 'Lepke' Buchalter had managed to infiltrate every part of Manhattan's clothing trade, from fur to leather, millinery and shirts. This led to frequent conflicts between hit men sent in by employers to squash union activity and union gangsters hired to retaliate against the bosses. These clashes reached the proportions of open warfare in the years immediately after the First World War. By the 1930s the Mafia had begun moving in to 'restore order' in the area of midtown Manhattan known as the Garment District. These were rich pickings for the gangsters, as this 18-block area supported more than 100,000 manufacturing jobs and produced nearly three-quarters of all women's and children's apparel in the United States. In the Depression years, Seventh Avenue stood for fashion in the same way that Wall Street symbolised finance.

Lepke and his henchmen took labour-extortion tactics in this industry to new heights: 'Instead of simply using their sluggers and gunmen to terrorize labor unions during strike periods, Lepke worked them directly into the unions and, by threat, violence and murder took control of one local after another.'[17] The Mafia was thus able to extract up to $10 million a year thanks to the infiltration of the garment industry.

On taking office on New Year's morning, 1934, New York's diminutive mob-busting mayor, Fiorello La Guardia, waded into this hornets' nest of organised crime, vice and gang violence. As far as the Little Flower was concerned, the city he had been called to govern was in a state of war with the mobsters. La Guardia lost no time in serving notice that his aim was to eradicate criminality from every nook and corner of New York City life. The man the mayor brought in to do the job was the tough and incorruptible Lewis J. Valentine, who later that year replaced Major General John F. O'Ryan as police commissioner.[18] O'Ryan resigned after a series of head-on exchanges with the mayor over La Guardia's alleged interference with policing tactics, a row it was said the mayor had himself instigated as an excuse to get rid of his truculent police chief. Valentine was famed as an implacable foe of corruption, especially within the NYPD. By 1938, he had personally sacked 221 police officers, while another 70 who were under suspicion of corrupt activities committed suicide.

The first year of La Guardia's administration saw a number of officers gunned down in clashes with the mobsters. In November 1934 Valentine reached the end of his tether when, in an identity parade at Police Headquarters, he came face-to-face with a particularly objectionable killer named Harry Strauss. The commissioner flew into a rage over Strauss's contemptuous smirk and even more so his natty suit and tie, topped by a velvet-collar Chesterfield overcoat. 'When you meet men like Strauss,' Valentine barked at his detectives, 'draw quickly and shoot accurately. Don't be afraid to muss 'em up. Blood should be smeared all over that velvet collar.'[19]

La Guardia heartily endorsed his commissioner's no-holds-barred attack on police killers. One year after taking office, the mayor made an impassioned pitch to bolster the NYPD's morale in an address to the annual Patrolmen's Benevolent Association's reception at Madison Square Garden: 'This is no time for sentimentality, this is no time for coddling crooks,' La Guardia proclaimed to a crowd of 22,000 police officers and their families. 'I say this: the war is on, and you cannot expect that a police officer is going to stand up and be shot down by a cowardly crook without defending his own life.'[20]

THE LITTLE FLOWER AND THE SLEDGEHAMMER

Sittman & Pitt, the Brooklyn-based manufacturer of coin-operated machines, was doing New York no favours when in 1891 it developed the precursor to the slot machine. The demise of bootlegged alcohol brought pressure on the Mafia to come up with money-spinner alternatives to the jewel in their criminal crown. In a very few years after the repeal of Prohibition, the 'slots', as they were known to the gambling public, proliferated in New York casinos, restaurants and even corner shops. This soon enabled the mobsters to pocket up to $60,000 a day from the slots racket, in total an illegal take of more than $20 million per year.

La Guardia loathed the slots as a particularly odious form of 'mechanical larceny', and the man behind this operation, the cunning Mafia boss Frank Costello, was targeted as his number-one enemy. Costello was not one to sully his hands, much less his expensively tailored pinstripe suits, with his enemies' blood. He instead acted as a smooth mediator in the Mafia's relations with officialdom, at least that segment of the police and politicians who were not disinclined to slip their hands under the table. Costello astutely took pains to keep aloof from hands-on criminal activities, and in this he proved an extremely slippery catch.

The mayor instructed police commissioner Valentine to open a vigorous offensive against Costello and his slot-machine enterprise, but the wily mafioso was one step ahead of his pursuers. When the NYPD staged a series of raids to confiscate slots, arresting hundreds of their operators and assorted criminals working the gambling rackets, Costello quickly had thousands of his machines converted into sweets dispensers. Following the wholesale seizure of slot machines at the Mills Novelty Company, at the time the world's leading manufacturer of slots, the company management obtained a court injunction against confiscation unless it could be proved the machines were used for gambling. A chewing-gum dispenser clearly did not fall into this category.

La Guardia was not one to be daunted by trifles like a court order, especially when the ruling ran contrary to his plans. In February 1934, the mayor strode angrily into the West 100th Street police station and announced that under the authority vested in him by the City Charter, he was sitting as a magistrate to take charge of the battle against the slot-machine racket. The first case heard was that of a woman charged with keeping a slot machine in her husband's shop. La Guardia labelled this a typical example of criminal exploitation of humble shopkeepers. He dismissed the woman in her husband's custody, until she could provide $5 bail. Then he turned to the police officers in the room and thundered, 'Get busy and arrest these racketeers!'[21] In a message to the general public, a month later the Little Flower sponsored a free exhibition of seized slot machines in the concourse of Rockefeller

Center. The purpose was to impress upon visitors that he meant business, in line with the NYPD's anti-slots slogan: 'You can't win.'

The mayor took his case to New York State's Supreme Court and then, in early May 1934, he expressed his delight on receiving a 'splendid' piece of news from the equally 'splendid officials' of the court, who backed his drive to rid New York of slot machines. In the end, New York State governor Herbert H. Lehman's enactment of the Esquirol Bill made it unnecessary for La Guardia to press his case, for the state legislature outlawed the slots and dismissed the Mills Novelty Company's suit.

Valentine immediately dispatched a fleet of Department of Sanitation trucks to round up the remaining machines. These were summarily dumped into Long Island Sound, where to this day they rest on the ocean floor. But not before La Guardia, with his irrepressible flair for theatrics, posed for the press at the waterfront, smashing up a pile of slots with a sledgehammer. Once the machines had been shoved from a scow off Eton Point, La Guardia told the assembled reporters, 'I'm going to City Hall to swing the sledge there. There's one reason why the politicians want to get control of the City of New York, and those hopes will go where the slot machines are going now.'[22]

La Guardia's crackdown on the one-armed bandits was hailed as one of the most spectacular triumphs of his early years in office. The mayor was notably less successful in his efforts to nail Costello, who quietly shifted his slot-machine operations to New Orleans, where they were promoted as 'charitable games'. Louisiana's flamboyant state governor Huey Long greeted Costello with open arms as well as pockets, in a deal that included a 10 per cent cut of the takings for the notorious Long, a politician who treated the state as his personal fiefdom.

Costello carried on wheeling and dealing for nearly another four decades, most of the time from his Waldorf-Astoria penthouse, in which he died of a heart attack in 1973 at the age of 82, having outlived La Guardia as well as Valentine by a quarter of a century. Informed gossip has it that for many years Costello was able to ply his trade unhindered thanks to the protection of FBI director J. Edgar Hoover, who was known to be an incorrigible racing addict. Through his agents, Hoover would place sizeable bets on horses, specifically those that Costello singled out as 'sure winners'. The mobster slipped his racetrack tips to Hoover through the good offices of newspaper columnist Walter Winchell, a mutual friend: 'There is considerable evidence from FBI agents about how pleasant Hoover could be after he had a satisfactory day at the track.'[23]

Having rid New York of the despised slot machines, La Guardia next trained his sights on the numbers operation. The New York policy racket was estimated to net the Mafia bosses in the region of $100 million a year, equivalent to roughly a sixth of the city's annual budget.[24] In Harlem, the Lower East Side, the Bronx and parts of Brooklyn, hundreds of small mom-and-pop tobacconists and grocers acted as collectors. They received the daily take on sales made by runners and passed the money on to a controller, who ran a district for the banker. In many instances, these corner stores made as much of an income from tickets as they did from retail merchandise sold off the shelf.

The business was put on a 'legitimate' footing by mobster Dutch Schultz, who made certain winners were paid in full at 600 to one, instead of deducting a cut for the controller. Before Schultz moved in on the racket, it was not uncommon for the controller to refuse to pay winners in full. Those who raised their voice in protest quite often had an unpleasant encounter at night with a truncheon or pair of knuckledusters.

La Guardia found the numbers a much tougher nut to crack than the slot machines, given the vast number of small operators involved. Ever the undaunted campaigner, the mayor unleashed his attack dog Valentine into the fray, with instructions to bring in as many offenders as he could round up. By March 1935, the police commissioner was able to report more than 7,000 arrests. To La Guardia's dismay, only a third of those who were hauled before the courts were convicted of their crimes, and the vast majority were given suspended sentences due to a lack of hard evidence. Fewer than 300 were handed short prison terms. La Guardia summoned up every device at his fingertips to bring the policy racket to book. He even requested the New York Stock Exchange to publish its daily sales totals only in round numbers, to prevent the racketeers using the last digits as the basis for their calculations. But his efforts were to prove of limited avail, for the numbers operation survives as a rival to the legitimate state lotteries and flourishes in New York today, as it did in the 1930s.

New York's fruit-and-vegetable market might seem an implausible target for La Guardia's anti-crime offensive. Yet this is where he struck next and it was also where the saturnine figure of Ciro Terranova appeared on the mayor's radar. Terranova was a leading member of the Morello gang, the oldest of New York's Mafia clans, pre-dating the setting up of the Five Families. As such, he lacked none of the bloodthirsty qualities of his brethren, though he preferred to take a more judicious approach to the business of dispensing Mafia justice. The day Joe Masseria was gunned down in a Coney Island restaurant, Terranova was happy to act as chauffeur for the killers, and crafty enough to abstain from taking part in the actual shooting.[25] That was very much Terranova's style. His interest lay more in manipulating the city's fresh-produce market to his personal gain, as a result of which he earned the nickname of the 'Artichoke King' of New York.

Terranova ran a straightforward swindle: his agents purchased crates of California artichokes – a delicacy for the city's Italian American community – for $6 a crate and sold them on to New York wholesalers at a 30 to 40 per cent mark-up. This was not a petty rip-off operation, since Valentine estimated that the racket netted Terranova and his cohorts upwards of $1 million a year. Retailers were hit with the usual surcharge above the wholesale price but they were terrified to stand up to Terranova's gangsters. Those few who mustered the courage to defy the extortionists soon came to regret their folly. Punishment was usually meted out in the form of a smashed stall and a personal roughing up for good measure.

On a bitterly cold December morning in 1935, La Guardia marched into the fray. At 6.50 a.m., two policemen sounded a trumpet fanfare in front of the Bronx Terminal Market, just as the shutters were going up on the stalls. At that moment the Little Flower, sheathed in his woollen overcoat, scarf and felt fedora, mounted the tailgate of a lorry to read out a proclamation outlawing the sale of artichokes, full stop. The ban would remain in force, he told the shivering crowd of greengrocers huddled around bonfires, until the mayor was satisfied that 'free and orderly wholesaling' of artichokes was restored to New York markets. Even as La Guardia spoke, police radio cars were receiving orders to post the edict wherever artichokes were sold in public markets.

The day La Guardia issued his proclamation, Terranova had little more than two years of life left in him. He suffered a massive stroke in 1938, at the early age of 49, though it might have come as consolation to him that he was the only one of the four Terranova brothers to die in bed. Ciro cut a pathetic figure in his final days, having been declared *persona non grata* in New York City. The once mighty Artichoke King was arrested for vagrancy whenever he was spotted roaming the streets of Manhattan. He was forced to surrender his Westchester County mansion in 1937, after which he took up residence in East Harlem. Shortly before his death, the dethroned monarch of the artichoke market claimed to be living on borrowed money.

But there were others waiting in the wings, notably Terranova's relative and acknowledged successor, Joseph Castaldo, who stepped into the Artichoke King's shoes even while the latter continued to draw breath. In February 1936 La Guardia had five men, including Castaldo, indicted on violation of anti-trust laws. This led to the 'artichoke trial', which collapsed in deadlock when, after 24 hours of deliberation, the jurors were unable to deliver a verdict. Castaldo walked free, but what the mayor did manage to achieve with his embargo was the closure of the Union Pacific Produce Company, which had been identified as the culprit behind the inflated sales of artichokes in New York markets.

The challenge of combating New York's organised crime syndicates was no less daunting than attempting to plug the proverbial dyke. If La Guardia fell short of his goal of cleansing the city of its mobsters, it can be said in his defence that he achieved better results in his efforts than any of his predecessors. During the La Guardia years, the Mafia families were unremittingly harassed and their criminal activities took an unprecedented battering, but they came through it far from defeated. The Five Families of the 1930s still dominate the New York rackets and their criminal activities continue to prosper, with the difference that today they have been redirected towards more sophisticated and opaque businesses. Gambling, loan-sharking, drugs and prostitution are still under tight Mafia control, only now the emphasis is on white-collar fraud, which earns the racketeers billions of dollars in stock market operations, the insurance industry and other financial services.

Although the rampant gangsterism that infected a multitude of the city's businesses should not be played down, New York in the 1930s was beset by more pressing threats than the numbers game and overpriced artichokes. As a result of the Great Depression, the city's credit rating had all but collapsed and officials were tearing out their hair trying to devise ways of raising the revenue needed to keep the city and its institutions afloat. New York City faced the spectre of joining the nearly 5,000 local governments in the United States that defaulted on their financial obligations between 1930 and 1939. The Depression had brought massive unemployment to the city, creating a vicious circle of a drastic reduction in tax receipts with a commensurate sharp rise in the need to provide basic social services, especially welfare payments, for the jobless. Those at City Hall tasked with formulating a plan for economic recovery found themselves swimming against the tide: property values continued to spiral downwards, year after year; municipal revenues were inadequate to cover the costs of spending required to stimulate growth and create jobs, and the credit markets remained hermetically shut to New York City bonds.

The Tammany clique La Guardia turned out of office in 1934 had left New York burdened with a $31 million budget deficit, almost a triviality when compared with the city's $82 million in debt obligations – equivalent to $14 billion in today's money – due and payable in the first year of the new administration. A month after the mayor took the oath of office, city chamberlain Adolf Augustus Berle Jr travelled to the state capital, Albany, to warn the lawmakers that New York City's fiscal crisis was tantamount to a full-blown financial emergency. Berle presented this $113 million sword hanging over New York's head as justification for quick passage of the Emergency Economy Bill, which would empower the city to enact swingeing job and wage cuts and bring in new taxes. Berle was a member of Roosevelt's 'Brain Trust' and therefore provided City Hall with the crucial direct link to the federal coffers.[26]

La Guardia threw himself fast and furious into the task of pulling New York back from the financial abyss. The mayor's resolve to rescue Gotham gave some reassurance to the markets. This was reflected in the yield on the city's long-term bonds, which gained seven percentage points in the first two months of his administration.

Balancing the budget was a prerequisite for obtaining federal loans and grants. Washington had so far refused to release the funds because the city had failed to demonstrate an ability to put its financial house in order. Even before La Guardia took office, he was forced to endure some finger-wagging, on a visit to Washington, from secretary of the interior Harold L. Ickes, the man in charge of the Public Works Administration (PWA).[27] Ickes warned La Guardia that no money would be forthcoming until he went to New York and balanced the books. The $132 million loan that the city sought was only marginally less than the $137 million in taxes Tammany had failed to collect in the year before La Guardia's election victory (the total was $2.6 million in 1927). New taxes and cutbacks were the touchstones of City Hall's hotly contested Emergency Economic Bill, which, after months of political vicissitudes and a good deal of acrimonious debate, was at last drafted into law by New York governor Herbert H. Lehman in April 1934.

It was the single most far-reaching piece of economic legislation in New York State's history, but a less uncompromising programme would never have succeeded in putting the city's financial affairs on an even keel. Banks now looked more favourably on requests for lower borrowing rates, thus providing the catalyst for increased bond sales. The Board of Estimate stepped in quickly to implement a draconian series of cuts to costs. Hundreds of civil servants lost their jobs – many, it must be said, were sinecures owed to nothing more than political patronage. Before the board finished wielding its pruning knife, a total of 1,225 jobs had been trimmed from the civil service payroll. The next step was a bid to introduce a 0.5 per cent tax on businesses with a gross turnover of more than $10,000 a year. Shortly after a meeting with Lehman, Berle and La Guardia got their way when the state legislature passed a measure approving this new tax and others as a means of helping to balance the budget.

The words of Michael J. Cruise might well have fallen on sceptical ears when, in a meeting of City Hall officials in August 1935, the city clerk solemnly pronounced the Great Depression 'over'. Cruise issued his declaration upon hearing the Board of Aldermen's 1936 budget, which asked for a $7,485 increase over the current year's $618,155 allowance. Cruise insisted that now was the time to restore pre-Depression salaries to those City Hall workers who had voluntarily accepted cuts 'during the emergency' (La Guardia set the example, having his salary reduced by half). It goes without saying that this entailed a $340 increase in Cruise's own wages, which would boost his earnings to $10,840 a year. In fairness, Cruise also suggested that salaries be raised for other clerks, examiners and stenographers, as well as for sergeants-at-arms, whose numbers had been slashed from 12 to three. While lodging the request, Cruise failed to notice budget director Rufus E. McGahen tighten his grip on the blue pencil he had been twirling in his fingers.

New York was far from out of the woods, but Cruise's confidence was by no means as preposterous as it might seem. By the mid-1930s just the vaguest hint of buoyancy could be detected in New York. People strolling along the streets of midtown might have been heard humming the tune of Cole Porter's 'Take Me Back to Manhattan', whose lyrics sang out an unabashed zest for Gotham.[28] The song was composed for the playwright's hit musical *The New Yorkers* in 1930, and then revived for another of his shows, *Anything Goes*, which took Broadway by storm in November 1934 and whose 420 performances made it one of the longest-running musicals of the decade. Despite the impact of the Depression on people's disposable income, including that of theatregoers, the comedy was a nightly sell-out, helped in no small measure by praise from the influential *New York Times* theatre critic Brooks Atkinson: 'hilarious and dynamic entertainment [...] a dashing score [...] a thundering good musical'.[29]

In stark contrast to the embryonic gaiety of Broadway, New York remained firmly in the grip of widespread unemployment, which continued to hover implacably over the 20 per cent mark. In addition to the jobless crisis, the city's benefits agencies were staring at bankruptcy; the budget deficit stood at a record $30 million; tenants were being evicted from their homes at a historic rate and the Mafia was sucking the lifeblood out of a wide range of businesses. Municipal revenues declined sharply when property owners found themselves unable to pay taxes. The city was forced to borrow on anticipated tax collections, piling up a public debt almost equal to the federal debt for the entire country. This created a vicious circle, in which New York's credit rating took a hammering as a result of increased borrowings. On the home-owner and tenant level, it was not unusual for the property crisis to result in scenes of street violence:

> In the Sunnyside area of middle Queens, eviction notices were fought by collective action. Doors were barricaded with barbed wire and sandbags. Householders bombarded sheriffs with pepper and flour. More than 60 percent of Sunnyside's home owners lost their houses through foreclosure. Families began doubling up in houses and apartments.[30]

The Little Flower had inherited the worst of the Depression years, and his predicament was aggravated by Tammany corruption and growing social unrest in the city's poorest neighbourhoods. Even the indefatigable Fiorello La Guardia could not hope to take on these enormous challenges single-handed, and he knew it. Fortunately, help was on the way.

5

ALL THAT JAZZ

n the late 1920s, Colonel H. Edmund Bullis of the US Army came up with an original proposal for cracking down on the nation's speakeasies. Bullis was executive secretary of the National Association for Chemical Defense. He was therefore acquainted with the latest developments in chemical warfare, one of which inspired him to suggest it as a substitute for padlocks. He explained that by spraying a speakeasy with a certain substance, the premises would be rendered uninhabitable for at least a month, such was the extreme irritation caused to eyes, nose, throat and skin. Bullis, who paradoxically served as secretary general of the International Committee for Mental Hygiene (ICMH), told a congressional committee that, in his view, this was 'the most effective and at the same time the most humane of weapons'.[1]

The authorities declined Bullis's proposal to launch a chemical attack on the speakeasies. Yet the colonel's plan mirrored the deep frustration felt by the ominously named Bureau of Prohibition about its failure to persuade a vast segment of the population to abide by a federal law.

The proliferation of speakeasies went hand-in-glove with an upsurge in crime and violence, as rival gangs battled for a bigger share of the lucrative alcohol trade. Nowhere was Prohibition-linked criminality more rampant than in Chicago, where, by the late 1920s, underworld killings topped 400 a year. Brooklyn boy Al Capone left New York for Chicago in 1920 at the invitation of fellow mobster Johnny Torrio, to help him run the bootlegging racket. He became Torrio's right-hand man, until his mentor was seriously wounded in an assassination attempt and fled to New York, leaving Capone to don the mantle of Chicago's chief racketeer. Capone built his 'Chicago Outfit' into the city's biggest importer and distributor of bootlegged alcohol. This was his chief source of income and he was not prepared to release his hold on the illicit trade without a bloody fight.

Police were being gunned down at a horrific rate: 40 per cent of Chicago's police officers were killed between 1920 and 1939. In 1928 the entire force, at least those who weren't on the Mafia's payroll, declared all-out war on the gangsters. The driving force behind the violence was the mobsters' resolve to protect at all costs their bootlegging racket. The city authorities adopted the strategy that by eliminating the client base you strike a death blow to the suppliers. In that year, 1928, the Chicago police launched a wave of raids on the city's bars that effectively put the speakeasies out of action. This marked a hard-won victory for the rule of law, but the gangsters and the speakeasy bosses (not to overlook the drinking public) were not the only ones to suffer.

Chicago's loss was New York's gain. The speakeasies' moneyed patrons demanded more from a night out than a mere furtive and expensive boozing session, especially if their carousing carried the risk of spending the wee hours in a police station. People expected to be entertained as well as watered. The Prohibition years overlapped with the rise of the hot jazz groups of the Roaring Twenties, along with a general awakening to this style of music and what it had to express. The early performers from New Orleans and the Midwest soon found their way to Chicago and New York, in search of national acclaim and the big money. Their music was a fusion of ragtime, Negro spirituals, blues and other genres, which came to be known as Dixieland. Small jazz ensembles became nightly features at Chicago's drinking clubs, fuelling the steady flow of alcohol with the beat of their drums and bouncy pianos, clarinets, guitars and trumpets.

The abrupt closure of the Chicago speakeasies left many young musicians jobless and, having had a taste of the big time, they could only ply their trade in one other big-time spot. Musical unemployment tempted many jazz players, almost all of them white, to board the Greyhound 'Supercoach' for the 700-mile journey to New York City, where a new style of music was being born: in the 1930s the jazz age gave way to the age of swing.

SWING AROUND THE CLOCK

The emergence of the big-band music of Duke Ellington and Benny Goodman, to name but two of the great bandleaders who dominated the New York dance stage in the 1930s, by no means resembled a Darwinian progression in the evolution of jazz. Those who seek a connecting line between the roots of jazz and the later big-band sound do so in vain, for the link is far from clear. During the jazz age, most of the big names were motivated by solo performances. They did not stand as leaders before great orchestras and they were more focused on improvisation than on orchestration. Their primary interest was the interplay between individual instruments, not that between sections. But it was almost inevitable that the big bands would take New York by storm. The 1930s was when jazz began to command audiences and attract figures who were to become the greats of the genre. Names like Artie Shaw, Jimmy Dorsey and Count Basie conjure up visions of a glittering bandstand, faultlessly attired musicians, glamorous female vocalists, dramatic lighting and a spectacle whose sound and sight dazzled its audiences.

The move to a new idiom of dance music, one that brought a historical break with the small combos of the past, was already in the making when these musical refugees from Chicago journeyed eastwards. Performers like guitarist Eddie Condon, bandleader Muggsy Spanier, pianist Joe Sullivan and the immortal drummer Gene Krupa found themselves in a city crippled by the Depression yet overflowing with musical energy. Harlem, between 118th and 142nd streets, boasted nearly 40 clubs, from the Alhambra Theatre, whose upstairs ballroom hosted evenings with the renowned Billie Holiday, to the Yeah Man Club, where in 1929 the 15-year-old future saxophone virtuoso Lonnie Simmons, with 50 cents in his pocket, turned up from South Carolina in search of a job. With this impressive array of venues dotting a strip less than one mile long, it was inevitable that New York should come to support the largest community of jazz musicians in the world.

By the end of the 1920s jazz represented a thriving component, if not the very lifeblood, of the New York entertainment world. In 1927 hundreds queued every night at the Warners' Theater in Broadway and 52nd Street, in a scramble for tickets to see the first 'talkie', bearing the appropriate title of *The Jazz Singer*. The film marked Al Jolson's screen debut, in which he played a young Jewish New York boy, Jakie Rabinowitz, who in defiance of his synagogue cantor father fulfils his ambition to become a jazz performer – a story based on Jolson's own life. Much of the film was still silent, though Jolson belted out several of his own jazz numbers, along with the Jewish hymn Kol Nidre. This liturgical song 'was received with rousing applause', wrote the film critic of the *New York Times*. Jolson was given a standing ovation at the premiere and came on stage afterwards to greet the audience, tears rolling down his cheeks. The film was modelled on New York playwright Samson Raphaelson's drama of the same name, which in turn was adapted from his short story 'The Day of Atonement'.

It was in the late 1920s that variations of jazz had proliferated in Harlem's nightspots, as well as further downtown in dance halls like the Roseland Ballroom, where New Yorkers wriggled, shimmied and jived to the Charleston, cakewalk and turkey trot. They were bending their knees and leaping high into the air to the rhythm of the 'Lindy Hop', named for aviator Charles Lindbergh's 1927 solo flight across the Atlantic, dubbed a 'hop' by the press. Jazz was everywhere and, for fun-seeking New York, there could be no more effective antidote to the Great Depression blues.

The Savoy Ballroom in Lenox Avenue was where couples headed to let off steam on the dance floor, known as 'the Track' because of the grooves worn through by the shuffling of dancing feet. The 1934 jazz standard 'Stompin' at the Savoy', a crowd-rousing number often played by Benny Goodman's big band, became the signature tune of the swing era. The Savoy was a huge rhythm factory, stretching from 140th to 141st streets, the place that set New York's jazz-fuelled tempo throughout the 1930s. On any given night, hundreds of couples packed the ballroom, swinging to the sounds of Duke Ellington, Ella Fitzgerald or Count Basie and inspiring the kind of gyrations that prompted the glamorous film star Lana Turner to call the club 'the home of happy feet'.

The Cotton Club, owned by mobster and convicted murderer Owney Madden, was New York's undisputed venue of choice for music. It was Harlem's acclaimed jazz Mecca, the spot where devotees gathered around tables laden with bootleg beer to listen to Duke Ellington, the master of showmanship. Ellington and his music are credited with masterminding the transition from 1920s jazz to 1930s swing, with Harlem as its focal point. Ellington had spent much of the jazz age in New York in the 1920s and was an enthusiastic advocate of the new wave, as expressed in a stanza from one of his featured tunes of 1932: 'It don't mean a thing if it ain't got that swing.'

Ellington secured the Cotton Club a top place in the New York jazz scene, and his name became a byword for the new style of music sweeping the clubs and dance halls of the city, as well as across the nation and abroad. This was the hub of Harlem nightlife, with the ironic twist that the club operated a 'whites only' policy, with bouncers at the door to deter any black people attempting to slip past the barrier. The management never specified how dark a customer's face needed to be before being turned away from the door. This bit of overt racism did not seem to trouble New York mayor Jimmy Walker, who was treated like visiting royalty on his regular visits to the club, where he was entertained by black musicians. Exceptions to the club's exclusionary policy were occasionally made to accommodate high-profile or wealthy black people, but even the performers' family members were assigned to a separate seating area. According to Langston Hughes, the black writer who became a leading figure of the Harlem Literary Renaissance: 'Harlem Negroes did not like the Cotton Club and never appreciated its Jim Crow policy in the very heart of the dark community.' He added that they also did not appreciate being gazed at by 'slumming whites' as if they were 'amusing animals in a zoo'.[2]

Ellington was himself far from happy with the Cotton Club's segregation policy, but he was well aware of his continuous rise to stardom at a time when many other entertainers were scratching about to make a living in the hard days of the Depression. The Cotton Club Band even featured in the 1930 film *Check and Double Check*, starring the blackface comedy duo Amos and

Andy. The following year Ellington became the first black bandleader in US history to be invited to the White House, where he was greeted by President Herbert Hoover.[3]

By 1933, Ellington's music had been eagerly taken up by European jazz fans. In that year the Ellington band embarked on what was to become a landmark foreign tour, playing at the London Palladium to audiences that one critic described as 'wildly enthusiastic'. So enthusiastic, in fact, that he was invited to give two extra concerts at the Trocadero, each night playing to a packed house of 4,300 fans. Afterwards, there was a complete breakdown of British phlegm when a clutch of frenzied admirers clung to Ellington's limousine as it left the concert.

The groundwork for this British jazz mania had been laid the previous year, albeit under different circumstances, when Ellington's fellow entertainer, the legendary trumpeter and vocalist Louis 'Satchmo' Armstrong, scored a triumph in performances in Britain and a number of European countries.[4] Armstrong's decision to embark on a tour abroad was partly driven by a desire to put some distance between himself and the mob. In Chicago, he fell afoul of some gangsters who had ordered him to go to New York the next day and play at Connie's Inn, a Harlem nightclub. With a gun pointed at his head, Armstrong had no choice but to acquiesce. However, the following morning he headed instead to his hometown of New Orleans, and from there he went to London, where he topped the bill at the Palladium, the first stop on what turned out to be an extended four-month tour of Europe.

And how the Europeans went for Satchmo's flamboyant charisma. On his visit to New York, the French architect Le Corbusier found himself in utter ecstasy after attending an Armstrong concert, eulogising what he had witnessed in the concert hall:

> Let's listen to Louis Armstrong on Broadway, the black Titan of the cry, of the apostrophe, of the burst of laughter, of thunder. He sings, he guffaws, he makes his silver trumpet spurt. He is mathematics, equilibrium on a tightrope. He is Shakespearean! [...] Nothing in our European experience can be compared to it.[5]

If the names Duke Ellington and the Cotton Club were regarded as synonymous by thousands of New York jazz enthusiasts, Louis Armstrong's realm was the Lenox Avenue club's competitor, Connie's Inn, located a few city blocks south in 7th Avenue. The venues both upheld a ban on black patrons and shared a heritage of murky links to the Mafia. Connie's Inn took its name from Conrad Immerman, one of three German immigrant brothers who had carved out lucrative vocations as bootleggers in their new country. They opened the club in 1923, in the halcyon days of the Roaring Twenties, along with their silent partner Dutch Schultz, the gangster who in 1935 was murdered for disobedience by his brother mobsters. That was the year before the club, which had taken a severe hammering in the Depression, as well as due to the repeal of Prohibition, moved its premises downtown and was eventually forced to shut its doors.

It is arguable that Harlem-born Thomas 'Fats' Waller achieved more than any of his contemporaries in spreading the gospel of the New York jazz scene to the American public. Waller was a regular attraction at Connie's Inn, where as a teenager he had been hired by the Immerman brothers as a delivery boy for a delicatessen business they ran in 125th Street. His early years paralleled those of Jakie Rabinowitz, portrayed by Al Jolson in *The Jazz Singer*, in that Waller had to overcome his clergyman father's opposition to his son taking up a musical career. The young Fats was not to be deterred: by the time he was six, the defiant Waller was to be found on Sunday mornings playing the harmonium to accompany his parents' singing at street-corner sermons in Harlem. Waller's genius was quickly recognised and he was soon performing as a soloist at Connie's Inn as well as with the house band. Waller was one of the most colourful artists in the Harlem jazz entourage of the 1930s, which says a lot in a world peopled by a raft of idiosyncratic characters. At the club, he would park his considerable bulk on a piano stool, a bottle of whiskey close at hand and a bowler hat or crumpled trilby perched on his head, as he flashed a pair of Eddie Cantor eyes as big as saucers at the audience. If by the end of the gig he found himself the worse for drink, which was often the case, rather than struggling to find his way home Waller would stumble across Seventh Avenue to a local flophouse or doss at the nearby Abyssinian Baptist Church.

Slapstick antics aside, it must not be forgotten that Waller, in collaboration with lyricist Andy Razaf, produced legendary compositions for New York stage revues, songs like 'Honeysuckle Rose' and the memorable 'Ain't Misbehavin'', which premiered in the musical *Hot Chocolates* (1929), the show in which Louis Armstrong made his Broadway debut.

Fats became a regular performer at Harlem rent parties, social festivities that were held during the Depression years. Solo musicians or groups would be hired to perform at these get-togethers, at which cash-strapped tenants would take up a collection to pay their rent. These Saturday-night revels often went on into the early hours of Sunday, and a halt was called to the jollity only when neighbours or the landlord threatened to call the police. The parties were advertised in the street by groups of youths passing out invitation cards. A typical one of the 1930s read:

> There'll be brown skin mammas
> High yallers, too
> And if you ain't got nothin' to do
> Come on up to Roy and Sadie's
> West 126th Street, Saturday night
> There'll be plenty of pig feet
> And lots of gin,
> Jus ring the bell
> And come on in.[6]

Many musicians, Fats Waller among them, found the rent party a useful venue for advancing their careers. It was at a more formal party at George Gershwin's Brooklyn home in 1934 that Waller got his big break. People were so captivated by his playing and singing that one of the guests, an executive of the RCA Victor record company, offered Fats a recording contract.

One evening Fats felt a revolver poked into his paunchy stomach. He found himself bundled into a black limousine, and for the better part of an hour, Waller thought his career had come to a premature end. On arrival at a fancy saloon, he was pushed toward a piano and told to play. Loudest in applause was a beefy man with an unmistakable scar: Al Capone was having a birthday party, and Fats Waller was a present from 'the boys'.

By the time of his death, brought on by alcohol-induced pneumonia in 1943 at the age of 39, Waller had triumphed in Europe, appeared in eight films, between 1930 and 1938, and composed prolifically for the Broadway stage. It can confidently be said that this jovial, corpulent native son of Harlem and its musical legacy was a leading precursor of modern jazz piano. Waller's output over the two decades of his short professional life was truly prodigious. His recordings alone numbered around 600; his name featured in many classical Broadway musicals and his beaming face appeared in many Hollywood films. His concerts abroad were hailed as tours de force. On the British stage his musical genius was in no way devalued by his habitual display of horseplay: 'In Scotland, wearing a Glengarry tartan, he dazzled the audience with a Harlem stride reworking of "Loch Lomond" and was brought back for ten curtain calls.'[7]

The swing era brought to prominence a number of black female vocalists, whose voices – at times purring and at others sheer dynamite – echoed across the nightclubs of Harlem. Singers like Ella Fitzgerald, heading the bill at the Savoy Ballroom with the Chick Webb Orchestra, or Ethel Waters, crooning at the Cotton Club, are remembered for songs still familiar more than 80 years later. Who today would not recognise the tune of 'A-tisket, a-tasket', whose lyrics were written by Fitzgerald in 1938, or 'Stormy Weather', first sung in 1933 by Waters at the Cotton Club?

The 26-year-old Chick Webb's big-band talent gained well-earned recognition in 1931, when his orchestra was hired as the Savoy Ballroom's house band. William James 'Count' Basie made New York his performing headquarters when he played at the Roseland Ballroom in 1937, and the following year engaged in a 'battle of the bands' with Webb at the Savoy. New York's music press pronounced Basie the winner at this event, in spite of Webb unveiling a secret weapon, in the person of Ella Fitzgerald. But the bandleader whose name will always be identified with the big-band music of that decade, and who by popular acclaim was crowned 'the King of Swing', is Benny Goodman.

Like many big-name musicians and vocalists of the New York jazz circuit Goodman was an outsider, born in the Chicago slums to poor Jewish immigrants from Poland. Unlike Fats Waller's, however, Goodman's father encouraged his son's musical ambitions, recognising in him the prodigy who was to give his first professional clarinet concert at the age of 12. Goodman is credited with having almost single-handedly brought off the transition from combo jazz to big-band swing. Wailing away on his bewitching clarinet, alongside virtuosos of genius like Gene Krupa on the drums and vibraphonist Lionel Hampton, Goodman set the swing era into motion at a pace that never slackened for a decade. He has been acclaimed as the bandleader who stood for the essence of the jazz clarinet, establishing standards which his peers struggled to match.

Goodman can claim the distinction of having presided over a defining moment in jazz history. New Orleans-style jazz was all the rage in New York up to the 1929 Crash, when for a large sector of the population it became synonymous with the unbridled decadence that had brought on the Wall Street debacle. It was around that time that record companies latched on to the word 'swing' as a marketing device aimed mainly at young audiences. Goodman, who had married into the ultra-genteel Vanderbilt family, came to be the envoy of this new white, middle-class dance music, which for the general public became the acceptable face of jazz.

In the summer of 1935 Goodman fired the starting gun on the swing era with an electrifying performance at the Palomar Ballroom in Los Angeles. The show drew a crowd of thousands to the concert hall and millions more who listened in to a live radio broadcast. The evening got off to an unpromising start: the audience was anything but impressed by the stock arrangements played in the first half. During the interval, Gene Krupa urged his bandleader to pull out hot swing numbers by Fletcher Henderson, the black pianist and songwriter who led one of New York's most popular bands – despite the fact that this was a predominantly white genre. The second half, with a little help from Henderson, Harlem's celebrated composer, brought down the house. Swing had become an overnight nationwide craze.

Goodman's Los Angeles performance placed swing in the limelight, but after three more years of spreading the gospel, he never expected to open the trade press to find a headline like this: 'The first formal swing concert in history. Short-hairs shag, long-hairs wag, walls sag, as Goodman's gang transforms ancient hall into modern swing emporium.'[8]

When Carnegie Hall on Seventh Avenue in midtown Manhattan opened its doors in 1891, the prestigious Italian Renaissance-style building showcased some of the most distinguished names in classical music, Pyotr Ilyich Tchaikovsky among them. Nearly half a century later the sedate concert hall – one might even venture to call it 'stuffy' – in 57th Street was swaying to the beat of the swing era.

A Benny Goodman concert at Carnegie Hall was the brainchild of the bandleader's publicist Wynn Nathanson, who put the idea forward mostly in the spirit of a media stunt to draw attention to his client. Goodman himself was worried that the proposal might be taken seriously, for this would take him down an untravelled road, making his the first jazz ensemble to appear on stage at Carnegie Hall. To the amazement of all, in late 1937 Nathanson was offered a contract for a session on 16 January 1938. In the days preceding the event, while Goodman and his band rehearsed in the hall to test its acoustics, the even more unexpected news was that tickets to the 2,760-seat hall had sold out weeks in advance.

On the night of the concert, a rather nervous Goodman began his performance with a version of Edgar Sampson's sweet and bouncy 'Don't Be that Way', which the audience found a bit lifeless, judging by the weak applause. Halfway through the number Gene Krupa, sensing the public's languor, suddenly let off a tremendous break on the drums that raised a tumultuous cheer from the crowd. Krupa's forelock tumbled across his eyes, the band fell into a groove, and the first half was saved by a rousing performance of Count Basie's 'One O'clock Jump'.

After that Martha Tilton, one of the few acclaimed white female jazz vocalists of the day, strutted onto the stage in a coquettish pink dress to sing 'Loch Lomond', a number that brought her back for five curtain calls. By now Goodman and his band had the house with them, and they knew it. When it came to the evening's climax, Goodman offered a belted-out rendition of Louis Prima's 'Sing, Sing, Sing', which virtually brought the house down. As the *New York Times* put it, 'Benny Goodman glorified swing music at Carnegie Hall.'[9]

It was a historic performance, after which most of the band, including Gene Krupa and Lionel Hampton, journeyed uptown to the Savoy to listen to Count Basie and Chick Webb slug it out on the bandstand. The rest of the group retired to a hotel room to work off nervous tension in a jam session that lasted until sunrise. As the ballroom lights dimmed at the Savoy and the lingering notes faded at that New York hotel-room jam session, swing had secured its place as the music of the 1930s. But events taking place in Europe would soon have people huddled round their radios to listen to news that had nothing to do with the latest dance tunes. This is how those carefree days of big-band gaiety were witnessed by one veteran jazz fan:

> I recall an evening in late summer of 1939, after a session at a place called Budd Lake where I first heard Artie Shaw and his wonderful orchestra. At the end of the evening Artie, his tenor man Tony Pastor and vocalist Billie Holiday repaired to Shaw's ancient Rolls-Royce. The trouble was, the car wouldn't start. They began pounding on the hood, kicking the tyres, swearing, threatening, but it just wouldn't start. As far as I know, the three of them may still be there. Driving home, I turned on the car radio to see how things were going in the outside world. The evening's main news item was that the next day, Sunday, 3 September 1939, Britain would consider herself at war with Germany. Thus did the 1930s end for all of us.[10]

LET'S FACE THE MUSIC

The lights were going out across Europe, but beneath the glittering marquees of Broadway the queues stretched round the block. It was a daily scramble to obtain tickets to the famed musicals of the 1930s. Throughout the last years of the Great Depression, with another world war on the horizon, Broadway remained a fixed point in a gathering storm. The prevailing spirit, more than ever, was one of a rousing 'Let's Face the Music and Dance', Irving Berlin's lead song for the 1936 film *Follow the Fleet*, which featured the celebrated dance duet of Fred Astaire and Ginger Rogers. An avalanche of famous musicals and revues served to distract audiences from their troubles, while also offering political commentary and social engagement: 'This is the Great

White Way, theatrical centre of America and wonder of the out-of-towner. Here midnight streets are more brilliant than noon, their crowds on ordinary evenings exceeding those of large town carnivals.'[11]

In good times and bad, Broadway reigned supreme, and it was ever thus:

> Our Broadway, ever changing, and yet the same old road, is perhaps our great historical monument, and the historical street of America by eminence [...] Thank heaven for old Broadway, noble type of American civilization, from the Battery to Harlem River, and may the ways of the city be as straight as the lines of its direction and as true to the march of the Providence of God.[12]

The allure of Broadway has not diminished in the nearly 150 years since these words were written by the nineteenth-century historian William L. Stone.

A subway ride to Broadway's Theater District took entertainment-starved New Yorkers into a magical world of escapism, a powerhouse of glamour unshaken by a decade of hardship and destitution, during which mighty banks and companies were toppled like houses of cards. The glittering thoroughfare's name figured in the titles of popular songs of the day: 'Broadway Rhythm', 'Your Broadway and My Broadway' and 'Broadway Melody', the last of which, from the 1929 play *The Broadway Melody*, treated audiences to Arthur Freed's upbeat lyrics: 'Broadway always wears a smile; / A million lights they flicker there; / a million hearts beat quicker there.' The type of entertainment the Depression-weary public sought was implicit in many of the titles: *Gay Divorce, Nymph Errant, Anything Goes, Jubilee, Red, Hot and Blue*.

Light-hearted musical comedy reached its moment of maximum splendour in the Great Depression and the plots did not always deal with romance. In 1937, the International Ladies' Garment Workers' Union (ILGWU) produced *Pins and Needles*, which brought to the stage union activism combined with scathing mockery of Hitler and Mussolini. A year later, the comedy team John Olsen and Harold Johnson premiered a slapstick lampoon of the growing fascist menace in Europe with *Hellzapoppin'*, a production in which Hitler makes an appearance, speaking in a Yiddish accent, and Mussolini is in blackface.

George and Ira Gershwin dominated the Broadway stage throughout the decade, turning out six productions in that period. The brothers started the ball rolling in 1930 with the political satire *Strike Up the Band*, a spoof that had the United States and Switzerland at war over high chocolate tariffs. That same year two of Broadway's most celebrated female performers, Ginger Rogers and Ethel Merman, starred in *Girl Crazy*. Merman's rendition of 'I Got Rhythm' never fails to set the feet tapping in dance-hall revivals. This was followed in 1931 by the political satire *Of Thee I Sing*, which became the longest running Broadway show of the 1930s and the first musical to win the Pulitzer Prize for drama.

Most memorable (and most frequently revived) of all Gershwin plays was *Porgy and Bess* from 1934, a work that marked a controversial departure from the light musicals of the past. This was in no way an attempt to set audiences laughing at the buffoonery of blockhead politicians or strutting dictators. Instead, this folk opera probes the depths of infidelity, rape and heartbreak, with the unprecedented feature of an all-black cast. George Gershwin's pioneering attempt to bring to the Broadway stage what he described in an interview as 'opera for the theatre, with drama, song and dance' met with mixed reviews. Critics could not make up their minds if the genre was too high- or too lowbrow, yet there was no disagreement over the work's hard-hitting power, and this is what made the show one of Broadway's most enduring productions.

Broadway gave the Great Depression public the chance to indulge in a few hours of carefree enjoyment, but this came at a price. A New York office worker earning on average $30 per week had to think twice about parting with $3, or twice that for a couple, on a Gershwin musical, not to mention the cost of transport and possibly dinner at the newly opened Carnegie Deli in Seventh Avenue.

Broadway audience turnout took a hit with the inauguration of the 1939 New York World's Fair, at which a 75-cent general admission pass provided a day of leisurely sightseeing for the entire family. But for New Yorkers on low incomes, a 25-cent cinema ticket became the most affordable alternative for a night on the town. This may have been hailed as Hollywood's 'Golden Age', but the film capital bowed to the fascination New York held for the nation by setting 42 films in Gotham in the 1930s. Broadway was at the time home to the world's greatest concentration of motion picture palaces, with Times Square at its centre. This lasted until the late 1920s, when the boom in movie-going led impresarios to start opening theatres in other neighbourhoods of Manhattan, as well as in the outer boroughs. Loew's Seventy-Second Street opened in 1932, a classic theatre built to resemble an Asian temple, complete with a lantern over the proscenium and an illuminated joss house that filled the auditorium with the fragrance of incense. Other cinemas of the era, like the art deco 99th Street Midtown Theater, were equally stylish in design.

The movies furnished New York cinema audiences with more than a quarter's worth of distraction from their Depression woes. Regular movie attendance was at a record high of 65 per cent of the population, a figure never matched since. *King Kong* (1933) enjoyed such immense popularity that it was shown simultaneously at Radio City Music Hall and the next-door RKO Roxy. The film was praised for its use of 'the most up-to-date camera tricks' and was acclaimed a triumph of 'make-believe with a vengeance'.[13] The filming was judged so realistic that several women fainted during the sequences depicting the monster on the rampage in the streets of Manhattan.

Comedy figured high on the agenda and it was the Marx Brothers who had their fellow New Yorkers rolling in the aisles with laughter. In the decade to 1940, the brothers – initially a foursome consisting of Groucho, Harpo, Chico and Zeppo, becoming a threesome after 1933 with the departure of Zeppo – starred in no fewer than eight films, and at least one of the Marxes had appeared in a similar number. Apart from the Marx Brothers' offerings, there were movies to titillate every emotion, from the feel-good *The Wizard of Oz* (1939) and Walt Disney's first feature film, *Snow White and the Seven Dwarfs* (1937), to the tear-jerker *Gone with the Wind* (1939).

Broadcasting had now come into its own and New York had become the home of the two nationwide radio stations, the National Broadcasting Company (NBC) and the Columbia Broadcasting System (CBS). This time the Great Depression served the consumer by driving down the price of the average radio set to less than half its pre-Crash level. For an investment of less than $50, New Yorkers were able to save the cost of a night out in Harlem to hear their favourite jazz band, many of which began to be broadcast live on the radio. Fans of George Gershwin could listen to his music on his own programme from 1934; the New York Philharmonic was on every week and even country music fans could tune in to the National Barn Dance, which in 1933 was picked up for transmission by NBC.

The popularity of radio was a double-edged sword for the jazz bands. As more fans tuned in from home to listen to live broadcasts from Harlem clubs, attendance suffered, as did the workload of the musicians. Bandleader Van Alexander complained that swing bands were spending so much time adapting their repertoire for radio listeners that they neglected other aspects of their music:

> Early-evening remotes are another factor in wearing out a band. The outfit broadcasts at about five o'clock, plays for dinner, a dinner show, some dancing, a supper show, more dancing, a late show, then finishes up about three in the morning. That's too stiff a schedule for anybody. This also has a detrimental effect on the quality of music.[14]

As the decade came to a close an even more powerful medium of entertainment made its debut at the World's Fair. Network television was introduced at the fair's grand opening on 30 April 1939.[15] On that day Franklin D. Roosevelt became the first president to make a televised appearance – albeit a low-definition, blurry one – when RCA unveiled their NBC television studios in Rockefeller Plaza. The first commercially produced sets were priced at nearly $200 for a five-inch screen encased in a polished mahogany cabinet. In less than a decade market demand had driven down the cost of a television console to a level that allowed thousands of hypnotised New York families to contemplate Arthur Godfrey twanging a ukulele on his *Talent Scouts* variety show, Groucho Marx treating the entire world as his fall guy on *You Bet Your Life*, the Cisco Kid and his jovial sidekick Pancho gunning down outlaws, and nail-biting contestants on *Beat the Clock* performing mental acrobatics for a $200 jackpot.

Who could ask for anything more?

6

GOTHAM GETS A FACELIFT

City parks commissioner Robert Moses, along with La Guardia and Roosevelt, stood as one of the pillars of New York's economic recovery. Roosevelt and his New Deal administrators controlled the purse strings; La Guardia provided the tireless dynamism, while Moses originated and executed the great public works projects that put the city back on its feet.

Moses was the antithesis of his boss La Guardia in almost every respect, with one notable exception: both men were possessed of an almost fanatical drive and ambition. In terms of social background, their lives were poles apart. Moses's parents were affluent German Jews, who took pains to ensure that their son benefited from the most exquisite upbringing money could buy. If anything, Moses's circumstances more closely resembled those of Roosevelt than La Guardia's. Yet it must be acknowledged that Roosevelt's patrician status owed more to class than affluence, while Moses gained entrance to New York's select society by virtue of family wealth.

The early life of New York's 'Master Builder', as he was popularly known, spoke of a background steeped in sybaritic privilege. Born in 1888, he sailed with his family to Europe every summer to ski in the Swiss Alps; he toured Italy's historical shrines, its artistic treasures, while indulging in the occasional tennis match on the shores of Lake Lucerne. Moses's university career followed this same elite trajectory, from Yale to Oxford to Columbia University, where he earned his PhD. His doctoral thesis argued in favour of the United States adopting the British civil service model, in those days a closed shop to all but Oxford and Cambridge graduates, and this clearly displayed Moses's contempt for those who had not enjoyed the benefit of an exalted upbringing such as his own. A year of mingling with the scions of British society at Oxford had transformed him into a committed snob.

Moses was a man of fighting spirit, though it must be said that he preferred to restrict his combat activities to the corridors of Washington and New York's City Hall. He never shied from taking on all comers in the many political battles waged during his career, but in the final months of the Great War he chose to turn down the offer of an army commission, which carried the rank of lieutenant. This was in stark contrast to La Guardia, who in 1917 took his fighting skills from Capitol Hill to Italy for a year-long tour of duty with the army.

Whatever resentment La Guardia may have harboured towards those who in his eyes assumed airs above their station – after all, the mayor was himself of Italian Jewish parentage, hardly a clubbable pedigree in the eyes of the Establishment – he was aware of Moses's talent for coming up with bold, innovative ideas, and above all of his will to implement them, while trampling to pieces any obstacles thrown in his path. So it was that, on 19 January 1934, Moses joined the administration as one of La Guardia's first high-profile office holders, with the title of city parks commissioner.[1]

Moses came to the job of parks commissioner with years of public service skills under his belt. His passion for urban green space began to bear fruit as early as the 1920s, during his tenure as president of two park commissions, an experience that brought about the extensive greening of blighted areas of Long Island. By the beginning of the 1930s Moses could claim as his own a number of projects, which taken together had created nearly 10,000 acres of parkland and added major road networks to Long Island. This was a prelude to the forthcoming task of giving New York a desperately needed makeover.

By 1930, the Chrysler Building and the Empire State Building had already spread their vast shadows across midtown Manhattan. Their silhouettes redefined the skyline above which they soared, yet what was seen from afar belied the reality of daily life in the streets beneath these two brick-and-steel sentinels. When Moses took office, more than 800,000 motor vehicles struggled daily to make headway on an arterial network which, in the previous 15 years, had not undergone any improvement or expansion. Traffic snarls were not unique to the gridlocked roadways of Manhattan: the thoroughfares of the outlying boroughs were proving equally inadequate to cope with the flow of commuter and commercial traffic to and from the city. At the beginning of the 1930s, New York's only road connections between the boroughs were via the Holland Tunnel (between Manhattan and Jersey City) and George Washington Bridge, both of which opened in 1931.

Almost from the outset, the mayor and his parks commissioner had a strained relationship. It was an alliance of convenience, one that, on more than one occasion, exploded into open belligerence. La Guardia and Moses were often photographed shaking hands at official ceremonies, their faces expressing uneasy and not very convincing grins. Moses was not troubled by this mutual hostility between himself and his boss. In almost every confrontation, which were usually touched off when La Guardia voiced objections to his plans, Moses would pull himself up to his full six-foot, one-inch height and threaten to resign. One day, La Guardia decided to call his bluff. The mayor had a pad of forms printed that read: 'I, Robert Moses, do hereby resign as _____ effective _____'. La Guardia's ploy achieved something resembling a victory. In their next altercation, La Guardia

> whipped out the pad, tore off the top form with a flourish and a broad – if forced – grin and handed it to him. Moses snatched the pad off the mayor's desk, hurled it across the room, stamped out the door – and used the threat more infrequently thereafter.[2]

Not for a moment did the parks commissioner doubt that he was destined for greatness. He was therefore unconcerned by those who resented his high-handed tactics, no matter how powerful the voice of criticism. This included Franklin D. Roosevelt, who made no attempt to conceal his contempt for Moses, of whom he once openly remarked: 'I don't trust him. I don't like him.' Roosevelt must have been rubbing his hands with glee when in 1934 Moses stood for New York State governor on the Republican ticket, only to suffer the most humiliating defeat in a contest for that office in the state's history. As for La Guardia, the mayor was at his wits' end over how to tackle the Moses–Roosevelt feud. Without an injection of New Deal public works subsidies, New York's road to recovery would be blocked, and now the president was threatening to withhold federal cash unless the mayor agreed to have Moses sacked. La Guardia exclaimed to an aide: 'Jesus Christ, of all the people in the City of New York, I had to pick the one man who Roosevelt won't stand for and he won't give me any more money unless I get rid of him.'[3]

The bad blood between Roosevelt and Moses had its origin in the 1920s, at a time when Roosevelt held a post with the Taconic State Parkway Commission and Moses presided over the Long Island State Parkway Commission. Moses was empowered to veto appointments to the Taconic commission, and as he had taken a dislike to the candidate Roosevelt had proposed for secretary, the future US president was obliged to endure the mortification of seeing his man rejected. As if to rub salt into the wound, Moses subsequently managed to divert funds that Roosevelt had earmarked for road building through the Hudson Valley into his own Long Island projects.

Roosevelt made one final and somewhat unbecoming attempt to break Moses's stranglehold on New York's building programmes. This man-oeuvre was carried out in connivance with PWA director Harold Ickes. La Guardia was handed an excuse for ousting Moses under the pretext of PWA 'Administrative Order 129', issued on 26 December 1934, which the mayor received as a belated Christmas present. This order stated that no PWA funds would be advanced for a project if any of the top officials connected with it held another public office. Moses was naturally not cited by name, but the order was clearly aimed at him in his dual role as parks commissioner and chairman of the Triborough Bridge Authority, the body set up to build and maintain a complex consisting of three bridges connecting the Bronx, Queens and Manhattan and that later took on the same role for New York's tunnels.

La Guardia jumped on what he interpreted as a watertight excuse to rid himself of his troublesome adversary. After the order was made public, the mayor announced that if the parks commissioner's departure from the

Triborough Bridge Authority was required to free up more than $300 million in federal funding for New York regeneration projects, Moses would have to go. The controversy was muddied by a tangle of legal ambiguities, but one fact remained clear: Moses had no intention of allowing himself to be bullied out of a job, not by the mayor, the secretary of the interior or the president of the United States.

While La Guardia was on a visit to Washington for talks with Ickes and Roosevelt, among other matters they discussed what was expected to be their common foe's imminent downfall. Moses had managed to turn the tables on his enemies by leaking Administrative Order 129 and the details of the whole row to the press. He revealed that only a year before the order was drafted, Ickes had signed an agreement to allocate $35 million to the Triborough Bridge Authority, and that this accord did not give the federal government jurisdiction over the organisation's governing board. Moses termed Ickes's new order 'a clear violation of the agreement', and for good measure he threw in a few unkind words about his antagonist.

This pre-emptive strike achieved the desired results. Roosevelt and Ickes were revealed in a most unflattering light: the two giants of Washington were suddenly cast as bullies in the public eye, abusing their power of office and money to tyrannise La Guardia and, by association, the people of New York. Ickes was torn to shreds when the dispute with Moses surfaced at a news conference. He later admitted that when asked if Roosevelt had ever discussed Robert Moses with him, he had had to lie to protect the president's reputation. When La Guardia returned to New York, he walked straight into a swarm of reporters shouting questions about Administrative Order 129, which he, along with Ickes and Roosevelt, believed remained under lock and key. Every New York broadsheet carried a leader in support of Moses: 'The public, that most fickle of lovers, embraced Robert Moses in January 1935 as fervently as it had pushed him away [in the gubernatorial elections] in November.'[4]

Leading the wolf pack was the influential Pulitzer Prize-winning political commentator Walter Lippmann. In a *New York Herald Tribune* opinion piece, Lippmann simultaneously lambasted Ickes and La Guardia, setting the tone for similar attacks from the other papers:

> It is of the greatest importance that Mr. Ickes should be com-
> pelled to come down off his high horse and explain himself.
> The mayor of New York will have bartered away not only his
> independence but the independence of all other local officials if
> he bows to Order 129 and dismisses Mr. Moses. The President
> [Roosevelt] will create an issue that will seriously embarrass
> him if he does not insist upon an accounting.[5]

The *New York Times* launched its offensive with a long-winded broadside implying that La Guardia had in fact squabbled with Ickes over the order. 'La Guardia fights to retain Moses' was the paper's somewhat distorted interpretation of events. The press campaign in support of Moses smacked of a deliberately concocted attempt to put the mayor on the back foot. This was reinforced by angry comments from Moses himself, who told journalists that 'Ickes had asked Mayor La Guardia to get me off the Triborough Bridge Authority on the grounds that I was not friendly to the recovery programme in Washington'. Furthermore, Moses asserted, he had made it clear to La Guardia that he would gladly give up all his posts in the administration, if that was the mayor's wish, 'but I would not take a back door out of the Triborough Authority merely because there was pressure to get me out for personal or political reasons'.[6]

When La Guardia was asked by reporters what he planned to do about Moses, now the cat was out of the bag and Administrative Order 129 in the public domain, the mayor replied, 'I'll think about it,' and walked away. That effectively drew a line under the affair, though there were several other head-to-heads still to follow. Needless to say, Moses stayed on at the Triborough Bridge Authority and saw this mammoth project through to completion.

Construction work on the Triborough Bridge had begun on the day of the October 1929 Stock Market Crash. The project faltered several times in the ensuing financial meltdown, until 1933, when Moses stepped in as head of the newly created Triborough Bridge Authority. In July 1936, less than two years after the dust had settled on the Moses–Ickes wrangle, what is arguably the greatest single achievement of the parks commissioner's career was opened to traffic.

Moses took his inspiration for the project from the Swiss-born architect Othmar Ammann, whose innovative concepts had earned him the job of chief engineer at New York's Port Authority. Ammann's most audacious accomplishment was the George Washington Bridge, the span that finally solved the century-old problem of building a road link connecting New York to New Jersey. On the day in 1931 when the 4,760-foot bridge over the Hudson was inaugurated, more than 55,000 vehicles and 33,000 pedestrians made the crossing between the two states. The renowned French architect Le Corbusier considered it 'the most beautiful bridge in the world'. Moses was impressed by Ammann's creativity and Swiss efficiency: when it opened to traffic in 1931, the George Washington was twice the length of any suspension bridge in existence. Moreover, it had been completed six months ahead of schedule and $15 million below the estimated $75 million construction budget. Moses lost no time in drafting Ammann into his Triborough Bridge Authority, for which the latter also built the Bronx–Whitestone, Throgs Neck and Verrazano–Narrows bridges.

The Triborough Bridge inauguration ceremony on 11 July 1936 was conducted with resounding flourish and fanfare: 3,000 police were drafted in to provide security, 1,000 of them to guard President Roosevelt and his entourage, among whom was Ickes – sweet revenge for Moses, one is tempted to assume. The police operation constituted New York's most elaborate security deployment since aviator Charles Lindbergh's triumphal return from Paris in June 1927.

In classic Robert Moses style, work continued at a frenzied pace and right down to the wire. More than 5,000 WPA workers laboured in round-the-clock shifts to ensure the bridge would be ready in time for the ceremony. It would still be several months until the final sections would be in place, but the bridge immediately allowed great volumes of traffic to flow smoothly for the first time between Manhattan, Queens and the Bronx. This was hailed as a historic step in breaking down the natural and man-made barriers that had blocked traffic moving in and out of Greater New York:

> In itself the Triborough is an underrated achievement only because we have grown accustomed to the thought that an

engineer, given enough time and enough money, can build a bridge from almost anywhere to almost anywhere else. Considered on its merits, it is as impressive as a Pyramid or a Colossus of Rhodes, and more useful.[7]

And, one might add, more profitable as well. Within two years of the dedication ceremony, the bridge was earning $1.3 million annually, with traffic volumes rising year-on-year. Moreover, the cost savings left the Triborough Bridge Authority with a $15 million surplus. The gigantic bridge, whose eight lanes now carry on average 200,000 vehicles a day, remains a money-making enterprise and continues to pay for a portion of the New York City Transit Authority's subsidy.

MOSES LAYS DOWN THE LAW

Given Robert Moses's bull-in-a-china-shop approach to anyone or anything that posed a threat to his plans, it would be ingenuous to assume that the morning of 11 July 1936 signalled the end of the Triborough Bridge melee. Less than a fortnight after the ribbon-cutting ceremony, La Guardia and Moses were once again at daggers drawn. This time the dispute involved demolition work Moses had ordered to open a right of way for the bridge from Manhattan to Queens.

On the afternoon of 22 July, an enraged La Guardia took the unprecedented step of sending in the police to stop Moses razing the Manhattan municipal ferry terminal at East 92nd Street and tearing up the street in front of the building. Moses had embarked on this extreme initiative, unannounced and without consulting any municipal authority, in order to make room for the East River Drive approach to the Triborough Bridge.

Many a Queens-bound commuter returning from work that afternoon found himself standing on the pier, flabbergasted to discover the ferry service from Manhattan had been cancelled for want of a terminal. Within hours, a large contingent of NYPD officers turned up to eject the demolition crew from the site. Officials from the Department of Plant and Structures were dazzled by the swiftness with which Moses had committed what they considered an unauthorised act of vandalism. They set to work with equal speed to send in a repair crew, which laboured throughout the night to rebuild the slips and the street in order to restore the ferry service, at least on a makeshift basis.

While La Guardia fulminated against what he denounced as 'this interference by force with the city's services', Moses calmly brought to his boss's attention their agreement to have the ferry service abolished once the bridge was opened. Granted, Moses had of his own accord brought forward the scheduled ferry closure, and perhaps a little precipitately at that. In his defence, he argued that this had been necessary in order to meet his own contractual deadline and avoid triggering a penalty clause for delayed completion of the access road. Moses reminded the mayor that he had been given notification of the ferry landing's demolition. This was to begin no later than three days after the Triborough Bridge opened, so in fact work to tear down the terminal was overdue. He further pointed out that the bridge was cheaper for drivers: 25 cents per vehicle versus 40 cents for the ferry crossing.

La Guardia was having none of it: he instructed police commissioner Lewis J. Valentine to arrest anyone who set foot on the property and ordered in city workers to tighten up bolts and replace timber that had been torn away from the ferry slips. After 24 hours of frantic negotiations, the great ferry battle had simmered down to a storm in a teacup. The peace treaty struck on 24 July between the two gigantic egos of Fiorello La Guardia and Robert Moses was settled on the usual terms of compromise: it was agreed that within a week's time, the last ferry would sail from Astoria in Queens to East 92nd Street. After that date commuter traffic was to be diverted to the new East River Drive entrance to the bridge. The mayor quietly cancelled a 60-day extension that had been granted at the request of commuters, when City Hall directed that ferry services were to be discontinued. Announcing the peace deal between himself and the parks commissioner, La Guardia quipped: 'All quiet on the Eastern Front.'

The Triborough Bridge saga revealed Robert Moses's potential for nastiness. The entire project, from its conception in 1929 to its completion seven years later, left in its wake a pile of mutilated egos and simmering resentment on the part of politicians, whose authority the Master Builder had trampled into the dust.

But this episode was small beer compared with the brouhaha that erupted over a proposed vehicular connection between Brooklyn and Lower Manhattan. The parks commissioner did not vacillate when La Guardia tasked him to come up with a proposal for a crossing from Brooklyn to Battery Park at the southern tip of Manhattan. The only sensible solution, he concluded, was a bridge. This was to be an integral part of an extensive road system he envisaged for connecting up every part of the city in one traversable unit.

Early in 1939, Moses submitted a typically monumental infrastructure plan, this time for a mile-long structure consisting of two suspension bridges, each the length of the Brooklyn Bridge.[8] He spelled out the details of his scheme in a letter to the mayor, explaining that the cost of a bridge, which he estimated at $41 million, would come in at half that of a tunnel. Moreover, the bridge would carry six lanes of traffic instead of the maximum of four for a tunnel, it would be completed in half the time and could be financed through a public bond issue – in Moses's words, 'without the contribution of a nickel of city or federal money'.[9]

To his amazement, this time Moses found that his perennial adversary had now become a staunch ally. Two days after Moses sent off his letter, La Guardia came out with warm praise for the bridge proposal – despite the fact that in 1936 City Hall had given $75,000 to the New York City Tunnel Authority to carry out a feasibility study for a tunnel connecting Battery Park to Brooklyn. It should be taken into account that La Guardia had failed the previous year to obtain PWA financing for a Brooklyn to Lower Manhattan tunnel, so to that extent his enthusiasm for Moses's plan rang a little hollow. But the mayor now hailed Moses's engineering design as 'clever', showing an 'ingenious utilisation of space'. La Guardia also liked the financial arrangements, given that the bridge would at once be self-supporting through the collection of tolls. The time element in construction was an added bonus. Brooklyn borough president Raymond V. Ingersoll threw his weight behind the bridge alternative, citing the lack of an adequate link between Brooklyn's wharves and factories and the markets of Manhattan.

Moses could scarcely believe it was all falling so neatly into place. But he detected a possible serious snag on the horizon when La Guardia made reference to an upcoming meeting with engineers of the US War Department, which exercised exclusive jurisdiction over New York's navigable waters. Indeed, this was to become the project's undoing. Moses cavalierly ignored the anti-bridge lobby, whose opposition centred mainly on aesthetic and local business concerns. They argued that a bridge would obliterate the view of the Lower Manhattan skyline as seen from the bay, and that the major casualty would be Battery Park itself when the bridge access road ploughed through its greenery and shopping streets. Sentimentality occupied at most 0.1 per cent of Moses's thoughts, but where he did come a cropper was in taking on the US military establishment. In the War Department, Moses had encountered an adversary which even the Master Builder was unable to bully into submission.

The US secretary of war Harry H. Woodring flatly turned down the request for a permit to build another bridge across a strategic waterway, which he argued, if destroyed in time of war would block sea access to the Brooklyn Navy Yard. Woodring pointed out that there were already two bridges across the East River seaward of the Navy Yard. These, he claimed, constituted potential security hazards in the event of an emergency. With this in mind, he went so far as to suggest having these bridges torn down and replaced with tunnels.

Moses fulminated against the War Department's ruling. He charged that his application had not been considered on its merits and that the War Department had refused to disclose its secret motives for rejecting the project. Moses's outburst fell on deaf ears. The bridge project was a dead issue the moment Woodring announced his decision, though it would be difficult to imagine an enemy air force bombing the city's bridges and not hitting the Navy Yard as well.[10]

Moses now found himself out in the cold. La Guardia, upon learning of Washington's decision, quickly threw his weight behind the tunnel. The War Department had the last word, the mayor reasoned, and they would now move on to 'the next thing'. It was a race against the clock to submit plans for the Brooklyn–Battery Tunnel and put in a bid for federal financing on the day the administration's $2.66 billion lending programme for self-financing projects became effective. Work on the tunnel commenced the following year, 1940, and in fulfilment of Moses's dire predictions, the final cost rose to $80 million. The construction overrun – work was interrupted by the war – meant that La Guardia was not able to preside at the completion ceremony until 1950, 21 years after the idea was first put forward for a bridge.

This was one of the greatest defeats Moses was to suffer in his career, rivalled only by his failure to wrest control of North Beach, later LaGuardia Airport, which was inaugurated on 15 October 1939. Operation of the new airport was placed under the auspices of the Port Authority of New York. Austin Tobin, the executive director of that organisation, was a lesser-known public authority figure but cast in the same ruthless mould as Moses when it came to consolidating his power base. The Lincoln Tunnel, Newark Metropolitan Airport and the World Trade Center were some of the massive projects executed by Tobin's agency.

In spite of the rancour Moses stirred up with officialdom, few would maintain that La Guardia had been mistaken in choosing him for the job. As one of Moses's biographers notes: 'No mayor shaped New York. No mayor, not even La Guardia, left upon its rolling surface more than the faintest of lasting imprints. But Robert Moses shaped New York. Physically, any map of the city proves it.'[11] The New York that today greets passengers disembarking at JFK, who are driven to their hotels in yellow cabs along the Van Wyck Expressway or Brooklyn–Queens Expressway, across the Triborough Bridge, along the road network from Brooklyn's Belt Parkway to the Henry Hudson Bridge linking Manhattan to the Bronx, north or southbound on the Harlem River Drive or West Side Highway, are benefiting from some of Robert Moses's many singular accomplishments.

There were those rare occasions when La Guardia and Moses sheathed their swords to collaborate on projects in which both found inspiration, whose end result was invariably the enhancement of the lives of New Yorkers. One of the undertakings that illustrates on the one hand La Guardia's clean-sweep principle, and on the other Moses's obsession with green space, was the demolition of Central Park Casino in 1936. When Moses was appointed parks commissioner in 1934, he was dismayed to find that the country's largest city, with nearly 7 million people, more than 5 per cent of the US population, could offer its children scarcely 100 playgrounds. Less than 20 years later this number had increased sixfold, and Moses was still acquiring land to build others. The Central Park Casino was one of the first and most headline-grabbing of his initiatives to spruce up the city.

The erstwhile venue for Mayor Jimmy Walker's nocturnal jamborees was replaced with a children's playground, but not without inciting the predictable furore that accompanied almost every Moses initiative. The civic-spiritedness that prompted the decision to tear down this pleasure palace seemed unassailable. Moses and La Guardia hated it: the Master Builder considered it a gross misuse of public space, while for the Little Flower it symbolised a remnant of the moral corruption that epitomised the Walker era, as well as an affront to the many citizens who were suffering the devastation of the Depression.

The Central Park Casino, which resembled an oversized gingerbread cottage, was built in 1863 on a site near 72nd Street. It was originally known as the Ladies' Refreshment Salon, a rest stop for unaccompanied women out for a stroll through the park. In 1929 Jimmy Walker had it converted into a nightclub (although it was not, it should be noted, a gambling casino), to which he was a frequent visitor. He was also known to use it as an unofficial workspace for entertaining his political cronies. The sybaritic decadence of the Casino during the early 1930s was in stark contrast to the plight of Central Park's homeless, curled up on nearby park benches under their 'Hoover blankets', piles of newspapers used by the destitute to help keep themselves warm in the park's shantytowns, known as 'Hoovervilles' – both terms referring to President Herbert Hoover, on whose watch the Depression had occurred.

This contrast recalled a remark uttered by financier and philanthropist Bernard Baruch, who, in 1933, at a meeting in his Madison Avenue office, reflected with regret on life's manifold injustices: 'In the presence of too much food, people are starving. Surrounded by vacant houses, they are homeless. And standing before unused bales of wool and cotton, they are dressed in rags.'[12] Those hit hard by the Depression saw their plight reflected not only in expressions of outrage by philanthropists like Baruch, but also in the cinema and popular comedy. In a sequence of the 1935 comedy-drama film *One More Spring*, Walter Baxter portrays a half-starved movie producer roasting a partridge in the Central Park maintenance shed he shares with two other paupers. Never at a loss to find the humour in any situation, Groucho Marx once remarked that he knew things were bad 'when I saw pigeons feeding the people in Central Park'.

'Is there anyone to stop him?' thundered appellate justice Francis Martin, presiding at a hearing convened in April 1936 to consider Moses's appeal against a state Supreme Court order halting the Casino's proposed demolition: 'There ought to be, in our opinion, some board to pass upon this before he becomes a Mussolini.'[13] There were strong arguments in favour of retaining the Casino as a historical monument. It was the first structure built after the city, in 1853, acquired the 700-acre plot of land that became a European-style park, modelled on London's Hyde Park and the Jardin de Luxembourg in Paris. But Moses was, as ever, resolved to have his way. The building was unsound, he remonstrated to his critics; it was not worth repairing, and the restaurant was too expensive for all but a small clique of New York's well-to-do. Moses would not hear of any compromise deals with the Casino's backers or, for that matter, the city authorities – the Casino would have to go, and in its place the children of New York would be given a playground.

For more than a month, the Master Builder stubbornly rebuffed every line of reasoning put to him by the Appellate Division of New York State's Supreme Court, until finally, on 1 May 1936, a weary bench of magistrates threw in the towel and unanimously agreed that Moses was empowered to raze the Casino. One year later, almost to the day, Moses unveiled a plaque inaugurating Central Park's two-acre Rumsey Playground, named for the social-welfare activist and consumer champion Mary Harriman Rumsey, who died in 1934.[14]

New York's 'Number one problem child', as one newspaper labelled Robert Moses, remained throughout his career a thorn in the sides of untold politicians, from his boss the mayor to Washington's highest authorities.[15] As is often the case with high-ranking public officials, Moses suffered from an insane relationship with his ego. Where he differed from many was in his deep-rooted belief in the cause he served. New York commuters are not alone in owing a debt of thanks to the man who, through his creativity and sheer doggedness, bequeathed to the city the great and lasting bridges, tunnels and roadways of the 1930s, without which New York's admittedly infuriating traffic would today be at a standstill. Thousands of children, from the 1930s to the present day, have benefited from the Master Builder's drive to create recreational facilities, which did not slacken after completion of Central Park's Rumsey Playground.

Moses's unconventional vision for building New York into a smooth-running global city earned him the enmity of those who watched in horror as one after another, long-established neighbourhoods and markets fell to make way for 14 expressways and more than 400 miles of parkways criss-crossing the boroughs. All of this, it stands to reason, was to the detriment of rail transport, which saw its volume of traffic decline significantly during the Moses years. In 1930, some 30,000 New Yorkers, roughly 10 per cent of commuters, travelled to work by car. Twenty years later, with Moses's vast road network in service, the numbers crossing bridges or driving along expressways every day had soared to nearly 120,000, or 30 per cent of total commuter traffic.

One can argue persuasively that much of the scathing criticism levelled at Robert Moses falls wide of the mark. New York, as the first half of its name implies, has always venerated the pursuit of originality. This was never truer than in the 1930s, when Gotham, guided by the hand of Robert Moses, embarked on the intrepid building programme that gave shape to a city beloved by its citizens and a good part of the world. Moses's public works projects virtually turned the city inside out. But New York is not Rome, London or Paris, cities whose millennial histories are embedded in every paving stone, tree-lined boulevard and church spire. New York, on the contrary, clings to comparatively few sacred cows. It is a metropolis whose physical appearance is in constant flux: this has been a truism since the city's earliest days. In the mid-nineteenth century, *Harper's Monthly* commented:

> A man born forty years ago finds nothing, absolutely nothing, of the New York he knew. If he chances to stumble upon a few old houses not yet leveled, he is fortunate. But the landmarks, the objects, which marked the city to him, as a city, are gone.[16]

The contradictions inherent in Moses's life and work will always serve as a subject for heated debate. Robert A. Caro's 1,169-page blockbuster, *The Power Broker: Robert Moses and the Fall of New York*, is assured of its place as the parks commissioner's definitive biography. Caro has many words of acclaim for his subject's remarkable legacy. Yet almost every example he cites is followed by a diatribe denouncing it as another step in 'the fall of New York', as stated in his book's subtitle. Thus Riverside Park was 'a beautiful park' but it deprived the city of its waterfront view. The Triborough Bridge, within two years of completion, was earning in excess of $1 million per year in net income. But building its approach ramps required the demolition of homes and sizeable apartment blocks, while the massive increase in road traffic caused unforeseen jams on the bridge and its approaches.

Slums were ruthlessly cleared to make way for parks and roadways; dilapidated tenements were unceremoniously demolished and, in their place, arose modern tower blocks. New York began to acquire the cohesive transport network it needed to keep traffic and the city's commercial lifeblood flowing. Yet it has to be acknowledged that when these hovels were razed a quarter of a million people were displaced from their homes, the majority of whom were among New York's poorest. These people, immigrants for the most part, found themselves forced to abandon derelict neighbourhoods that, when all is said and done, were rich in community spirit and cultural traditions. Beginning in 1948, to clear space for the 6.5-mile Cross Bronx Expressway, 1,500 homes were flattened on the autocratic principle that the slums must be destroyed and damn the inhabitants, for these people would later be housed in the new, albeit uninspiring brick towers. The high-rise blocks were undeniably tidy and functional dwellings, replete with lifts and modern kitchen and bathroom facilities. But they were also soulless, disorientating abodes in the eyes of their new tenants, the majority of whom were foreign-born and had grown accustomed to what might have been perceived by the gentrified classes, with paternalistic disdain, as a poor but cheerful existence. Furthermore, the profusion of multi-lane roads and bridge approaches that entombed the old neighbourhoods had the effect of swelling the volume of traffic to levels which to this day have consigned parts of Manhattan to semi-permanent gridlock. And so on ad infinitum, as the legions of Moses denigrators would have it.

Those who sit in judgement of Robert Moses might do well to ponder the question of what would have been the consequences for New York, its economy and its infrastructure, if the Master Builder had not sent 84,000 workers out to construct parks, bridges, playgrounds, homes, tunnels and roadways. During his tumultuous term of office as parks commissioner, and with the exception of the East River Drive, Moses planned and built major motorable roads across the length and breadth of New York, as well as the city's main tunnels and bridges. By the time he stepped down in 1968, after more than 40 years as the city's Master Builder, he had spent in excess of $150 billion in today's money on bridges, tunnels and roadways connecting Manhattan with the outer boroughs and the latter with one another.

In spite of Moses's character failings – his detractors would almost certainly place an egocentric aloofness, which all too easily tipped over into sneering arrogance, at the top of the list – in his first year in office the parks commissioner, true to his job title, channelled $26 million of federal funds into New York's parks and multiplied their number by a third. But as was reflected in his vast infrastructure initiatives, Moses's vision went well beyond offering New Yorkers a scattering of new recreational resources. Here too, as suggested above, we find a man obsessed with housing, one who embarked on a three-year tower-block construction programme to the colossal tune of $245 million, involving ten slum-clearance projects in Manhattan, the Bronx, Brooklyn and Queens. It might be added parenthetically that Moses came up with the forward-looking idea of funding part of the work with an additional one-cent tax on a packet of cigarettes. He also advanced a scheme for massive housing developments for those on low incomes, which would be financed by commercial companies such as insurers.

This was the era of slum destruction with a vengeance, whose aim was to make way for the high-rise blocks that dominate the skyline of the Lower East Side and neighbourhoods of the outer boroughs. One of the most colossal and outstandingly lifeless of these projects was Knickerbocker Village, completed in 1934, which stands between the Brooklyn and Manhattan bridges. However, as the developers tended to set rentals above the means of most blue-collar workers, there were limits on the number of such enterprises.

This problem was addressed in the same year as the inauguration of Knickerbocker Village. The New York State Legislature took the matter in hand by issuing a ruling that sanctioned the use of public money to acquire private property, thus sidestepping the property developers. As one contemporary journal highlighted: 'The significance of this recent declaration of the legislature is the proposition that slums cannot be eliminated by private enterprise alone. This is now a truism.'[17] At the same time, the legislature recognised that certain areas of the city were blighted by unsanitary or substandard housing conditions, owing to overcrowding and tenant density. It further acknowledged an inadequate supply of safe and salubrious accommodation for low-income families.

The answer to this dilemma came in the guise of the so-called 'First Houses'. Over the course of several years, many people living in New York's more than 80,000 tenement buildings moved into these public-housing units, which opened for tenancy in 1935 and each contained more than 100 flats, in a row of four- or five-storey nondescript redbrick buildings on the Lower East Side. This was the first completed project of the New York City Housing Authority (NYCHA), formed in 1934, as well as the first municipally built public-housing project in the United States. The NYCHA prospered in partnership with Moses, as an integral part of the parks commissioner's plan to rid the city of run-down neighbourhoods.

The *New York Times* is not normally given to lavishing praise on City Hall officialdom. Nonetheless, in a tribute to the Master Builder, the paper echoed the sentiments of many residents of Gotham in words of guarded admiration: 'Anything that Mr Moses has to say deserves a hearing. His ability, his surprising energy and his unswerving devotion to the public good cannot be doubted.'[18] It must not be forgotten that in 1898, the year in which the City of Greater New York was founded, there were only three ways into Manhattan: by sea, by motoring across the Brooklyn Bridge or overland through the Bronx on the New York Central Railroad.

Moses's ambitious bridge- and road-building projects achieved their objective, by easing automobile congestion and facilitating flows in and out of Manhattan and across the outer boroughs. Equally critical was the need to open up Manhattan's commercial arteries, which from the earliest days and throughout the 1920s had been a bottleneck to traffic. City Hall had engaged the engineering firm Day & Zimmermann to provide a report on traffic conditions in the heart of Manhattan's commercial district, roughly along a three-mile strip with Fifth Avenue as its central axis, running from Washington Square in the south of Manhattan to 59th Street, which runs along the southern edge of Central Park. This route takes in all the city's great retail emporiums, entertainment venues and grand hotels. The report, which was completed in October 1929, had urged the construction of a $200 million tunnel (nearly $3 billion today) under Fifth Avenue. In addition, the firm proposed a comprehensive scheme of street widening, tunnels and bridges to link the five boroughs and take traffic away from the congested heart of Manhattan.

The Triborough Bridge, the West Side Highway, the Eighth Avenue subway and other great infrastructure initiatives were instrumental in bringing an improvement in transport facilities south of 59th Street. Even as the stock market went into freefall, in 1930 new building and renovation applications to the tune of $150 million were being submitted for Fifth Avenue, an increase of $50 million on any previous year. It is worth bearing in mind that this took in a district comprising only 1.5 square miles of New York City's more than 300 square miles of land area. Plans were laid out to dismantle the Sixth Avenue elevated subway line (the 'El') and the Madison Avenue tramline, along with the removal of the 34th Street El, to make way for a new Sixth Avenue subway, which would replace those above-street-level obstacles to traffic.

The La Guardia–Moses partnership of the 1930s, if that term is applicable to what more often resembled a bare-knuckle boxing match than a political alliance, represented a decisive era in New York City's history. These two men, each in his own way, left an indelible imprint on the city's landscape and character. What the lofty, dour Moses and the minute, peppery La Guardia had in common, apart from a mercurial temper and an addiction to their bloated and irreconcilable egos, was a love of New York: La Guardia the man concerned with the people's welfare, and Moses the builder of the city's infrastructure.

Moses stood head and shoulders above La Guardia in a physical sense. He was a giant of a man alongside his boss, and he also had the gift of longevity.

The Little Flower died in 1947 at age 65, two years after completing a record three terms of office. He slipped into a coma shortly after giving a lecture to a boys' school in the Bronx and died peacefully in his sleep four days later. Moses soldiered on to 1981, dying of heart failure at the age of 92. One might think that Moses had fortune on his side, in granting him more than another three decades of life in which to vindicate his controversial career. Yet he never managed to achieve this aim, nor did he lose any sleep over it: 'Those who can, build,' he once said. 'Those who can't, criticise.' When La Guardia appointed Moses parks commissioner in 1934, he had unleashed a demon obsessed with remaking New York in his image, from top to bottom. Within a few months of taking on the job, the Master Builder had completed 1,700 projects, from park-bench repairs to rebuilding Central Park Zoo.

The Master Builder's ambiguous legacy could not have contrasted more sharply with that of La Guardia, who predeceased Moses by 34 years. On the morning of 21 September 1947, the day following the mayor's death, more than 45,000 people from every walk of life passed through the Cathedral of St John the Divine, appropriately located near La Guardia's Harlem residence. They came to pay tribute to the man whom most New Yorkers hold up as their city's greatest ever mayor, and certainly the most distinguished since Peter Stuyvesant. By arm-twisting Washington into funding the creation of 200,000 jobs within weeks of taking office, by creating more than 4,000 city works projects aimed mainly at improving the lives of the neediest and by running a clean and transparent administration throughout his three terms of office, La Guardia endeared himself to the hearts of all New Yorkers.[19] 'Dynamite and aggressive, he appeared to be everywhere at once, rushing to fires at times and at other times flying all over the country by airplane,' was the *New York Times* testimonial. 'A fighter by nature, he was always ready to take on all comers, big or little, from Hitler to the man in the street.'[20]

7

THE THING ABOUT SKYSCRAPERS

The skyscraper can trace its ancestry back many years, millennia in fact, before the existence of New York City. The book of Genesis tells the story of Babel, the Babylonian city in which Noah's descendants tried to erect the mythological tower: 'Come, let us build for ourselves a city, and a tower whose top will reach into Heaven' (Genesis 11:4). For their presumption the people were punished: their words were made incomprehensible to one another. This aetiological tale of the diversity of speech could easily be applied to New York, home to the speakers of some 800 languages, a city in which cab drivers routinely set their satnavs to Russian, Bengali, Serbo-Croatian or any of a myriad of other tongues.

When Greater New York came into being in 1898, the island of Manhattan accounted for half the inhabitants of the newly amalgamated five boroughs. The advent of new, affordable rental accommodation kicked off a migratory move to the outer boroughs, in particular Queens and Brooklyn. A case in point was Queensbridge Houses, the nation's largest public-housing complex, built under the auspices of the NYCHA, which La Guardia set up in 1934 to provide affordable homes for the city's low-income families.[1] As a result of this demographic shift, by the end of the Second World War Manhattan's population had fallen to a quarter of the total for New York City.

What Manhattan had lost in numerical superiority it more than made up for in stature – quite literally. The notion of a building soaring hundreds of feet above the pavement was in the nineteenth century given the name 'skyscraper', originally a nautical term referring to a small triangular sail set above the skysail on a sailing ship. In time, such edifices came to be seen as an intrinsic feature of Gotham's landscape. By the 1930s, the Manhattan landscape was dotted with about 100 buildings worthy of the name skyscraper, albeit ones that responded to an early twentieth-century definition of the term, from the 373-foot Woodstock Tower luxury apartment block in 42nd Street to the recently inaugurated 1,454-foot Empire State Building. The British architect Alfred Charles Bossom, who worked in the United States in the 1920s, considered the skyscraper to be a wholly new and revolutionary form and type of building, one that is characteristically and absolutely American. Writing in 1934, he said:

> If all of America were wiped out except the skyscrapers of New York, the archaeologist would be able to reconstruct, with a minimum of error, the character, the intellectual qualities and the ideals of the nation that produced them. All of those mighty structures proclaim the daring, the inventiveness, the self-confident power of their creators and the more recent and best of them proclaim also their delight in the beauty of design and effect. The Titans might have built them. The Renaissance would not have disowned them.[2]

But how did this phenomenon come about – and why? The answer to the first question can be found in two events that took place in the nineteenth century, each of which contributed to the formation of a radically new Manhattan landscape. At the 1853 Crystal Palace Exhibition, on the grounds where the New York Public Library now stands, the master mechanic Elisha Graves Otis stood on a platform suspended by a cable above a crowd of onlookers. On a given signal, he ordered the cable to be severed. To the spectators' amazement the platform dropped a few inches and then held fast, thanks to a safety device Otis had installed to prevent it from crashing to the ground.

Thus was born the precursor of the modern elevator, which in turn was to give birth to the Otis Elevator Company, the world's largest manufacturer of vertical transport systems. This meant that apartment dwellers and office workers could now ascend to great heights in a building without having to climb stairs.

While Otis was dazzling audiences with his failsafe hoist, in Europe a revolution had begun in the steel-making industry. Until the mid-nineteenth century steel was almost regarded as something of a precious metal, used mostly for cutlery and weaponry. But technological advances imported from Britain, where Sheffield mills had moved into the vanguard of the industrial revolution with inventions like crucible and stainless steel, greatly reduced manufacturing costs in America. By the late nineteenth century, having incorporated these developments and due to the sheer size of its industrial base, the United States had become the world leader in steel manufacturing. This meant that not only could people be transported up and down buildings in safety, but it was now possible to erect tall structures without having to rest them on enormously thick and space-consuming masonry walls.

The Egyptians had to build their pyramids stone by stone. The Greeks and Romans needed columns to support their roofs. The churches of the Renaissance, with their huge stained-glass windows, would have collapsed but for the buttresses that provided support against lateral forces. Now a structural steel frame could be raised like an umbrella and a building draped over it. Thanks to the advances in steel production, the skyscraper of the 1930s became as great a departure from the traditions and practices of the past as the internal combustion engine of the mid-nineteenth century. In theory, the sky was now the limit. Raymond Hood, an architect closely associated with Rockefeller Center, declared in 1932 that with the use of steel and lift technology, it was theoretically possible to construct a skyscraper 7,000 feet tall. The only obstacles to putting up a Fritz Lang-type monster of this sort were economic considerations, such as the great space required for lift shafts, which would make it impractical to service such high buildings.

The acclaimed Swiss-born French architect Charles-Édouard Jeanneret-Gris, better known as Le Corbusier, made his first visit to New York in 1935. He expressed boundless enthusiasm for the city's skyscrapers, which he proclaimed to be 'signs of unchained power', and its grid system, superior in design to the cramped buildings and narrow, twisted streets of Paris. It is noteworthy that after inspecting the Chrysler and Empire State buildings, among others, Le Corbusier considered them *too small*:

> The skyscraper is built of steel, a skeleton woven like a filigree in the sky, a spidery thing, marvelously clear and free. There are no *walls* in the skyscraper [as opposed to structural supports], since a wall is not easily put in place at six hundred and fifty feet. Why have one anyway? Until the introduction of new methods of construction in reinforced concrete or steel, a wall served to *support floors*. Today they are carried by posts which do not take up a thousandth part of the surface of the ground, and not by walls. The exterior of the skyscraper, the facade – the facades – can be a film of glass, a skin of glass. Why repudiate richness itself: floods of light coming in. The skyscraper should be large. It can contain ten thousand, twenty thousand, thirty thousand, forty thousand occupants easily.[3]

The power-driven lift and the steel skeleton were the enablers, the crucial elements that came into existence to cater to the demand for ever more towering structures. But as for the *why*, it is not coincidental that almost all of Manhattan's early skyscrapers arose as testimonials to commercial enterprise. America in the early twentieth century was a rising power in the worlds of finance and industry. In 1913 Henry Ford had introduced the world's first electric-powered assembly line; during the First World War New York Harbor was abuzz day and night with shipments of commodities and war material for Britain and her allies, and by 1920 the United States had become the world's supreme financial power. New York, more than any other US city, was now the nation's gateway for the export of goods, as well as a magnet for human capital.

The birth of the modern skyscraper corresponds in time to the founding of large American corporations, many of which, like Singer, Woolworth and Bankers Trust, were New York companies or chose to set up headquarters in the country's leading business centre. With a massive increase in the number of white-collar workers in clerical and management jobs, the need for sprawling factory floor space was overtaken by a demand for verticality:

> These were the years when the skyscraper was born and grew
> to maturity, when architecture was put securely in the service
> of engineering and the profit motive, and when the identity
> of New York became inextricably associated with its skyline.[4]

On 30 April 1939, New York City took a big leap forward in its claim to international industrial prominence when it welcomed the first of 44 million American and foreign visitors to the World's Fair. With this lavish celebration of material progress – which, one might say, had been symbolically erected on the site of a rubbish tip – the city turned its back on the Great Depression. Robert Moses selected a 1,216-acre field in Flushing Meadows, in the borough of Queens, for the $591 million project. The site's pastoral name was deceptive, for the future fairground was in fact a vast landfill site inhabited by an assortment of vermin, including swarms of giant river rats.

Thanks to the parks commissioner's road-building efforts, Queens was by that time within easy reach of travellers from any part of the city. As had been the case with other large, complex projects of the 1930s, such as North Beach Airport and the Empire State Building, the World's Fair was built in record time, in fact in just two years, a feat that few developers would today consider possible to replicate. The ground-breaking ceremony took place on 29 June 1936, and the fair's doors opened to the public before the end of the decade. This was no surprise, given the omnipotent presence of Moses, who wielded his whip at every step in the construction process. Even before work began, the Master Builder was putting out warnings that delays in preparing the site would prove 'fatal'. At one critical point in the planning schedule Moses threw down the gauntlet to La Guardia and the Board of Estimate: either they wished him to complete the contracts on the assumption that the fair was to go ahead, or they could adopt an alternative plan that he had already prepared, which was to develop the meadows as yet another of his parks. Moses offhandedly told City Hall officialdom that it mattered little to him which alternative they chose – he was determined to get one project or the other moving without delay.

The city got its World's Fair, and moreover it was ready in time for the scheduled grand opening on the 150th anniversary of George Washington's New York inauguration as the first US president. The event was celebrated under brilliant sunshine and the proceedings were enlivened by massed military bands, in the presence of President Roosevelt, Governor Lehman, Mayor La Guardia and 206,000 spectators.

As had been anticipated, the chief beneficiary of this enterprise was the city's transport system, with the construction of new approach roads and modernised subway carriages to transport visitors to and from the fairground. Some of the more notable works carried out in connection with the World's Fair were the Bronx–Whitestone Bridge, the Whitestone Expressway, the extension of a subway line to nearby Kew Gardens, a new station at Willets Point Avenue and a station of the Long Island Railroad. For once, La Guardia and Moses had worked hand-in-hand on a project in near perfect harmony, the only glitch being a spate of industrial action during the construction process, something with which the parks commissioner was admirably equipped to deal.

A particularly awkward moment arose in 1936 when Hermann Goering threatened to dispatch the Luftwaffe to bomb New York City. The Reichsmarschall ordered the German aircraft industry to design planes capable of transporting a load of five-ton bombs across the Atlantic. After the war the Allies captured a German map of Lower Manhattan, pinpointing the target areas, which stretched from Governors Island to Rockefeller Center.[5] The Nazi chieftain's hackles had been raised when La Guardia rejected a request by Germany to be allotted exhibition space at the World's Fair. The mayor had also spoken of Hitler in less than flattering terms, telling a group of Jewish women that he was of a mind to place an effigy of the Führer in the Chamber of Horrors pavilion. When this story got about, the German consulate in New York requested police protection against a feared attack by Jews seeking revenge for Nazi atrocities committed against their European brethren. The mayor was only too happy to oblige, supplying an all-Jewish

1. Protesters put out of work by the Depression rally outside the Bank of United States to demand jobs and aid from City Hall.

2. New Yorkers resorted to every imaginable means, from polishing shoes to selling apples, in order to eke out a living in the dark days of the Depression. A street band strikes up a tune in Yorkville, in Upper Manhattan.

3. Federal Hall in Wall Street, which was to become a gathering
spot for panicked investors after the 1929 Crash.

4. Mayor Fiorello La Guardia (left) and parks commissioner Robert Moses in a rare photo together. In spite of the smiles, their personal relationship was uneasy, to put it mildly.

5. The newspaper and gossip columnist Walter Winchell (left) interviews the 1930s comedian and juggler W. C. Fields on NBC radio. Winchell was a frequent patron of the 21 Club speakeasy, until he was blacklisted for leaking stories about the club's clandestine activities.

6. Police at the scene of one of New York's frequent gangland murders in the mid-1930s. It was commonplace for feuds between mobsters to be settled in the city's streets.

7. World heavyweight champion boxer Jack Dempsey (crouching, left) celebrates the end of Prohibition in 1933. The 1920 law banning the sale of alcoholic beverages gave rise to more than a decade of criminal activity and public protests.

8. Duke Ellington in his dressing room at the New York Paramount Theater, a top venue for swing music.

9. The view of the Chrysler Building from the Empire State Building, which usurped the Chrysler Building as the world's tallest skyscraper on its completion in April 1931.

10. The Waldorf-Astoria rises above the skyline in art deco magnificence. The hotel was the favoured residence of celebrities, tycoons, socialites and the occasional Mafia boss.

11. Builders on the Waldorf-Astoria take a 'lunch break'. The hotel launched the concept of room service, though not necessarily to this extreme.

12. It's back to work after lunch, the men well nourished and filled with enthusiasm.

13. The Lower East Side was the abode of New York's largest community of Jewish immigrants. They created a self-contained world of kosher delicatessens, synagogues, social clubs and Yiddish theatre companies.

14. A restaurant on the Bowery offering Depression fare.

15. The 21 Club was a thriving speakeasy and watering hole for the doyens of New York high society, some of whom ended their evening in a police van after a raid by federal agents. It remains an iconic Manhattan bar and restaurant.

16. The 21 Club's famed jockeys still adorn the balcony above the West 52nd Street entrance. They were presented by affluent customers to represent the racing colours of the stables they owned.

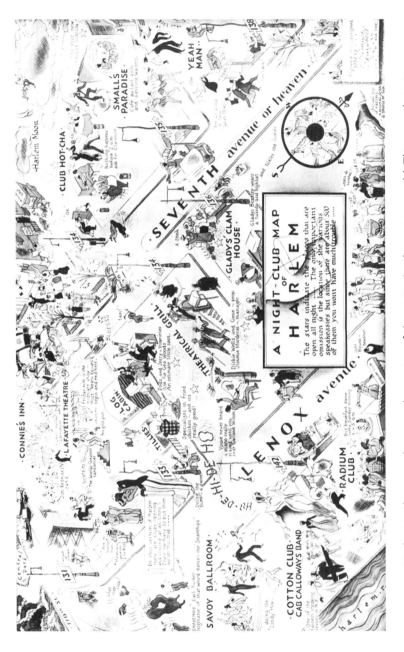

17. Harlem in the 1930s became the centre of the nation's vibrant jazz world. This map depicts some of the hottest venues in town, like the Cotton Club and the Savoy Ballroom.

18. Jitterbug dancers hop and bounce to the music of the big bands of the 1930s.

19. Grand Central Terminal played a key role in developing midtown Manhattan's commercial life in the 1930s. Thanks to this splendid railway terminus, thousands of workers were able to commute to their jobs in Manhattan's new office buildings and skyscrapers.

20. The Third Avenue 'El' ran from Manhattan all the way to the Bronx and was one of the last of the elevated subway lines to be demolished. The disappearance of the El helped to relieve traffic congestion and reduce vagrancy in New York streets.

21. Slum clearance was high on the agenda of parks commissioner Robert Moses. These tenements were on the demolition list to make way for high-rise apartment blocks.

22. With the completion of the Chrysler and Empire State buildings in 1931, Manhattan acquired the silhouette for which it is admired today.

23. Jewish refugee children from Nazi Germany and other totalitarian regimes of Europe get their first view of the Statue of Liberty on entering New York Harbor.

security detachment led by Captain Max Finkelstein, president of the NYPD's Jewish fraternal organisation, the Shomrin Society.[6]

The World's Fair could not by any measure be considered a financial success. The 45 million visitors who flocked to Flushing Meadows in its 18-month duration amounted to less than half the number the event's planners had anticipated. Likewise, the $48 million it generated in revenue represented an almost $20 million shortfall (excluding external infrastructure expenditures) against total investment.

It was nevertheless an extraordinary farewell to a remarkable decade, one that opened under the shadow of despair, witnessed years of struggle for recovery and saw in its closing days a sense of deep apprehension at what the European war might augur for America. Designed to be everything from an economic catalyst for a Depression-laden New York to a harbinger of a worldwide peace movement, the fair came to stand for a turning point in history. By its opening day in 1939, the world was already preparing itself for what would be, for most, the second major war of their lifetimes. Above all, thanks to the fair New York secured its membership in the fraternity of international exhibition organisers. In all, 60 countries were represented, more than twice the number who came to fly the flag at the 1851 Great Exhibition in London, the city that at that time was considered the global centre of culture and commerce. The New York World's Fair was a symbol of the hope that beyond the looming European conflict a future lay ahead for mankind, one in which the miracles of technology would make people free to enjoy an existence of ease and leisure.

Twenty-five years later, in 1964, a second World's Fair was erected on the same Flushing Meadows site, with a by-now-elderly Robert Moses once more at the helm. Today all that is left of the original fairground is the granite monument marking the spot where the two bullet-shaped Westinghouse Time Capsules were buried, in 1939 and 1964 respectively. The first capsule is an 800-pound cylinder assembled from a corrosion-resistant non-ferrous alloy called Cupaloy, created especially for the project. It was lowered 50 feet underground at precisely 12 noon on 23 September 1938, the moment of the autumnal equinox, bearing instructions for it to be opened in 6939, 5,000 years in the future. It is filled with an eclectic assortment of gadgets, artefacts and documents from the 1930s, from swatches of textiles, a Waterman fountain pen, an alarm clock and a toothbrush, to the writings of Albert Einstein and Thomas Mann.

It could be said that the 1939 World's Fair, with the surge of self-confidence and promise of material progress it was intended to display, reflected New York's emergence from the darkest days of that decade. On the other hand, while the hardship and economic devastation brought on by the Depression years cannot be overstated, it would be wrong to conclude that the city's life had come to a total standstill in the 1930s.

PLANTING THE SEEDS OF GIGANTISM

A hectic overhaul of Manhattan's commercial heartland was taking place against a backdrop of ballyhooing by Captain William J. Pedrick, vice president of the Fifth Avenue Association:

> The momentum of American business is too great to be checked by any condition except one that strikes at the root of business, and there is no evidence to support the belief that the Stock Market depression mirrors the industrial or business history of our country.[7]

That was in early January 1930, less than three months after 'Black Tuesday', the day of the Crash, which brought the Roaring Twenties to a screeching halt. But in contrast with the stock market collapse, which was followed by the wider economy's slide into depression, New York's modernisation and construction boom did not grind to a halt in the 1930s.

A stroll through the canyons of the city's financial district, to a junction where Broadway meets Wall Street, takes one into a spacious garden enclosure set in the shadow of surrounding skyscrapers. Within this secluded spot stands Trinity Church, a classic example of Gothic Revival architecture. Until 1890, this Episcopalian church's 284-foot spire dominated the Manhattan skyline. Indeed, for nearly half a century Trinity stood unchallenged as the city's tallest building. But then, in 1888 the Hungarian immigrant turned publishing magnate Joseph Pulitzer purchased French's Hotel, situated at Park Row and the now-defunct Frankfort Street. He promptly had the building demolished to make way for the Renaissance Revival-style headquarters of his newspaper the *New York World*.[8] Two years later Pulitzer and a host of dignitaries, including the mayor and the state governor, presided at the opening ceremony of the 20-storey edifice, christened appropriately enough the New York World Building. At 309 feet this was now the world's tallest building, crowned by a futuristic gilded dome. The building had also become the first landmark to greet passengers arriving by sea into New York Harbor. It was a symbol, one might argue, of the rise of secular capitalism as New York's predominant faith.

The 'tower' considered by many to be the forerunner of the true skyscraper pre-dated the New York World Building by 20 years. The Equitable Life Assurance Building in Lower Broadway opened for business in 1870. What is especially significant about this neoclassical structure is that it was the first to be erected around a skeletal steel frame and to incorporate Otis hydraulic lifts. The seven-storey office block had a short lifespan, however, for in 1912 it was gutted by a massive blaze, which gave the lie to the architects' assurances that it was completely fireproof. Even more tragic was that this occurred on a bitterly cold January morning, a day so frosty that the water pumped on the fire froze in the hoses. Six people perished in the flames.

Within three years, a new Equitable Building had arisen on the same spot as its predecessor, becoming the world's largest office building, occupying 1.2 million square feet of floor space and casting a seven-acre shadow over the city. The unveiling of this 40-storey tower triggered a flurry of controversy and it was no coincidence that one year after its inauguration, the city authorities enacted their first 'zoning resolution', which changed the rules governing skyscraper design.

The Equitable Building resembles a mammoth cube rising straight up without setbacks, thus preventing light and air from reaching the street below. Taking this into account, the 1916 law divided the city into zones of usage: commercial, residential and unrestricted. The impact on skyscrapers was almost immediately felt in planning circles and ushered in the advent of the setback design. While the regulations did not impose a limit on height, front walls of buildings were limited to a specific number of storeys. Above that height, buildings were required to 'set back' the facade at intervals. This stepped architectural style evoked the Babylonian ziggurat tradition of successively receding levels.

As we have seen, the steam-powered lift and low-cost steel were the two key factors that enabled New York's skyscraper boom to get under way in the late nineteenth century and flourish over the next 50 years. But a number of innovations came along in the 1870s that made skyscraper living desirable as well as feasible. Central heating, the electric light bulb and the telephone provided creature comforts and efficiency in the work environment.

The growth of skyscrapers was determined by the US economy, which experienced a spectacular transformation between the time Otis unveiled his pioneering machine and the opening in 1909 of the 50-storey Metropolitan Life Insurance Company Tower (known as the 'Met Life Tower') in Madison Avenue, a landmark skyscraper which briefly held the title of the world's tallest building. In the space of roughly half a century, industry and services had overtaken agriculture as the nation's dominant economic activities. The combined output of manufacturing and key businesses like banking and retailing grew from 58 to 79 per cent of the total in this period, while the number of people employed in these two sectors rose from 40 to 59 per cent of the workforce. Behind the form of the new skyscrapers lay the economic reality which made them economically viable.

The American economy experienced a decade of rapid expansion in the 1880s. The multinationals of the future began to appear on the scene, giants like Standard Oil, American Tobacco, Pullman, I. M. Singer, Woolworth and Metropolitan Life Insurance. The one thing these companies had in common was the need for large headquarters to accommodate hundreds, and in some instances thousands, of office workers: 'A major factor in Gotham's primacy was its matchless array of investment banks: J. P. Morgan, the Rockefellers' National City Bank, Kuhn Loeb, the U.S. Trust and the Bank of New York, to name but a few.'[9]

In the days of peace and stability that followed the end of the Civil War in 1865, up to the outbreak of the Spanish–American War in 1898, New

York experienced a surge in business growth and the spread of the arts. An increasingly leisured society began to develop an interest in promoting and enjoying cultural activities in music and the visual arts. The Metropolitan Museum of Art, whose collection today comprises more than 2 million works, had opened its doors in Fifth Avenue in 1880. Three years later, opera buffs began to flock to Broadway's original Metropolitan Opera House, a symbol of the great wave of artistic endeavour that was sweeping the city. Less than a decade after that, 57th Street was graced by the Italian Renaissance-style Carnegie Hall, inaugurated in 1891 with a five-day music festival in which Pyotor Ilych Tchaikovsky conducted several of his own works.

These venerable establishments came about thanks to the generosity of leading New York citizens, the new moneyed elite who endowed their city with grand monuments to match in splendour the great cultural institutions of Europe. In the case of Carnegie Hall, this is implicit in its namesake, the steel tycoon and philanthropist Andrew Carnegie, who invested $2 million (about $45 million in today's money) in the enterprise. The Metropolitan Museum of Art's co-founders included the investment banker and industrialist Howard Potter, the railway executive John Taylor Johnston and the publishing baron George Palmer Putnam. The German-born banker Otto Hermann Kahn served as chairman and benefactor of the Metropolitan Opera House, whose home today, Lincoln Center, replaced the original building in 1966. These men shared a collective conviction that if New York could not rival the capitals of Europe in historical depth, it could certainly dazzle them in boldness of style. Furthermore, in undertaking these great projects, New York's magnates of commerce and banking had an eye on their personal legacies, seeing these great structures that would rise up across Manhattan as monuments in steel and brick to their achievements in the business world.

By the late nineteenth century, the streets of New York's financial district were becoming overcrowded with 'skyscrapers', and hence after the turn of the century there was a shift of construction activity to the north of Wall Street into some of the less developed parts of midtown Manhattan. One of the men who led this shift was George A. Fuller, who is credited with having 'invented' the true skyscraper, and whose striking Flatiron Building kicked off Manhattan's twentieth-century race to the sky.[10]

New Year's Eve 1899 brought the city's first snowfall of the year. It was substantial enough to robe the streets in white as revellers wended their way towards Trinity Church to ring in the turn of the century, while ice skaters waited for the all-clear to dash down to the frozen ponds of Central Park. By the next morning, even with the streets blanketed in snow and the temperature at a glacial 16° Fahrenheit, the clanging of picks and shovels could be heard at 175 Fifth Avenue. Braving the Arctic cold, hundreds of workers were busily laying the foundations for the headquarters of the George A. Fuller Company. When completed in 1902, the beguiling 22-storey triangular icon was likened to a steamship fashioned out of stone. A forerunner of the modern skyscraper, the Flatiron Building, with its undulating French Renaissance terracotta cladding, speaks of a classical past while also heralding the dawn of the great steel structures of the future.

It did not take long for New Yorkers to rechristen the Fuller Building the 'Flatiron', for reasons that become obvious when viewing the building's narrow, six-foot-wide apex from the junction of Fifth Avenue and Broadway. Fuller died two years before completion of his superb creation, but his company went on to execute some of New York's most famous buildings, among them Macy's in Herald Square, the 1904 reincarnation of the New York Times Building and the French chateau-style Plaza Hotel, opened in 1907.

The Flatiron was the forebear of an eclectic collection of buildings that were to shape Manhattan's visual iconography in future decades. It even found its way into New York's popular lexicon, with the now obsolete expression '23 skidoo', a term used to banish someone from sight. The building stands on what was once the city's windiest street corner and, on particularly breezy days, men would cluster at 23rd Street to gape at ladies passing by in the hope of seeing their petticoats lifted by the wind. When the lecherous crowds were dispersed by policemen, they were said to have been given the '23 skidoo'.[11]

In 1913 the king of America's retail trade, New Yorker Frank W. Woolworth, celebrated the success of his 'five-and-dime' empire with the opening of the Lower Broadway headquarters bearing his name. As was the case with Fuller's Flatiron, this precursor of the modernist masterpieces of the 1930s arose as a tribute to the commercial narcissism embodied in many of the city's skyscrapers. It was at once, like the Chrysler Building and others that preceded it, as well as those that were to follow, a tribute to personal vanity and an obsession with laying claim to ownership of the world's tallest building.[12] The architect Cass Gilbert, an early proponent of the skyscraper, claimed that Frank Woolworth was determined to build his headquarters higher than the Metropolitan Life Insurance Company Tower. This was largely in reprisal for Woolworth's having once been turned down for a loan by the insurer. He came across a postcard from India, of all places, with a photo of the Met Life Tower. He calculated its height and ordered his architect to build one higher.

The Woolworth Building was a prominent example of corporate advertising and personal ego, combined in one of Manhattan's early skyscrapers. The stepped medieval spire rising 55 storeys above the street was acclaimed as a tour de force of New York architecture. The building, which was paid for out of its namesake's pocket, held the record for the world's tallest for 16 years until it was surpassed by the Chrysler Building, also financed by the man whose name it bears. Soaring to nearly 800 feet, the Woolworth tower so closely evoked a great European basilica that it was soon dubbed the 'cathedral of commerce'.

This was an apt tribute to the man who paid $11.5 million of his own money for its construction and acquired sole ownership of the 57-storey structure. On 24 April 1913, President Woodrow Wilson officially opened the building from Washington, on the evening Woolworth was hosting a lavish dinner for 900 guests on the twenty-seventh floor of his tower. At a signal, a Western Union telegrapher notified the White House that all was ready: a minute later Wilson conveyed his congratulations to Woolworth and his guests, their glasses raised in the banquet hall. At a given moment, a bell rang and for the first time lights flashed from every floor.

On a drizzly November morning in 1932, Abraham E. Lefcourt was laid to rest in Brooklyn's Salem Fields Cemetery. This classic rags-to-riches entrepreneur, a Russian Jewish immigrant from Britain who in 1928 owned Manhattan skyscrapers collectively valued at $100 million, had died suddenly of a heart attack at the age of 55 in his Savoy-Plaza Hotel residence, leaving an estate of $2,500 and an empty property folio. It is nothing short of astonishing that Lefcourt, once the most renowned of New York's developers, who in the space of 20 years erected no fewer than 31 buildings, should today be all but forgotten.

Lefcourt blanketed almost 150 acres of Manhattan's land mass with steel and bricks, on which he erected structures totalling 477 storeys in height, nearly five times that of the Empire State Building. One of his acquisitions was the old Hotel Normandie at Broadway and 38th Street. It was on this corner that in 1886 the nine-year-old Abraham from the Lower East Side had spent his mornings selling newspapers to earn the few pennies that started him on his career. 'In all my life I have never received the thrill that I got in taking title to this corner,' he reflected after signing the purchase agreement. 'I remember so clearly the days when I stood on this corner selling newspapers, and little did I think that the day would ever come when I would own such a valuable piece of property.'[13]

Lefcourt served a ten-year apprenticeship in New York's garment industry, as did many Jewish immigrants of the time.[14] Unlike most of his co-religionists, who spent their working days in front of a sewing machine, Lefcourt became a powerful figure in the industry's hierarchy and went on to assume control of his employer's wholesale business. At 33, he decided to embark on the career that would make him one of the most influential developers in Manhattan's fast-growing property market. He inscribed his name on the New York skyline with a loft building in 25th Street that was to become his first company headquarters.

Lefcourt spent the next two decades putting up skyscrapers at a frantic pace. He founded his own bank, Lefcourt National Bank & Trust Company, to help finance an empire that eventually comprised seven property companies. In 1927 he single-handedly relocated the hub of the garment trade uptown when he built the 27-storey Lefcourt Clothing Center, in recognition of the huge commercial value of this business. This vast industry was at the time turning over some $200 million a year, roughly equivalent to $16 billion in today's money. Two years later the stylish Lefcourt Colonial Building opened in Madison Avenue and 41st Street. This represented a shift further north in the Manhattan skyline, which in the following decade was to acquire its classic silhouette. That same year saw the completion of another office block, the 21-storey Lefcourt Empire Building in 30th Street. Nearly a dozen more buildings bearing the Lefcourt name went up in the year just before the 1929 Crash. In keeping with the chest-thumping spirit of the Roaring Twenties' business world, almost all of his enterprises display 'Lefcourt' on the dedication plaque.

As for Lefcourt himself, rarely has anyone at the peak of his career suffered so sudden and vertiginous a fall, almost as if he had been toppled from the roof of one of his skyscrapers. Lefcourt's property companies crumbled to pieces in the wake of the Wall Street Crash, forcing him to place his entire portfolio into liquidation in order to repay investors. But the legacy he left amounts to more than the story of a Horatio Alger character whose luck turned sour. Every pinnacled tower, every streamlined facade, chevron, rectangle and sunburst that adorned the creations of Lefcourt and his fellow developers of the Roaring Twenties, foreshadowed the coming of the classic art deco giants of the 1930s.

It would have come as a consolation to the ruined Lefcourt, in the final days of his life, to recognise the imprint of his innovations on the skyline taking form across midtown Manhattan, for the 1930s architectural concepts shared by these skyscrapers are rooted in many of Lefcourt's earlier buildings. When he died in 1932, the Empire State Building, the Chrysler Building and the Waldorf-Astoria were already permanent fixtures on the Manhattan landscape, while construction on the 19 buildings that comprise Rockefeller Center was well under way.

SEVENTY-SEVENTH FLOOR, PLEASE

A t the time of writing in 2016, a dozen buildings in Manhattan stand more than 60 storeys in height. Four of these – the Chrysler Building, the Empire State Building, 40 Wall Street and 70 Pine Street[1] – were inaugurated between 1930 and 1932.

It was always going to be only a matter of time before Manhattan's skyscrapers pushed through to new plateaus. By the 1930s, the New York business world was firmly rooted in midtown Manhattan, where construction space was at a premium. Hence architects and their entrepreneur clientele were champing at the bit to achieve ever greater verticality. The technical challenges of *how* had been mastered. Crucially, the issue of stability posed no obstacle to erecting skyscrapers of several hundred storeys, as architect Paul Starrett asserted in 1931 after the completion of the Empire State Building. In theory, at least, Manhattan could easily support structures of almost limitless height. Large areas of the island sit on what is known as Manhattan schist, basically bedrock of a highly solid composition. Starrett, the head of the firm of contractors that built the Empire State Building, pointed out that a building weighing 308,000 tons required no anchorage on a solid foundation like Manhattan's.

The 'skyscrapers' that began to appear in the early part of the twentieth century were pygmies, completely overshadowed in later years by the titans of midtown. New Yorkers gazed in wonder at the 30-storey twin-tower Park Row Building that ushered in the new century. Scarcely had they been given a chance to catch their breath when in 1908 along came the Singer Tower. It had been commissioned by Frederick Bourne, who headed the company founded by Isaac Merritt Singer in the mid-nineteenth century. At 47 storeys, this Beaux Arts-style building set a new record for construction height, but retained the title for only one year.

In 1909, not to be eclipsed by a common sewing-machine manufacturer, the Metropolitan Life Insurance Company, the world's biggest insurer of its day, opened its headquarters in 23rd Street. The pinnacled clock tower, modelled after St Mark's Campanile in Venice, soared to a giddy 50 storeys. This now ranked as the world's tallest building, but the competition was ratcheting up and, four years later, Woolworth snatched away the title with its 57-storey neo-Gothic tower in Lower Broadway.

By now, the odds would be long on the New York skyline having achieved its definitive silhouette, yet for more than a decade after the completion of the Woolworth Building not a single new challenger appeared on the horizon. Then, suddenly, in the heady days of the late 1920s, several projects of colossal proportion began to emerge from the depths of Manhattan's bedrock. These were the mould-breakers, the first in the line of 1930s office structures truly worthy to bear the title of skyscraper.

The first hint of something momentous in the works for Manhattan's profile came on 4 October 1928, in a brief three-paragraph article in the *New York Times*. Walter P. Chrysler and former state senator William H. Reynolds were away from New York at the time. They were unavailable to comment on persistent rumours that the former, an automobile magnate, was negotiating the purchase from the latter of the leasehold to a property in Lexington Avenue, between 42nd and 43rd streets:

> The report is that Mr Chrysler, if he obtained the property, would use the building to be erected there for the main offices of his automobile interests [...] Whether he would erect the

67 storey building planned by Senator Reynolds or revise the plans is also problematical.[2]

It had been announced a few weeks earlier that the mortgage specialist S. W. Straus & Company had struck a deal to finance the building with a $7.5 million loan to Chrysler. The tenants on the site had vacated the premises, but no move had yet been made to demolish the structures. However, in October 1928 Chrysler began marketing mortgage bonds for his proposed Manhattan tower through Straus, the company that since 1886 had financed the construction of some of New York's grandest buildings. What exactly was on the cards for that piece of prime midtown property – and why all the mystery?

Reynolds had made it known as early as 1921 that he intended to erect a skyscraper on that spot, which was all the more attractive given its location behind Grand Central Terminal, which had been inaugurated in 1903. Another leading player in this commercial drama was the distinguished Brooklyn-born architect William Van Alen, who had been hired by Reynolds to design an enormous structure for the site, first as an office building, then in a change of mind as a hotel. Reynolds had envisaged a building flowing with romantic imagery: 'The initial sketch was self-consciously Modernist, boasting glazed, curved corners [...] But the final version was vaguely Oriental.'[3] Before Van Alen could begin unfurling his rolls of blueprint, his client was obliged to withdraw from the project for lack of financial backing. Reynolds was a shady individual who in 1917 had been hauled before a grand jury, charged with perjury over an allegedly fraudulent property sale.[4] He served one term as a senator and spent most of the rest of his working life as a property developer. His parlous financial situation made him easy prey for well-heeled, ambitious businessmen, and hence the lease on the property passed smoothly into Chrysler's hands, who was able to obtain a completion bond on the site and construction project.

The automobile magnate had different thoughts about the building's design. Decorativeness was replaced by an unabashed portrayal in cold metal of America's supreme symbol of success, the automobile, with boastful representations of spokes, hubcaps and radiator caps, set at various levels and sides of the tower.

GOING UP

Nineteen months later, on 18 June 1930, New York's newspapers heralded the opening of yet another tallest skyscraper in the world, this time hailing it as the most daring example of stylistic experimentation of the decade. The 1,046-foot Chrysler Building, the expression of its owner's whims and Van Alen's art deco genius, was the great game changer of its day. It was acclaimed as an audacious triumph of modern architecture and acknowledged as a tribute to its namesake's commercial acumen. In the space of a decade, from 1921 to 1931, the site and surrounding area on which the building stands soared in value from $143 million to $355 million.

Walter P. Chrysler, the person who stamped his identity on what many consider the most sublime edifice to adorn the Manhattan skyline, traced his origins somewhat whimsically to the royal families of Scotland and Saxony. That, at least, was the conclusion drawn from a costly genealogical research study commissioned by Chrysler's daughters, which was incorporated into a sumptuous gold-embossed leather volume of their family history. A less romantic though probably more factual version links Chrysler's forebears to immigrants from the Palatinate (a former territory of the Holy Roman Empire, now part of modern Germany), who joined a wave of emigration to the American colonies in the early eighteenth century.

Chrysler was born the son of a railway engineer in the town of Wamego, Kansas, which is serendipitously located near the city of Manhattan. He came into the world in 1875, almost ten years before Wamego got its first post office. In faraway New York City, circus impresario P. T. Barnum had yet to march 21 elephants across the Brooklyn Bridge to demonstrate its sturdiness, and it would be several more years before the dedication ceremony in New York Harbor for the Statue of Liberty, a gift from France in honour of the centenary of the Declaration of Independence.

Chrysler first demonstrated his mechanical skills at the age of 26. The jobless railway enthusiast was given the urgent task of repairing a broken locomotive cylinder head for the Denver and Rio Grande Western Railroad, as a result of which he was taken on as the company's roundhouse foreman. Six years later he had moved up to the position of master mechanic at the Chicago Great Western Railway. His career was now firmly rooted in the expanding American railway industry, and indeed he dreamed of following in the footsteps of his father. But then, as Chrysler tells it, another fast-rising US mode of transport caught his attention:

> Frequently I had to travel over to Chicago on business, but in 1908 I went to Chicago to see the automobile show. That is where it happened. I saw this Locomobile touring car; it was painted ivory white and the cushions and trim were red. The top was khaki, supported on wood bows. Straps ran from that top to anchorages on either side of the hood. On the running board there was a handsome tool box that my fingers itched to open. Beside it was a tank of gas to feed the front head lamps; just behind the hood on either side of the cowling was an oil lamp, shaped quite like those on horse drawn carriages. I spent four days hanging around the show, held by that automobile as by a siren's song.[5]

It was love at first sight. The $5,000 price tag was well beyond his means – Chrysler had only $700 in his bank account. So he borrowed $4,300 and, not knowing how to drive the sleek car, had it shipped home by rail.

The unexpected turn of events that would eventually lead to Chrysler featuring on the cover of *Time* as the magazine's 1928 Man of the Year came in 1911 in a meeting with Charles W. Nash, president of the Buick Motor Corp. Chrysler was 36 and had spent the valuable years of his youth roaming the American West and holding down middle-ranking posts at various railway companies. Nash had been briefed on Chrysler's machinist skills and his talent for lateral thinking. Over drinks and panatela cigars, he was offered a job as Buick's works manager in charge of production. During his eight-year tenure at the assembly plant in Flint, Michigan, Chrysler gained a reputation for finding ways to reduce production costs. Eight years later, Chrysler left Buick to take charge of Willys-Overland Motors and Maxwell Motor Company. He set about restoring Maxwell to profitability and, in 1924, introduced the automobile that bears his name, the Chrysler Six, during the New York Automobile Show. The following year Maxwell was reorganised into the Chrysler Corporation.

In 1928 Chrysler purchased another car company, Dodge Brothers, and later that year introduced the first Plymouth model to compete with modestly priced Fords and Chevrolets. He now found himself at the helm of the world's third-largest automobile manufacturer, surpassed in output only by General Motors (GM) and the Ford Motor Company.

A year later, the moment had arrived for Chrysler to embrace the tradition of America's great business leaders and start thinking about securing himself a niche in the pantheon of immortals: 'Something that I had seen in Paris recurred to me. I said to the architects: "Make this building higher than the Eiffel Tower." That was the beginning of the seventy-seven storey Chrysler Building.'[6] For a while it looked like architect H. Craig Severance had seized pole position in the race to build the next in the series of the world's tallest skyscrapers. Van Alen's former partner and now professional rival had been commissioned to design the headquarters of the Manhattan Company, New York's second-oldest bank at 40 Wall Street.[7] Keeping a watchful eye on the progress at the Chrysler Building nearly four miles north of Wall Street, Severance concluded that his project was going to stop at 925 feet. This would fall short of the 1,063-foot Eiffel Tower which, though not a building, was the world's tallest man-made structure, and that Chrysler had set out to upstage with his skyscraper.

Severance never suspected that Van Alen was holding a trump card up his sleeve or, more accurately, hidden in a locked storeroom. The architect of 40 Wall Street was certain his building would snatch the crown, so much so that he and his associate, the Japanese-born architect Yasuo Matsui, decided to call a halt at 927 feet of useable space. The two master architects must have been gnashing their teeth in despair on that October morning in 1929 when Van Alen unveiled his secret weapon. In the space of 90 minutes, a specially trained team selected from the 2,400 builders employed on the site hoisted into place four sections of the 27-ton, obelisk-shaped, sunburst-patterned silver spire that pushed the Chrysler Building majestically to its record-breaking height, and which on a clear day can be seen from a distance of more than 50 miles. The spire caused a sensation in the architectural world. The pinnacle had been assembled inside the building and then hoisted into place and secured through an aperture in the roof. The steel cladding achieved its purpose of catching the sunlight and drawing people's eyes from the street more than 1,000 feet below.

One of Chrysler's most dramatic innovations also stood as a reflection of his lifelong passion for metal and its creative uses. The Chrysler dome and spire, together the building's *pièce de résistance*, were clad in a revolutionary metal that looked like an alloy of steel and light. This was diamond-honed 'Enduro KA-2' steel, a form of stainless steel developed by the German steel (and arms) manufacturer Krupp after the First World War under the trade name 'Nirosta'. It was exhibited for the first time in 1926 and its use has been hailed by many architects as Chrysler's most significant achievement. It was very much in keeping with Chrysler's hands-on approach to this monument to his own person. The alloy used to clad the dome was extensively tested in his company's laboratories, until he was satisfied that its platinum colour and anti-corrosive qualities made it a suitable coating. In almost 90 years of exposure to the extremes of New York weather, no part of the spire has ever needed to be replaced.

The spire's unveiling was fervently acclaimed by the press, in professional circles and among passers-by, who craned their necks to gaze up at this tower thrusting its dazzling spear towards the heavens: 'The sudden appearance of the hidden, secret vertex was the culmination of the whole Chrysler Building project. One of the most astonishing occurrences in New York history, there has never been anything like it, before or since.'[8] Manhattan's newest symbol of architectural glory even served as inspiration for screenwriter Madeleine Ruthven's poem 'Chrysler Building':

> Never again in our time
> Shall such pinnacles leap to the sky.

These fabulous towering spires,
These airy mountains of glass,
Are the signatures of an age –
A way of life that must pass.

The delicate petals of stone,
The leaves of silvered steel,
The brassy gargoyles that fling
Their snouts to the imminent sky
Are praise of a greatness that lied,
Are wreaths for a world that has died.[9]

This was a celebration of capitalist triumph, a cocktail shaker of a building showing off the greatness of a Midwest railway mechanic who had risen to become, along with Henry Ford and the chairman of GM, Alfred P. Sloan, a household name among US automakers. The building shouts its bravado far and wide, from the whimsical frieze of hubcaps halfway up the facade to the gleaming eagle gargoyles with their 15-foot wingspans, jutting from the corners of the sixty-first floor and the crown of steel above. They are gigantic replicas of the 1929 Chrysler bonnet ornament, while the spire itself bears a playful resemblance to a car's radiator grille.

Until 1945, visitors could pay a 50-cent entry fee to ascend to the seventy-first-floor observation deck for a privileged view of Gotham and beyond. The first sight to greet tourists alighting from one of the building's 32 lifts was a picture of the site in the 1870s, when it was a goat farm; another showed the old four-storey buildings that were demolished to make way for the present structure. Between them stood a glass case containing a box of mechanics' tools, which Chrysler had made with his own hands and placed on display to illustrate his rise to power:

Years after I ceased to need them to earn a living those tools I made [...] were placed on display in a glass case on the observatory floor, seventy-one stories up in the tower of the Chrysler Building. There, on a clear day, a visitor may look to a horizon nearly 50 miles away, and by strolling around a corridor see in one quick panorama hundreds of densely populated square miles of this great land. Yet I am sure that one who neglects the view to gaze, with understanding, into that chest of tools I made, will have learned more about America than one who looks from an observatory window down into the uneven mass of steel, stone and brick that forms the city.[10]

On a steamy New York July afternoon, three months after the building's completion, a select group of business leaders, politicians and celebrities gathered for lunch at a breezy 733 feet above street level. The occasion was the opening of the Cloud Club on the Chrysler Building's sixty-seventh storey, located just at the base of the dome. This was New York's newest and most exclusive dining venue, in its design a fantasy of four blue marble columns supporting a vaulted ceiling decorated with paintings of clouds. From here, the likes of publishing mogul Condé Nast, financier Edward F. Hutton and prominent socialite Cornelius Vanderbilt Whitney could enjoy a panoramic 360° view of the city, as well as a quiet drink at the bar in the waning days of Prohibition.

The Cloud Club was a popular page filler in the gossip magazines, but there were also secrets embedded in the Chrysler Building. One of these unresolved mysteries concerned a private duplex apartment that Chrysler was said to keep just below the three-storey observation dome. If this pied-à-terre in the clouds did exist, it would undoubtedly have served as a haunt for its tenant's not-infrequent extramarital trysts. When it came to glamour, Walter Chrysler was as much an aficionado of attractive women as he was of stylish architecture. There was little of the puritanical Midwesterner in his after-hours activities, most conspicuously in his undisguised affair with the six-times-married Ziegfeld Follies starlet Peggy Hopkins Joyce, on whom he bestowed $2 million in jewellery.

Chrysler's biographer Vincent Curcio recounts an anecdote that illustrates his subject's voracious appetite for the ladies. Chrysler was once accosted by a gaggle of reporters when he alighted from a train at Grand Central Terminal. The press had got wind of his alleged frolicking with party girls in a hotel suite:

Notebooks out and flashbulbs popping, they asked him if it was true he had a girl in his sleeping compartment during the trip. He categorically denied that this was so. As he walked away [...] he told a very close associate, 'Actually, I had two.'[11]

NOT LONG AT THE TOP

In May 1930 the job was done: 21,000 tons of structural steel, nearly 4 million bricks, 794,000 partition blocks and 750 miles of electric conductor wiring, all assembled without a single mishap on the scaffolding that rose hundreds of feet above the ground. As Chrysler pointed out with pride, those 19 months of work by more than 2,000 bricklayers, electricians, glaziers and craftsmen of various trades passed with a flawless safety record. This was the first time any structure in recorded history had reached such a height with no loss of life on the building site.

The observation deck was shut to the public more than 70 years ago, when the dome was converted into office premises. Visitors are not allowed to ride the opulent Otis lifts to the upper floors, but their rare wood marquetry doors are there to dazzle the visitor. The lobby is open to sightseers and ranks as one of Gotham's most captivating art deco attractions. This is every inch a 1930s film set, one that conjures up an image of Fred Astaire and Ginger Rogers gliding across the polished marble floor. This fantasy masterpiece is clad in various marbles, onyx and amber. It is sumptuously decorated with Egyptian motifs and a ceiling fresco by Edward Trumbull entitled *Transport and Human Endeavor*. The mural depicts buildings, aeroplanes, decorative patterns and, it goes without saying, scenes from the Chrysler car plant assembly line. At 100 by 76 feet, it is reputed to be the world's largest ceiling fresco and was executed to express the spirit of the mechanical age.

The Chrysler Building became something of an overnight celebrity, heralding its future status as one of New York's best-loved architectural icons. The skyscraper has appeared in a number of movies and stage productions, including David Butler's 1930 science-fiction musical comedy *Just Imagine*, and as the Shangri-La lamasery in Frank Capra's 1937 film version of *Lost*

Horizon, which starred Ronald Colman and Jane Wyatt. More recently, in 1978, no fewer than five Chrysler Buildings were used to represent the fugitive Emerald City in Sidney Lumet's *The Wiz*, an all-African American reimagining of *The Wizard of Oz*.

The reflection from the Chrysler Building's terraced crown can cast an overwhelming, almost hypnotic spell when viewed from street level, yet this spectacular addition to Manhattan's skyline was not to everyone's liking. Two months after the opening the *New Yorker's* architecture critic, George S. Chappell, pronounced it a stunt conceived to make the man in the street look up: 'To our mind, however, it has no significance as serious design, and even if it is merely advertising architecture, we regret that Mr Van Alen did not arrange a more subtle and gracious combination for his Pelion-on-Ossa parabolic curves.'[12] In 1932, the founding director of the Museum of Modern Art (MoMA), Alfred H. Barr Jr, saw reflected in its design, as he put it, the taste of 'property speculators, rental agents and mortgage brokers'. Be that as it may, for the vast majority of people who marvel at the grandeur of the Chrysler Building's gleaming metal-clad facade and triumphal spire piercing the clouds, it is difficult to resist the urge to shout, 'Yes!'

Regardless of one's personal critique of the building's design, what cannot be denied is Chrysler's ability to pull in the paying tenants, who made this venture a commercial success from the very start. This was all the more noteworthy given the year in which it was opened for business. By mid-1930 it had become apparent that the Stock Market Crash was not a passing thunderstorm but a portent of something far worse: few now harboured any doubts that a prolonged economic disaster was in the making.

The May 1930 opening was held as an unofficial ceremony, given that construction work was still in progress on the observatory room, the Cloud Club and several other features of the upper storeys. The formal inauguration was planned for July, but by that time the building had already been 65 per cent rented, largely due to the fact that the city had yet to feel the full impact of the Depression. The first big-name tenant to take up residence was the Texas Corporation, the oil giant later known as Texaco, which leased three floors of office space. Chrysler's own company became a rent-paying customer, along with Time Inc.'s magazine empire.

Walter Chrysler was riding the crest of his career, basking in accolades from almost all quarters, hosting luncheons for the cream of New York society and banking considerable sums of rental income. The aftermath was a less joyous occasion for Van Alen, however, whose relationship with his employer ended in the law courts. In June 1930, Van Alen filed a lien against the Chrysler Building Corporation for non-payment of $725,000, which he was allegedly owed. This was part of the $865,000 he claimed as the standard 6 per cent fee of the building's cost, as stipulated under the code of the American Institute of Architects. Not only did Chrysler refuse to acknowledge Van Alen's claim, he tried to turn the tables on his chief architect in a rather nasty way by accusing him of taking kickbacks from contractors. After a protracted and acrimonious legal battle, the courts ruled in Van Alen's favour. But he had only scored a pyrrhic victory, for the affair tarnished his reputation so badly that he found himself boycotted from all major New York projects. Not to be deterred by this unfortunate turn of events, Van Alen put in an appearance at the 1931 Beaux Arts Architectural Ball dressed as a model of the Chrysler Building, sporting a black and silver tower on his head.

Chrysler Corporation's vice president Frank Rogers, whose role in the project was that of construction supervisor, expressed his belief that the Chrysler Building had all but breached the limits of skyscraper height. Rogers argued that office structures could not rise higher until new transportation technology, requiring a proportionately smaller amount of lift space, was devised. Yet he saw no prospect of this becoming a reality, at least not in the near future. The Chrysler Building's Otis lifts were designed to reach a speed of 1,000 feet per minute, but they were held back by a limit of 700 feet per minute set under the New York building code.

That said, even as Walter Chrysler was greeting the great and the good at his Cloud Club restaurant on that July afternoon in 1930, eight city blocks to the south work had already got under way on the building that was to relegate the apple of his eye to the second division among skyscrapers.

ANYTHING YOU CAN DO

On 1 October 1929, demolition work began on the old Waldorf-Astoria, New York's most stylish hotel, which consisted of two buildings, the Waldorf and the Astoria, opened in 1893 and 1897 respectively. In all, it required 16,000 loads of debris to be carted away and dumped into the sea. The gaping hole left in Fifth Avenue between 33rd and 34th streets was earmarked to accommodate the Empire State Building, which would surpass the Chrysler Building in height by 204 nose-thumbing feet.

Initially, the project was not intended to be a record-breaker in height. Property developer Floyd de L. Brown had acquired the Waldorf-Astoria with a 50-storey multi-use complex of shops and offices in mind. Brown had borrowed heavily to purchase the hotel and the land it stood on for $14 million. What he envisaged for the site was a large but modest loft-style building. He engaged an architect, drew up a feasibility study and then went about trying to raise the cash needed to consummate the deal. The Chatham & Phoenix Bank granted him a $900,000 loan to meet his first payment, but he failed to come up with enough investors who shared his enthusiasm for the project. As a result, Brown found himself in arrears on the second mortgage payment and he was forced to default. That was when two of the wealthiest men in the United States stepped into the picture: Pierre S. du Pont, of the giant chemical firm DuPont, and the financier and former DuPont treasurer John Jakob Raskob. In August 1928 they sent a memorandum of understanding to Brown's banker, Louis Kaufman, with details of their plans to build the Empire State Building.

Bad news was in store for Walter Chrysler: only two months after the pinnacle was set in place atop his building, former New York State governor Alfred E. 'Al' Smith announced that New York City was to have the greatest skyscraper of all time, rising a vertiginous 102 storeys. The building's record height would be attained by adding the unorthodox, not to say fanciful feature of a dirigible mooring's mast. This white elephant in the sky was never used for the purpose for which it was intended, but it did achieve the same objective as Chrysler's shining spire. However:

> This was utter folly. Not only does a dirigible need to be anchored by both the nose and the tail […] the updrafts in midtown were so strong that a zeppelin the length of two city blocks would have whipped around in the wind like a child's toy.[1]

More to the point, a dirigible's gondola was situated in the centre of the ship's underbelly. People would never have been able to exit from the helium-filled balloon straight into the waiting room on the 102nd floor.

Nevertheless, the Empire State Building's promoters were determined to prove the sceptics wrong, and they set out to do so in a most imaginative way. On one extraordinarily lucky occasion in 1931, a dirigible successfully anchored itself to the mooring. Somewhat in the spirit of a stunt, it had been sent to deliver a bundle of newspapers to the roof. Raskob and his colleagues were satisfied at having silenced their critics, though the exploit was never repeated.

Like the Chrysler Building, the plan to build the world's tallest skyscraper was conceived and put into execution in the ebullient days of New York City's property boom. From 1920 to 1930, the city's available office space increased from 74 million to 112 million square feet. Property developers had unlimited confidence in the market's resilience, for even the obvious glut of commercial space in the second half of the decade failed to slow the pace of construction. Other imperatives needed to be factored into the decision to build to a record height, specifically escalating land prices, which forced developers to make maximum use of the sites purchased, and the easy availability of financing before the Crash.

In 1928, few could foresee the disaster which lay in store, namely that an overheated stock market was on the brink of imploding. In that year, New Yorker Al Smith had been defeated in the US presidential election, having been the first Catholic to stand for the nation's highest office. Smith was born into a working-class Irish family. He grew up in Manhattan's Lower East Side where, before entering politics, he had worked as a lorry driver's assistant, a fishmonger and a shipping clerk. Despite having to repel a barrage of attacks by the Republican Party and newspaper mogul William Randolph Hearst, he was elected four times governor of New York State on a progressive and anti-Prohibition ticket. Now, at the age of 55 and having lost his bid for the White House to Herbert Hoover, he found himself out of a job. The anti-Catholic vote, especially in the Deep South, had been an instrumental factor in handing victory to his Republican opponent. He would never have suspected that having failed in his attempt to reach the White House, his future was entwined with an entirely different type of 'house', as president of Empire State, Inc., the syndicate launched in September 1929 to finance and promote the Empire State Building.[2]

When Walter Chrysler received the news of the plans for a new and even taller skyscraper, it must have come as a severe irritant to learn that John Jakob Raskob, finance director of his rival, GM, had become the driving force behind Empire State, Inc. Even more dispiriting was the news that Raskob had sold his GM shares at a handsome profit to help cover the cost of the venture. Chrysler was saved from what would have been the coup de grâce when the syndicate vetoed Raskob's proposal to christen the project the GM Building. There was yet another bizarre twist when Smith accepted an invitation by Raskob, who had worked as campaign manager for his failed presidential bid, to head the financial syndicate. Once at the helm of the project, Smith attended to his Roman Catholic pride by arranging for the first day of construction to take place on 17 March 1930, St Patrick's Day. Both he and Raskob were the sons of Irish mothers.

The site chosen for the skyscraper could boast a noteworthy historical heritage, having played a crucial role in the American War of Independence. It was here, at the foot of 34th Street, that in September 1776 the British succeeded in massing an army at Kips Bay Farm. On learning of this development, a distressed George Washington rushed down from his headquarters at 160th Street to take up a position on a knoll today occupied by the New York Public Library. Washington succeeded in leading his trapped soldiers, numbering more than 3,000, safely back to his north-Manhattan barracks. The retreat was organised near the Murray Hill Farm, which gave its name to the present-day neighbourhood. This is where the Quaker farmer's wife, Mary Lindley Murray, came to prominence as the alleged saviour of the Continental Army. She invited the British officers in for cakes and wine and distracted them so effectively that Washington's troops were able to slip past the redcoats and make their way safely back to Harlem Heights.

In the nineteenth century Scottish immigrant John Thomson built a picturesque farm, with a brook meandering across the property, on the site where more than a century later the 102-storey brick and steel colossus would be erected. At that time, the nearest sign of life was the occasional wagon rumbling along the dusty Bloomingdale Road, the trail that led to Broadway. Manhattan's transition to verticality is vividly illustrated by the fact that the Empire State Building occupies only a tenth of the original 20-acre farm, yet there are more than 50 acres of office space under its roof.

Apart from cheap financing and the soaring cost of land, the decision to erect a great office tower on this spot was in response to the steady migration of businesses from downtown to midtown Manhattan. Developers had begun to realise that this was destined to be the city's commercial hub. Starting in the early twentieth century, fashion outlets and large retailers like Bonwit Teller, B. Altman & Co., Macy's and Tiffany's had moved from the Union Square and 23rd Street area to the vicinity of 34th Street and Herald Square. By the 1930s, this junction could claim the dubious fame of being the most congested traffic corner in the world. Below Herald Square ran the Pennsylvania Railroad and the 6th Avenue IND and BMT subway lines, along with the Hudson Tubes that connected New York and Jersey City, which crossed one another at varying angles 65 feet underground.[3] Buses, taxis, automobiles, trucks and pedestrians clogged the intersection during working hours. A network of water mains, gas and electric lines, telephone and telegraph cables and sewers completed the tangle.

Other businesses followed the exodus from downtown. The fur trade relocated from Canal Street to Manhattan's up-and-coming commercial centre, taking with it 5,000 firms and 12,000 workers. The garment trade and textile industry followed suit, while the inauguration of Pennsylvania Station in 1910 opened up rail access for suburban commuters to midtown Manhattan and was likewise a major factor in the area's business development.[4]

Raskob, who was the building's leading promoter, appointed the prestigious architectural partnership of Shreve, Lamb & Harmon to design and construct the world's tallest skyscraper. The firm was more than up to the task: they managed to put up the 59-storey 500 Fifth Avenue Building concurrently with the Empire State Building, and in 1931 the firm was awarded the Architectural League's gold medal for its achievements. Urban folklore credits Raskob for having come up with the basic design concept. The story goes that in a meeting with William F. Lamb, he stood a four-sided sharpened pencil on end to illustrate his idea and asked Lamb how high he could build without risk of the building tipping over. Lamb established several basic priorities in order not to exceed the $50 million budget allocated for construction. The distance from window to corridor in an office was limited to 28 feet and as many storeys as possible would need to conform to those parameters. He required a cost estimate of the limestone facade and set delivery of the completed structure at one and a half years, or at the latest by 1 May 1931.

Richmond Harold Shreve was the architect tasked with putting his planning skills to work on the tower. A year later, he declared that it had required feats of organisation never before attempted in the trade. The 60,000 tons of steel used in construction were brought in on a daily basis by rail from mills in Pennsylvania. The cargo was offloaded at a depot in New Jersey, whence the girders were loaded onto a convoy of lorries that rumbled into New York City through the Holland Tunnel. Most of the deliveries were driven directly into a special entrance to the building in 34th Street. It was a truly remarkable feat of construction planning and execution. In a single working day, the steel beams were transported from the mills to midtown Manhattan and riveted into place, sometimes in eight hours or less.

The building materials were distributed by open railway carriages on narrow-gauge tracks that ran completely around each floor of the building's perimeter. Cars loaded in the basement could be hoisted up to the relevant floor and delivered to the spot where the material was to be used. One car could bring up 400 bricks per trip, compared with 100 under the old wheelbarrow system. During the summer of 1930, more than 3,400 men were on the site daily. The builders made four trips up and down per day, to and from the floors on which they worked: up in the morning, down for lunch and back up and down in the afternoon. Remarkably, in all those months of labouring in unsafe working conditions hundreds of feet above ground, only six workers and one passer-by lost their lives during the entire process – although, as we have seen, this was a significantly higher casualty rate than was experienced during the construction of the Chrysler Building, where there was not a single death. The luckless pedestrian was Elizabeth Eagher, who in July 1930 was struck on the ankle by a section of broken plank that fell from the building. The injury became infected and she later died of blood poisoning.

BRICKS FLY TO THE SKY

The timeline for one of history's most extraordinary examples of engineering work speaks for itself: on 1 October 1929, demolition crews began tearing down the Waldorf-Astoria. A little more than a year and a half later, Al Smith formally opened the Empire State Building. Five days after the hotel's demolition, the first steel girders for the new tower were set in place. In terms of construction time alone, the colossus had been erected in one year and 45 days. It was an achievement that could never be replicated today. It would require at least five years, taking into account today's layers of governmental bureaucracy and health-and-safety constraints, to construct a building of comparable scale. It had been a touch-and-go affair and one that caused Raskob and his associates many long days of anxiety. The directors had successfully dealt with the financial and technical challenges of the project, but the stumbling block that threatened to throw their plans into disarray surfaced in the guise of the 1916 New York zoning resolution.

The architects had taken pains to ensure that the Empire State Building's design complied with the requirement for setbacks at a specific height above street level. New York's building code differed from those of other US cities on one key issue: the maximum allowable stress for steel girders. If Raskob and his partners failed to persuade Mayor Jimmy Walker to amend the existing legislation and raise the limit from 16,000 to 18,000 tons of stress per square inch, the amount of steel required would take them at least 10 per cent over budget, adding some $500,000 to construction costs. A proposed revision of the law had been sitting on the mayor's desk for almost two years, but Walker had twice vetoed any changes. Finally, for reasons and in circumstances unknown, the mayor relented, though he had managed to keep the promoters on tenterhooks right up to the last moment. A plausible explanation of what might have persuaded Walker to change his mind is put forward in fictional form, in Thomas Kelly's 2005 novel about the Empire State Building:

> Walker stared out the window and said, 'So, Deputy Commissioner of Buildings, did the little code changes make my constituents happy?'
>
> 'Pleased as punch.' Farrell smiled at the rare use of his official government title.
>
> 'A small price to pay for the ability to construct such a monument to their own greed.'
>
> 'Business as usual.'[5]

At a stroke, the fears of delays and added costs had become history. Almost within hours of the revised statute obtaining official clearance, the first steel girders were being hoisted into place.

Ten million bricks and 60,000 tons of steel were all put in place in a breathtaking six months, along with 200,000 cubic feet of stone, 300 tons of exterior chrome-nickel steel, 450 tons of cast aluminium, 10,000 tons of plaster, nearly seven miles of shafts for 67 lifts capable of running at a speed of 1,200 feet per minute to serve 1,239 entrances, more than 17 million cubic feet of telephone and telegraph wire, 6,400 windows, 6,700 radiators, 51 miles of plumbing, 396 openings into mail chutes and a ventilating system delivering 725,000 feet of air per minute.

The construction system in itself was an amazing triumph of coordination, efficiency and sheer human energy. The *New York Times* dispatched one of its columnists to the Fifth Avenue building site to report on progress, when the structure was roughly at the halfway stage. He followed one of the flatbed lorries delivering its load into the building, where he found himself surrounded by a forest of concrete-covered piers. The journalist gazed on a swarm of human activity, probably not dissimilar to the raising of the Great Pyramid of Giza. He wrote:

> Here there is an infinity of operations. Truckloads of bricks are being unloaded with a roar as the truck chassis tips up and the load goes thundering down through the floor into a basement hopper. Sheet iron, metal parts, bales of wire and coils of cable, sand and cinders and lumber and pipes arrive. Each is unloaded in a special corner of the block-wide floor, presently to go shooting up in elevators to the floor where each is needed.[6]

People on their way to work, passing along Fifth Avenue and 34th Street, could not fail to halt and contemplate the wondrous tower rising before their eyes. With good reason they might have asked, why so quick, why so high?

Never before had a structure on this scale been put up at so dizzying a speed. A mere 20 months had elapsed between the signing on of Shreve, Lamb & Harmon as architects and the opening day on 1 May 1931. At one stage, workers set in place enough steel, concrete and stone to race 50 per cent ahead of their one-storey-a-day schedule. As one foreman on the site commented to the *New York Times*, 'We ran trucks the way they run trains in and out of Grand Central. If a truck missed its place in the line on Tuesday, it had to wait until Wednesday to get back in.'[7]

Not a moment of working time was wasted on the job, not even for lunch breaks. Mobile kitchens were set up at various levels of the building to avoid the need for the builders to climb down and back up for their midday meal.

Each storey had a miniature railway system, equipped with turntables, for carrying equipment and building materials from the central work lift to the outposts of each floor.

It was this clockwork vertical assembly line that enabled the project to be completed ahead of schedule. Everyone involved in the process – from equipment and building-material suppliers to promoters, architects and contractors – worked in close round-the-clock collaboration. It is obvious that without skilled and unremitting direction and microscopic attention to detail, nothing but chaos would have ensued. This was a well-oiled construction machine, which on an average day could seamlessly deliver 500 loads of materials, machinery and equipment to the site, on most days within eight hours. The site itself was the equivalent of a small railway marshalling yard, with rails laid on the first basement and street-level floors, an overhead monorail for delivering equipment and material to a required construction spot, 17 internal hoists operating at 600 feet per minute and nine cages independent of the lifts for transporting builders up and down the structure.

The finished building was a masterpiece of discipline and organisation, a testimony to the need for teamwork and flawless coordination. It was through this determination to forge ahead tirelessly but always according to a meticulously designed master plan that the stupendous feat of finishing the Empire State Building was accomplished within a year of the erection of the first steel stanchion.

The consummate performers in this drama were the contractors Starrett Brothers & Eken, a firm set up in the early 1920s by Paul and William Starrett and joined in 1929 by Andrew Eken, who in later years took over as chairman. The Starretts and Eken, separately or in partnership, were responsible for building some of New York's most eminent structures, including the Flatiron Building, Pennsylvania Station and the New York Life Insurance Building. Eken could take credit for another record-breaking skyscraper, the 70-storey Bank of Manhattan Trust Building at 40 Wall Street. For two months before the inauguration of the Chrysler Building, this tower had dominated Gotham's skyline.

As Paul Starrett tells it, he and his brother William were called to the office of former state governor Al Smith, president of Empire State, Inc., at the Biltmore Hotel to present their case for the Empire State Building contract. Starrett knew he was up against stiff competition from a handful of well-established firms: 'This was to be the most magnificent skyscraper ever erected in the world. I felt that I had been working towards the job all my life. I *must* get it.' Starrett's strategy was to convince Smith and his partners that he could put up the structure in record time, matching his performance on the Bank of Manhattan Trust Building. Smith asked how much he wanted for the job. Starrett said his fee was $600,000, to which Smith retorted that he was prepared to offer $500,000 at most. He encouraged Starrett to consider the status attached to having his firm's name on the project. Smith explained that whenever he gave a speech, he held up his bowler, given him by Dobbs, a millinery firm, with the label conspicuously facing the crowd. 'That shows what value Dobbs puts on advertising.' Starrett demurred, assuring the syndicate members he could complete the job in 18 months. With that, he got up and left the meeting.

That same afternoon, when Starrett had returned to his office, Smith and Shreve turned up at his door to congratulate him: they had decided to award him the contract, albeit for a fee of $500,000. Starrett hesitated, bickered for a few minutes and then accepted the commission with resignation: 'I was very glad to get the job at any price. The Depression came, all construction in New York had dropped to zero, but we were at work on the biggest building in the world.'[8]

Above and beyond whatever glory might be harvested from having put up the world's tallest building, as far as its investors were concerned the chief purpose of this undertaking was to turn a profit. Smith, Raskob, du Pont and the rest of the syndicate had taken an enormous gamble on the Empire State Building. The Depression was biting deeper by the day; rental prospects grew gloomier with each storey that was added to the tower and, by the time of completion, the calculated return on investment had been slashed by 20 per cent. Land costs in midtown were at a premium; hence good business sense dictated that the bigger the building, the greater the potential for rental income, in this case for a population of 25,000 housed in office premises. The promoters worked tirelessly to advertise the status attached to having the Empire State Building as a corporate headquarters address.

It has been estimated that above a certain height of paying occupancy, roughly equivalent to that of the Chrysler Building, the law of diminishing returns on investment begins to take effect. Profitability usually kicks in at eight storeys and each additional floor spreads the cost of land thinner across the total investment, thus enhancing returns. Where land is extremely expensive, as is the case in the Wall Street district or midtown Manhattan, with property costs averaging $200 per square foot in the 1930s (roughly $3,000 in today's value), the skyscraper is the only solution for achieving an acceptable rate of return from the cost of land – but only up to a point. At a determined level a series of negatives need to be factored into the equation, such as property-tax rates and the cost of added construction materials. When the Chrysler and Empire State buildings were erected, for instance, steel accounted for some 7.7 per cent of the total cost of an eight-storey structure, rising to 14.8 per cent for a 75-storey tower. In 1930, a multi-discipline commission of professional builders calculated 63 storeys as the limit for obtaining an optimum annual income on capital outlay. In the case of the Empire State Building, commercial office space occupied 80 storeys, 17 above the financial threshold.[9] These equations were to prove ominous for Raskob and his colleagues, but for 13 months promoters and builders alike pushed relentlessly on, their sights set on a single objective: the completion and unveiling of the greatest architectural triumph in Gotham's history.

THE LEVIATHAN ARISES

The great day finally arrived. At 11.30 a.m. on 1 May 1931, President Herbert Hoover – who like Woodrow Wilson in the earlier part of the century, had become something of a practitioner in inaugurating skyscrapers remotely – pressed a button in the White House that switched on the lights in this 1,250-foot, 102-storey behemoth. While Al Smith's two grandchildren cut the ribbons at the 350 Fifth Avenue entrance, patrolmen and mounted officers struggled to hold back a throng of spectators in their thousands, who surged forward to rush the police lines. Far above the crowd, a buffet lunch for 350 guests was in progress in the splendid eighty-sixth-floor observation deck, from which the visitors could see the boundaries of three states: New York, Connecticut and New Jersey.

It was equally a day of jubilation for the more than 3,000-strong construction team, a large number of them Irish Americans, who took obvious pride in being a part of this historic undertaking. As one of the building's architects, Richmond Shreve, remarked when the job was done: 'When we were in full swing going up the main tower, things clicked with such precision that we once erected 14 and a half floors in one working day – steel, concrete, stone and all.'

The Empire State Building was now officially open for business: only there was none to be found. Paul Starrett, along with the partners of Empire State, Inc., observed with a heavy heart the darkened windows of unrented offices in the tower. The US economy had gone into freefall. The final dark days of 1929 were followed by an even bleaker 1930. The Empire State Building had been completed, was ready for occupancy but stood ominously empty.[10] Building permits, which between 1925 and 1929 had averaged more than $850 million a year in value in New York, by 1933 had fallen to $50 million. Starrett himself suffered a severe nervous breakdown, but managed to hang on and keep his scaled-down company afloat. Not so his friend Harry S. Black, chairman of the giant George A. Fuller Company, America's largest construction firm, which had given its name to what became known as the Flatiron Building. Black's primary residence was on the eighteenth floor of the Plaza Hotel, which he had helped to build. One summer morning in 1930, he walked out of the revolving doors on Fifth Avenue and drove to his exclusive Long Island estate where he put a gun to his head in his bedroom.

In 1934, the *New York Times* had occasion to reflect on the future of the skyscraper as a commercial venture. The paper ran an editorial the week following the death of legendary New York architect Raymond Hood, whose last great commission had been Rockefeller Center's Radio City, another colossal enterprise of the Depression that had suffered through a good deal of financial pain:

> How many years will it be before builders set out once more to
> out-top their neighbours' towers? Or has an era which began

about 25 years ago with the Singer Tower and the Woolworth Building come to an end with the Empire State and Rockefeller Center? Even before the Great Crash and the Great Depression, the skyscraper was under suspicion from the standpoint of sound economics. It did not always pay for itself as a renting enterprise.[11]

The risks inherent in an undertaking of this magnitude were a matter of unassailable commercial logic. A large part of the financial return would depend on the success of a campaign to advertise the project's sheer size or uniqueness. But to achieve this purpose, a skyscraper needed to be more than tall. It had to be taller, or indeed the tallest. In the early 1930s, developers were not erecting high buildings, but higher buildings, primarily for the world to look at and talk about, and only subsequently for tenants to rent. The collapse of the US economy turned this into a very costly publicity exercise.

The Empire State Building might have stood a chance of benefiting from the slow recovery of the US economy, which showed signs of improvement in the years following its inauguration. By the middle of the decade, production, corporate profits and wages had regained their pre-Crash levels. But the hopes of better times ahead were dashed in 1937 when the country slipped into a double-dip recession. Unemployment rose nearly 5 per cent, while manufacturing plummeted 37 per cent, back to its 1934 level. There is no consensus among pundits to explain this unforeseen collapse, but most lay the blame at the door of the federal government's spending cuts and tax increases, as well as the Treasury's tightening of the money supply in the quixotic anticipation of a sustained rally.

The Empire State Building's 2.1 million square feet of rentable commercial space considerably exceeded that of the Chrysler and Manhattan Life Insurance buildings combined.[12] For more than two decades the syndicate teetered on the verge of bankruptcy, unable to fill the empty offices. It was a nerve-racking time for investors. Five years after completion only a quarter of the building's available office space had been rented, with 56 floors remaining empty. Raskob could only look on in dismay as the Chrysler Building's letting agent celebrated a 70 per cent occupancy rate. In desperation, Raskob instructed the maintenance staff to go about switching on lights in vacant offices at night, the idea being to send out an appearance of activity behind the building's aluminium-panelled curtain walls.

In the context of this near collapse in economic activity, the Chrysler Building was ready for occupancy just under the wire. In contrast, by the time its giant downtown rival opened its doors, the Depression was biting with a vengeance. Proximity to Pennsylvania Station, which served mostly longer-distance travellers, turned out to be less of a boon than the Empire State Building's letting agents had anticipated. The Chrysler's Building's location at 42nd Street put it a stone's throw from Grand Central Terminal, a far more practical station for commuters from the outer boroughs and nearby towns of New Jersey and Connecticut.

The Empire State Building's one profitable source of income in those days of financial famine was the observation deck, which earned $1 million in 1930 alone and by 1935 had brought in 2.1 million paying visitors. The massive, austere lobby was an attraction in itself, with its 15,000 square feet of aluminium panelling and 1,300-square foot, 23-carat gold leaf celestial ceiling mural, painted by Edward Turnbull in the art deco style. The subject matter chosen is that of the defining symbol of the American success story: the family car. In keeping with the public's adulation of the automobile, the sun and planets that cover the mural are executed to resemble gears and wheels.

It was not until after the Second World War, when the country's economy reverted from war-related manufacturing, that a significant number of commercial tenants began signing leases. Around that time, as if to drive home the building's sorry state, on a Saturday morning in July 1945 a US Air Force B-25 bomber crashed into the seventy-ninth floor while coming in to land at Newark Metropolitan Airport in thick fog. Tragically, the plane had banked right instead of left when passing (irony of ironies) the Chrysler Building, taking it on a direct collision course with the Empire State Building. The crash killed 14 people and ignited what was and remains the highest blaze ever extinguished by firefighters. The building's owners were nonetheless determined to shrug off the disaster and, in the absence of today's health-and-safety authorities, on Monday morning the Empire State Building was open for business as usual.

The corporate world may have turned its back on the Empire State Building, but not so the entertainment industry. Whatever its financial misfortunes, this skyscraper was destined to become a (many would say *the*) Gotham landmark. Since the 1930s its distinctive contours have featured in some 90 films. The most famous of all is *King Kong*, the 1933 classic starring Fay Wray as the archetypal damsel in distress. With its cataclysmic, heart-breaking finale, the film gives the impression that director Merian C. Cooper placed the great lovestruck ape on the mast (dirigibles beware), swiping its fist at dive-bombing aeroplanes, and worked his way back from there to develop the rest of the story. The film acquired cinema-icon status, with Hollywood follow-ups in 1976 and 2005.[13]

The building also features in the 1939 film *Love Affair*, with Charles Boyer, and the 1994 remake starring Katharine Hepburn and Warren Beatty. In the 1957 movie *An Affair to Remember*, the glamorous nightclub singer Terry McKay (Deborah Kerr) and Nickie Ferrante (Cary Grant) fall in love while returning from Europe to New York on a cruise ship. Despite both being engaged, they agree to meet in six months' time on the observation deck of the Empire State Building, which a gushing McKay calls 'the closest thing to heaven in this city'. The 1993 romantic comedy *Sleepless in Seattle* has Tom Hanks and Meg Ryan meeting one night on that same observation deck. Television viewers on the other side of the Atlantic even witnessed the collapse of the great tower of the Empire State Building in an early episode of the British series *Thunderbirds*.

The Empire State Building, as the undisputed embodiment of New York's skyscraper phenomenon, nevertheless generated criticism from some quarters. As far back as the late nineteenth century, the Brooklyn-born architect Ernest Flagg had warned of the alleged perils of tall buildings in general. He highlighted the risk of fire engulfing anybody trying to escape a burning building, unable to flee in the narrow, crowded streets below. Flagg's foreboding rings with a certain degree of hypocrisy, as it was he who designed the Singer Tower in Broadway, which at 47 storeys held the title of the world's tallest building in 1908–9. Other opponents railed against what they saw as a violation of the city's aesthetics. The flamboyantly bewhiskered art critic Montgomery Schuyler denounced skyscrapers as destroyers of New York's low-rise skyline, plunging the streets below into gloom under a 'horribly jagged sierra'.[14] Schuyler's bluster arguably contains a degree of legitimacy, for the Empire State Building does cast an extensive shadow over swathes of midtown. But with the passing hours of day, no one segment of city blocks is consigned to permanent darkness.

Like it or not, the Empire State Building, more than any structure in Manhattan, has come to symbolise the energy and singularity of Gotham. To put this into perspective, today many New Yorkers are voicing their outrage not against this treasured icon, but the fact that the 1,775-foot Nordstrom Tower commercial and residential project in West 57th Street, due to be completed in 2018, will block their view of the Empire State Building.

Snobbery and groundless health warnings aside, when viewed from the waterfronts of Long Island Sound or Brooklyn Heights, from the back seat of a yellow cab grinding its way from JFK towards Manhattan, or from the deck of a ferry chugging to Battery Park from the Statue of Liberty, for much of the world, the Empire State Building stands as the most evocative symbol of New York City. The Manhattan skyline and its most emblematic building inspire awe, a promise of excitement, even a sense of reverence. The Russian-born writer and philosopher Ayn Rand expressed it in her 1943 novel *The Fountainhead*:

> I would give the greatest sunset in the world for one sight of New York's skyline [...] The shapes and the thought that made them. The sky over New York and the will of Man made visible [...] Let them come to New York, stand on the shore of the Hudson, look and kneel.[15]

10

YOU'RE THE TOP

L ate on the evening of 13 December 1931, an event took place in Manhattan that could have altered the course of the Second World War. That afternoon, Winston Churchill left his suite at the Waldorf-Astoria to pay a visit to his close friend, the American financier and philanthropist Bernard Baruch. Churchill stepped out of the hotel's gilded Park Avenue exit and climbed into a waiting yellow cab for the uptown drive to Baruch's Fifth Avenue mansion.

On alighting from the taxi into two-way traffic, perhaps in a distracted state of mind at having recently been excluded from Ramsay MacDonald's coalition government, Churchill seemed to have forgotten the difference between the British and American rule of the road. He looked left, without taking notice of a car approaching on his right. The only vehicle in the street was another cab and, as bad luck would have it, it slammed straight into Britain's future wartime prime minister. Churchill was rushed to Lenox Hill Hospital, suffering from severe shock and concussion, along with heavy bruises on his arm, chest and legs, and deep cuts on his forehead and nose. Had he not been wearing a thick fur-lined overcoat, the accident could easily have ended Churchill's life. In reporting this near tragedy, the New York papers drew attention to Churchill's sporting gesture in exonerating the cab driver from all blame. For his part, the mortified cabbie made it a point to visit the patient every day during his stay in hospital.

A limping, badly bruised Churchill returned to the Waldorf-Astoria after several weeks in hospital for the start of a two-month period of convalescence. The incident did not fail to arouse his Fleet Street instinct for a good story. As a former war correspondent, he managed to squeeze a well-paid article out of his accident for William Randolph Hearst's *New York Journal-American*. The impression Churchill left with the hotel staff, especially bearing in mind his battered state, is at variance with Yousuf Karsh's memorable 1941 bull-dog-scowl photograph. Frank Kelly, who was bell captain of 'the Towers', the most exclusive floors of the hotel, where Churchill had his suite, remembered him as 'a grand old man' (Churchill was 57 at the time), always with a cigar, a smile and something nice to say.[1]

The new Waldorf-Astoria, where the British politician and a multitude of other world statesmen and celebrities were to reside on their visits to New York, had opened its doors for business only three months previous to Churchill's mishap. The inspiration behind the hotel's origins can be traced to the town of Walldorf in the German state of Baden-Württemberg. Walldorf today ranks as one of the most prosperous towns in Europe, thanks largely to its status as the headquarters of SAP, the world's third-largest software manufacturer. The town can also lay claim to being the birthplace of Johann Jakob Astor, who, unlike his namesake father, the local butcher, was an adventurous-spirited soul, living the life of a merchant and fur trader. In 1784 he arrived in America, where he anglicised his name to John Jacob, invested in New York City property and died in 1848 at the age of 84, the richest man in the United States and the country's first multimillionaire, leaving a fortune calculated at more than $100 billion in today's money.

Two of Astor's sons, John Jacob Astor Jr and William Backhouse Astor (later Sr), established themselves in Fifth Avenue and its soon-to-become fashionable streets in the 1830s. In 1827, the latter purchased the land on what would become 33rd Street and Fifth Avenue for $20,500. By the 1890s, and two generations of the Astor family later, William Waldorf Astor and his cousin John Jacob Astor IV (both grandsons of William Backhouse Astor

Sr) shared the property, William on the 33rd Street side and John on the frontage facing 34th Street.

It was William who came up with the idea of building an opulent, European-style hotel in midtown Manhattan. Thus in 1893 arose the original Waldorf, which as we saw earlier was torn down 36 years later to make way for the Empire State Building. The site chosen for the original pleasure palace was William's 33rd Street family home, a sprawling Victorian mansion every bit as imposing as that of his cousin and next-door neighbour John Jacob Astor IV, who in 1912 was to be lost with the sinking of the *Titanic*.

The Astor family's two elegant townhouses were quite a radical venture, for in the mid-nineteenth century Fifth Avenue was little more than an unpaved road: Manhattan maps of the day catalogued numbered houses only up to 23rd Street. This is where the avenue crosses Broadway, in those days the bustling thoroughfare linking the downtown financial and commercial district with the burgeoning residential community north of Wall Street. Now Fifth Avenue's social profile was starting to undergo a transformation, one in which the Astor family played a key role. The avenue acted as a natural magnet for New York's affluent set. Unlike the tumult and congestion generated by the Broadway tramline that began running in 1884, the roadway to the east remained an undeveloped haven of genteel tranquillity.

The arrival of the Astor clan and their magnificent abodes heralded Fifth Avenue's coming of age. The two stately homes that stood on 33rd and 34th streets became the much-solicited rendezvous for New York's 'Four Hundred', an exclusive tribe consisting mainly of old money with a smattering of new. Among them, it was the arrivistes who fought to have their names pinned to the guest list of New York's prime socialite, Caroline Webster Schermerhorn. The self-proclaimed '*the* Mrs Astor' was the wife of William Backhouse Astor Jr (father of John Jacob Astor IV), the next-door neighbour of his older brother John Jacob Astor III (father of William Waldorf Astor). It was said the Schermerhorn ballroom could comfortably fit 400 select guests.

William Waldorf Astor provided the money and location for the first incarnation of the hotel that was to bear the name of his home town in the Old World. The concept was simple yet revolutionary for the New York (and American) hotel industry, a sector distinguished by the uninspiring sameness of the travelling salesman's overnight rest stop. This was to be something out of the ordinary, quite a cut above the drab piles that had begun to dot Fifth Avenue and, in 1890, New York's social-gossip grapevine was buzzing with rumours that 'Willy' Waldorf was thinking of building a great luxury hotel. Waldorf had been in talks with his estate agent Abner Bartlett, which led to the demolishing of the Waldorf family mansion and the moving in of steam shovels. This development was observed with concern by Willy's cousin John Jacob Astor IV, whose red-brick home stood on the adjoining plot of land.

ENTER THE HOTEL GRANDEES

Two men shortly came on the scene, both destined to become immortal names in the New York hotel industry. George C. Boldt and Oscar Tschirky were to characterise the personality and luxurious standards of not only this, but also the second and definitive incarnation of the Waldorf-Astoria, which opened in Park Avenue in 1931. Boldt, a German immigrant and self-made millionaire who brought with him a solid track record as a hotelier, was chosen by Astor to guide the Waldorf's destiny. He took over the original 17-storey tower and raised the standards of hospitality to hitherto unimagined heights, right from the very afternoon of its grand opening ceremony on 14 March 1893. On that day:

> Sweet and gentle Charity was the honoured guest at the formal opening of the sumptuous new Waldorf Hotel, Fifth Avenue and 33rd Street. The hand of Society greeted cordially all persons who entered the portals of that regal establishment and led them, not only into a realm of splendour and luxury, but into a genial atmosphere of restful enjoyment.[2]

The ceremony got off to a touch-and-go start, thanks to a morning of torrential rain, a last-minute walkout by kitchen employees and a fatal staff accident. Kate McNierney, a 23-year-old storeroom worker, on her way to bed shortly before midnight, suffered the misfortune of stepping into the open door of the elevator shaft without checking that the lift was actually at the floor. She fell eleven storeys to her death.

Most of the guests would not learn of this mishap until the next day, but the suave, bespectacled and goatee-bearded Boldt was there to take all these problems in hand, with the exception of the weather. The day went down as one of Gotham's most memorable society events of the season. The New York Philharmonic played Liszt, Rossini and Wagner for the great families of New York, as well as for the patricians who figured on the Social Registers of Philadelphia, Boston and Baltimore. The Vanderbilt family turned it into a charity event in aid of New York's St Mary's Free Hospital for Children.

By the 1890s, Boldt's fame as the gracious manager of the Bellevue-Stratford Hotel in Philadelphia had reached New York City. His first fortuitous encounter with William Waldorf Astor took place in that hotel, when Boldt moved himself and his family out of his own suite to make room for Waldorf, who had failed to find accommodation elsewhere on a trip to Philadelphia. Boldt's most providential recruit was Oscar Tschirky, a 27-year-old Swiss who became the creator of the Waldorf salad and was immortalised in Manhattan's smart circles as 'Oscar of the Waldorf'. Tschirky had arrived in New York as a rugged, lantern-jawed youth of 17, imbued with the Calvinist work ethic of his homeland and with an unambiguous vision of the path his career was to follow. He immediately set his sights on America's burgeoning hotel and catering industry, taking a job as a humble kitchen assistant in what was then New York's leading hotel, the Hoffman House at Broadway and 25th Street. His starting pay was $18 a month, a far cry from the $250 he would be drawing a few years later as the Waldorf's head waiter.

Tschirky's reputation as a tireless and talented hotelier eventually landed him a six-year stint at Delmonico's, the New York restaurant favoured by Charles Dickens and Theodore Roosevelt, among other eminences. Out for a stroll one day, Tschirky came across a great hole in the ground at Fifth Avenue and 33rd Street, the spot where the Waldorf family mansion had stood. When he was told this was to be the site of a great hotel, he lost no time in firing off a job application to Boldt. The hotel owner replied, saying it was early days to be looking for a maître d'hôtel, but that he would be happy to consider a few letters of recommendation. Tschirky was equally happy to oblige and, a few days later, he delivered a ten-page document bearing the testimonials of, among others, businessman 'Diamond' Jim Brady, Pennsylvania Railroad president Samuel Rea, actress Lillian Russell, financier George Gould, industrialist and silver-mine magnate John William Mackay and celebrated war reporter and novelist Richard Harding Davis.

Tschirky got the job.

The Swiss are not generally noted for being mould-breakers. However, Tschirky could rank as an exception, given the innovations he brought to the hotel business. During his tenure at the old Waldorf-Astoria, Tschirky introduced the institution of room service to the hotel trade. Though lacking in culinary skills, he organised and presided over untold dinners and banquets in the 50 years he was employed at the old and new hotels. Tschirky capitalised on New Yorkers' fondness for dining and seeking entertainment outside their homes. Among the wealthier and socially exclusive classes, the Waldorf-Astoria brought popularity to the art of 'dining out'. This idiosyncrasy was noted in the late 1930s by the British photographer and designer Cecil Beaton, during a visit to New York: 'One of the greatest upheavals that befell the city was when, during a strike, no one could go out to the cinema or a restaurant, and the radio advised everyone to stay at home by his own hearth.'[3] It was ingrained in Tschirky's egalitarian Swiss DNA to abolish the ban on women dining on their own in a restaurant and, not to be accused of reverse sexism, he did away with the rule that forbade men from smoking in front of ladies in a public place. The hotel also had a salon reserved for women to play billiards and table tennis. In a word, he paved the way for modern standards in catering and hotel service. Tschirky shrugged off critics of his liberalising policies with unassailable Swiss logic: 'We do not regulate the public taste. Public taste does and should regulate us.'[4]

Not to be outdone by his enterprising cousin, within two years of the inauguration of the Waldorf in 1893 John Jacob Astor IV had likewise reduced his home on the adjoining property to a pile of rubble in order to clear the land for development of the 13-storey Astoria, four floors higher than Willy's building. The name Astoria was chosen in memory of the first trading post established by his great-grandfather in 1811, at the mouth of the Columbia River in Oregon. The opening ceremony for the new hotel took place on 1 November 1897, with fairy lights and a children's dance in aid of charity organised by the dowagers of New York high society.

The combined Waldorf-Astoria ushered in the era of the skyscraper hotel: 'In this enormous caravansary [...] every personal desire could be fulfilled without ever venturing outside its walls: lectures, receptions in one of 40 different rooms, spectacles and vaudeville entertainment on the rooftop were common features of the hotel.'[5] In addition, the two buildings could accommodate 1,500 guests, serviced by almost as large a staff, which included 150 hall boys, 400 waiters and 250 chambermaids. The hotel was equipped with an enormous electric plant using 16 tons of coal a day, powering 16 lifts, a plant making 50 tons of ice daily and a huge set of boilers providing hot water for all the suites.

By mutual consent of the Astor cousins, Boldt was appointed owner of the Waldorf-Astoria Hotel Company, which held the lease on the property, and with Prussian determination, he spared no effort to ensure that the new hotel measured up to the Waldorf's standards of luxury. The rooms were furnished with lace curtains from Switzerland, Arabian and Renaissance hangings from Paris and polished walnut furniture built by French as well as American craftsmen. The most eye-catching salon was the Louis XV-style Astor Gallery, a coquettish copy of the Hall of Mirrors at Versailles.

But it was Peacock Alley that stole the show, hands down.

That the ground floors of both hotels stood at the same level, enabling them to be joined by a marble corridor, known as 'Peacock Alley', was a result of Boldt's foresight: he caused the Waldorf's ground floor to be set high enough above 33rd Street to meet the pavement in 34th Street, which stands several feet higher. Peacock Alley gave access to two of the most fashionable restaurants in New York, the Palm Room (in the Astoria) and the Empire Room (in the Waldorf). In its original guise it boasted Corinthian columns, mosaic floors and richly appointed benches lining the promenade. Its name came from the *New York Herald Tribune* newspaper, which used the term after a journalist overheard a guest remark that the 980-foot corridor – a society catwalk where ladies of fashion strolled in order to display their gowns, jewellery and plumed hats – was like an alley of peacocks. It was not unusual for 25,000 people to walk the length of Peacock Alley in a single day.[6]

The Waldorf-Astoria, joined together in 1897, suffered a devastating blow 19 years later, shortly after the staff had taken down the last of the Christmas party decorations, with the sudden death of Boldt at the age of 65. For a while it was hoped that his son and heir to the job, George C. Boldt Jr, would strive to keep alive the intimate touch that had made his father the Waldorf-Astoria's guiding spirit. In nearly a quarter of a century at the hotel, George Sr had developed personal friendships with many of the hotel's eminent guests, and his affable personality enabled him to retain old acquaintances and easily make new ones. But George Jr, by his own admission, had no particular interest in hotel management and after three years he withdrew from the business.

In 1918 the hotel, which operated under a lease from the Astor family, was passed on to a property partnership set up by the hotelier Lucius Boomer and the industrialist Thomas Coleman du Pont. Boomer was appointed president of Boomer–du Pont Properties Corporation, which carried with it responsibility for managing the hotel. The Waldorf-Astoria was valued at $20 million, though at the time the sale price was not revealed.

The new owners were not in for an easy ride, for despite its widespread fame and grandeur, the Waldorf-Astoria faced tough times ahead. For the one thing, Manhattan's gentrified classes had been steadily migrating further north, fleeing the increasingly commercialised area of midtown. This trend had been foreseen by a handful of property developers and hoteliers. The Plaza Hotel opened its doors a decade before the Waldorf-Astoria changed hands. This grandiose, French Renaissance-style building stands in 59th Street facing Central Park, a location closer to Manhattan's new affluent residential centre. The Plaza was within easy walking distance for local residents, a convenient place for them to stop for tea or dinner, avoiding the necessity of battling through the traffic more than a mile downtown to the Waldorf-Astoria.

There were another two threats lurking on the horizon, both of which were to make 1920 a crunch year for the hotel. The post-First World War economic depression was by no means as severe or prolonged as the collapse that was to follow a decade later. But a combination of the wrenching readjustment to a peacetime economy, a spike in trade union militancy and a sharp rise in interest rates hit business activity hard enough to bring a sharp fall in GDP, estimated by some economists to be as high as 6.9 per cent. Concurrent with the postwar downturn, in the same year Prohibition came into effect when Congress passed the Eighteenth Amendment. This represented a devastating blow for the Waldorf-Astoria – for any hotel, for that matter, whose bars and restaurants provided a flow of substantial income from the sale of wine and spirits.

With elite society turning its back on the spreading commercialism of the Herald Square–Pennsylvania Station district, the nearby Waldorf-Astoria found itself on the cusp of the slippery slope. The grand hotel was no longer the centre of Manhattan high life, a turn of events that understandably did not escape Boldt's attention. But he and the rest of the management were spared the agony of watching this queen of hotels decline into financial ruin.

The hotel was sold to Bethlehem Engineering Corporation in 1928, while Boomer went scouting about for a suitable location uptown to which to relocate. The site selected did not seem at first glance the most auspicious of settings. The Park and Lexington avenues enclave between 49th and 50th streets was occupied by a YMCA, a boiler works, a brewer and a piano manufacturer. Nevertheless, Boomer saw promise in this new home and he especially liked the Empire State Building's promoters' offer of $13.5 million for the old hotel. The financial package for the new Waldorf-Astoria was signed on 3 October 1929. Investors estimated the cost of the 47-storey building at $28 million. Two railway companies agreed to put up $10 million in financing, while the Waldorf-Astoria Corporation issued $11 million in bonds. A syndicate of 21 banks provided another $7 million on 28 October, the day before the Stock Market Crash.

A GRAND REINCARNATION

The first rivet was driven into what was to become the world's largest hotel on 24 March 1930. The new Waldorf-Astoria would be more than twice the size of its predecessor, occupying an entire city block between Park and Lexington avenues. Boomer's dream was on its way towards fulfilment, and not a moment too soon, for by now his was not the only show in town.

Apart from the Plaza, several other grand hotels had opened premises along the fashionable Upper East Side. The most eye-catching of the lot was the Pierre in Fifth Avenue and 61st Street. This svelte, 41-storey tower offered its guests unmatched views of Central Park and a panorama of Manhattan's most prominent landmarks. Walter P. Chrysler had joined the group of investors who financed the $15 million French chateau-style project, while the firm of architects Schultze & Weaver had also been engaged by Boomer to design the new Waldorf-Astoria.

The Pierre opened for business on 1 October 1930, boasting magnificently appointed rooms for 700 guests and with France's legendary 85-year-old chef Auguste Escoffier at the kitchen helm. With the Pierre's opening, this soaring 525-foot tower in Fifth Avenue, its neighbour the Plaza and others had planted their standards in the turf Boomer set out to claim as his own, with the Waldorf-Astoria still a year away from completion.[7]

The opening-day ceremony proved that the Waldorf-Astoria name had lost none of its magic for New Yorkers during the years it remained shut to society's upper crust. On the morning of 1 October 1931, a year to the day after the Pierre's opening, a crowd of 20,000 visitors gathered in front of the new Waldorf-Astoria's Park Avenue entrance. Shortly before midday, northbound traffic was stopped in the avenue to make room for the largest hand-tufted carpet ever woven in a single piece to be carried into the foyer by 50 fitters. This carpet, 70 feet in length and 50 in width, had required the work of 30 Czech craftsmen, who had laboured for ten months, tying 12.6 million knots to fashion a sumptuous Persian garden scene. A detachment of officers from the NYPD formed a cordon at the entrance, while the hotel crew swung the carpet far out into a freshly swept street. They then aimed the two-and-a-half-ton colossus at the entrance door and hauled it into the foyer.

President Hoover was once more drafted in to deliver a message of congratulations from the White House. His words were received by the hotel's own mast antenna and broadcast across the United States to a nation struggling to keep despair at bay, as they watched the country's economy crumble to pieces. Hoover praised the hotel as 'an exhibition of courage and confidence to the whole nation'. Indeed, the Waldorf-Astoria could be said to be a symbol of defiance of the Depression, its massive limestone-and-brick facade surmounted by twin chrome-capped towers that dispelled any notion of hardship and despondency. The determination to set one's face against hard times was embodied in the winged art deco statue *Spirit of Achievement*, the work of Icelandic sculptress Nina Saemundsson, which rises over the hotel's Park Avenue entrance.

The polished brass-framed revolving doors led guests into a fantasy land that dispelled any thoughts of despondency and despair. The new Waldorf-Astoria was a fairy-tale castle rising in the midst of a desiccated landscape. Oscar Tschirky was as always on hand to greet his distinguished guests, from US presidents and foreign heads of state to Hollywood film stars, just as he had done for nearly 40 years.[8] Tschirky brought in further groundbreaking innovations, which he had not had time to introduce at the old hotel. For instance, thanks to his efforts in 1931 the Waldorf-Astoria became the world's first major hostelry to employ women chefs. The hotel's total staff numbered some 2,000, nearly one employee for every guest room. The interior was skilfully decorated with rare marbles, selected stones and nickel-and-bronze-alloy cornices. The furniture was eighteenth-century and colonial design. The two-ton grand clock from the Astoria in 34th Street became the centrepiece of the new Edwardian-design lobby, its diagonal base emblazoned with commemorative plaques of six US presidents, Benjamin Franklin and Queen Victoria. The Spanish painter Josep Maria Sert was commissioned to execute a series of murals for the room that bore his name. He chose as his theme for the 15 panels an episode in Cervantes' *Don Quixote*: the marriage of Quiteria, with its attendant scenes of bucolic entertainment. The crystal and silver lobby decor transported the visitor into a Jean Cocteau fantasy film. No effort or cost was spared to import furnishings from any part of the world, including a reconstructed eighteenth-century salon from Basildon Park, a country house in England, complete with painted cornices, fine wood panelling, a marble mantle attributed to the sculptor John Flaxman and oil paintings by the Austrian neoclassical painter Angelica Kauffman. Peacock Alley was back, at least in name, now in the guise of a lavish lounge and restaurant. A dazzling 100-square-foot chandelier hung in the main foyer, equipped with an automatic lift for raising and lowering the giant fixture.

The arrival of the second Waldorf-Astoria was heralded with a fanfare evocative of Peter Paul Rubens's opulent tapestry *Constantine's Triumphal Entry into Rome*. But there was no disguising the fact that the hotel had made its debut at a time of rapidly dwindling fortunes for the majority of New Yorkers, the affluent classes not excepted. On one occasion, it served as a backdrop to the despondency experienced by those who had lost their fortunes in the Crash. On a January morning in 1934, the chambermaid entered the bathroom of a room on the fourteenth floor, to discover the body of Ross E. Young, a 56-year-old stockbroker, sprawled on the floor with a bullet wound in his temple. Young had shot himself, leaving a note for his wife on hotel stationery which read: 'I got a dirty deal.'

As for the hotel's revenue shortfall, the repeal of Prohibition in December 1933 was anything but an instant panacea for the damage done. In a gesture remindful of Raskob's action at the Empire State Building, Boomer instructed the chambermaids to switch on lamps in empty rooms from twilight to midnight, to give the appearance of full occupancy. The staff continued to parade about in immaculately starched uniforms and, to the casual observer's eye, it was business as usual at the Waldorf-Astoria.

The hotel's precarious cash-flow situation revealed a different reality. On the occasion of the Waldorf-Astoria's forty-first anniversary in March 1934, Boomer had some good tidings to convey to a staff meeting. Income from room occupancy had soared 60 per cent from the previous year:

> We have been greatly encouraged by the effects of Repeal in restoring to hotels the legal right to sell alcoholic beverages, and especially by the passing of the speakeasy. In other words, we think New Yorkers and visitors to New York are in the mood to get more out of life and its amenities than they have been.[9]

Boomer then proceeded to throw a jug of cold water on what had begun to sound like a hopeful report: the renewed sales of alcoholic drinks had not been the cure-all for the hotel's financial ills. On the contrary, a depressed dollar exchange rate and a sharp rise in taxation had pushed sales below pre-Prohibition levels. Despite the welcome increase in food and drink consumption a return to profitability was not in sight in the near future.

Almost inevitably, in late June 1934 the Waldorf-Astoria's management company filed a district court petition requesting permission for a financial restructuring under the New York Bankruptcy Act. Boomer stated that the company had liquid assets of less than $552,000 to meet $5.4 million in current liabilities. The following day the hotel's three top executives announced that they were taking voluntary pay cuts. Boomer's salary went from $60,000 to $36,000, and Tschirky's from $30,000 to $20,726, while company secretary and treasurer August Miller's pay was reduced from $36,000 to $23,085. It was a goodwill gesture initiated by Boomer after he had taken the painful step of eliminating 500 staff jobs. The courts deliberated for almost six months before granting approval for the hotel's financial-restructuring plan, which entailed a debenture issue that was taken up by the requisite two-thirds of bondholders.

The Waldorf-Astoria managed to pull back from the brink of financial collapse, a trifle that went unnoticed by hotel guests who, throughout the crisis, continued to dine on china trimmed with gold leaf and piled high with pheasant, quail and choice cuts of beef. It was nearly a decade after the opening-day ceremony that the hotel finally managed to inch its way into the black, in tandem with the bumpy but steady recovery of the US economy – despite the fact that the country suffered a second economic setback beginning in 1937. Boldt believed that what kept the Waldorf from capsizing during all those turbulent years was its dedication to a tradition. He was determined to see it remain independent, yet secure enough for people to trust it in a crisis, and it had to carry on offering the same level of service that had been so painstakingly crafted under his stewardship.[10]

Newspaper readers in the early 1930s would have been aware of the Waldorf-Astoria's balance sheet woes, but New Yorkers were far keener to follow stories of the hotel's gala events and visiting celebrities, all of which continued unabated and served to enliven the papers' society columns. One of Boldt's masterstrokes was to give the celebrated gossip columnist Elsa Maxwell a free suite at the Waldorf-Astoria Towers, correctly reasoning that she would sing the hotel's praises to her many rich and famous acquaintances.

People flocked to Broadway to see the 1934 Cole Porter musical *Anything Goes,* in which the song 'You're the Top' featured the line 'You're a Waldorf salad.' The play opened in London's West End the following year and was made into a film in 1936. Porter, an intimate friend of Elsa Maxwell, was another long-term resident of the Towers. His Steinway piano still graces the Cocktail Terrace overlooking Park Avenue's art deco splendour. In 1945, the Waldorf-Astoria became the first hotel to be used as a film set. It served as the backdrop to the Robert Z. Leonard movie *Weekend at the Waldorf,* starring Ginger Rogers and Lana Turner.

No hotel in New York could rival the Waldorf-Astoria in the assemblage of glamorous and influential visitors who were spotted parading through its art deco corridors and salons. Every US president has stayed there, starting with Herbert Hoover, who made it his home for 30 years after he left the White House. Very few people were aware that Franklin D. Roosevelt, paralysed from the waist down by polio, had a private railway siding beneath the hotel, so that he could arrive unnoticed without revealing his disability. Other notable guests with private railcars also used that semi-secret entrance. The hotel's lost property office is a treasure trove of peculiar occurrences involving some of the biggest names of the era. Gregory Peck once left his X-rays in his suite, while crooner Eddie Cantor had his slippers returned, as did travel writer Lowell Thomas his overlooked underwear, folded in a discreetly wrapped box. Cary Grant, Elizabeth Taylor, Frank Sinatra, Grace Kelly – all were regulars, to be found sipping a cocktail in Peacock Alley or another of the hotel's lounges.

The cost of meeting the demands of these distinguished guests, in terms of service and cuisine, kept the hotel in the red almost perpetually, with just the occasional break-even year. It was not until 1939 that the first profit was reported. A decade later, in stepped Conrad Hilton, who had once written on a photograph of the Waldorf-Astoria, 'the greatest of them all'. The most successful of American hoteliers came as a saviour for under its new owner, who paid $3 million in the takeover deal, the Waldorf-Astoria was at last able to keep its head above water. Sixty-five years later the Hilton Group decided to seek a buyer for the hotel and, in 2014, China's Anbang Insurance Group dug into their deep pockets to pay $1.95 billion for the Waldorf-Astoria.

Sentimentalists may wring their hands in anguish over a foreign firm acquiring ownership of this most notable of New York hotels. That is understandable, but at the same time they would do well to recall that of the two men who made the Waldorf-Astoria a grand institution, one was Prussian and the other Swiss. Standing in the handsomely appointed lobby with its mammoth clock centrepiece, or admiring the Empire Room's Napoleonic blue-and-gold themes and French crystal chandeliers, or the Vanderbilt Room with its deep green marble wainscoting and pilasters capped with gold-leaf cornices, one cannot fail to detect the presence, in spirit if not in body, of Lucius Boomer and Oscar Tschirky, attending with flawless efficiency to their guests' every whim and requirement.

THEY ALL LAUGHED AT ROCKEFELLER CENTER

A casual stroller through midtown Manhattan in 1929 would have been tempted to pick up the pace when passing the area bounded by 48th to 51st streets, between Fifth and Sixth avenues. The neighbourhood was a cluster of speakeasies, brothels and more than 200 crumbling four-storey brownstones dating from the mid-nineteenth century, with an additional note of decrepitude provided by the overhead rumble of the Sixth Avenue 'El'.[1] A decade later, John D. Rockefeller Jr, with a 60-pound riveting hammer in hand, drove a silver rivet into the steel-beamed lobby of an unfinished structure at 48th Street and Sixth Avenue, now known as 10 Rockefeller Plaza. It was the last of the 10 million rivets used in this project, the fourteenth building of the vast business and entertainment complex that bears his family's name.

Discussing Rockefeller Center calls for a recital of superlatives: it is the world's largest privately owned commercial development, now visited each year by more than 50 million people, making it the most popular sightseeing and shopping attraction on the planet. This undertaking can be regarded as the culmination of the building boom of the 1920s. It is a city within a city, and during nearly a decade of construction work it carried on expanding under its own momentum, with the Damocles sword of contractual obligations hanging over the heads of its promoters, even as the Great Depression was shutting down the New York property market. The irony is that the development of these 22 acres of land in the centre of Manhattan came about as a product of circumstance, almost haphazardly, owing little to preconceived commercial development strategy.

The Rockefeller family member behind the Fifth Avenue centre was the son of the dynasty's founder, John D. Rockefeller Sr, a name that stands for the quintessence of American capitalism. After occupying himself for more than 50 years with building an oil empire, which made him the richest person in US history, Rockefeller Sr spent the last four decades of his life setting up philanthropic enterprises and funding universities. The same urge to do good works also raced through the veins of his fifth child, John D. Rockefeller Jr, an avid conservationist, a supporter of the League of Nations, a restorer of Europe's war-damaged monuments and a financier of hospitals and cultural institutions from Stratford-upon-Avon to Tokyo. There was never a suggestion of self-aggrandisement or egotism in these philanthropic endeavours, or in his attaching his name to what would be New York's – as well as the world's – greatest urban complex. It was from the outset a business venture, pure and simple, one that came into being in fits and starts, and only through happenstance did it evolve into the multifaceted Rockefeller Center as we know it today.

The project as originally conceived turned out to be an abject failure. In the boom times of the late 1920s, New Yorkers with a surfeit of disposable income – and they numbered in the thousands – filled the boxes and stalls of the Metropolitan Opera House, an Italian Renaissance-style building that had opened its doors in Broadway and 40th Street in 1883. The level of attendance by opera buffs of old and new money made the opera house an unqualified financial success. As such, in 1925 the institution's trustees began to consider a move to more spacious quarters. Above all, they saw no reason why so exalted a cultural institution should sit within the Garment District, with its sweatshops and air of crass commercialism, at a time when the city's affluent were moving uptown. This was no longer deemed a suitable location for the likes of the Goulds, Vanderbilts or Morgans to roll up outside of an evening in their gleaming chauffeured Cadillacs and Rolls-Royces.

The first idea put forward for the Met's new home was the brainchild of Otto Kahn, its director. In 1925, Kahn put together a $3 million financing package with which to acquire premises a good distance uptown, in West 57th Street, between Eighth and Ninth avenues. Kahn could count on the support of the Met's board of directors, who wholeheartedly endorsed the proposal to seek a new home. What they sought was to create a worthy rival to the great opera houses of Paris or Milan, in capacity and architectural distinctiveness. However, this was somewhat at odds with Kahn's vision for a simpler design, one based more on functionality than ostentation.

That was one stumbling block: another was the location itself, which several board members adjudged a trifle too close to the Ninth Avenue El, whose shadowy corners and doorways had become a haunt for vagrants and drunks. In addition, Kahn's German Jewish origins did not endear him to some of New York's blue-blooded elite, such as the Vanderbilts, who took advantage of their considerable social influence to heap criticism on the project.

Kahn brought together two distinguished architects, Joseph Urban and Benjamin Wistar Morris, with the idea of a collaboration on the new opera house. Both men went off on a trip to Europe, albeit separately, to refresh their knowledge of modern theatre design. They returned at daggers drawn, each claiming his proposal to be superior to that of his rival. This row eventually led to Urban dropping out of the project in a huff. There was further discouragement in store for Kahn when elements of the Establishment closed ranks against him and persuaded the Met's board to seek a different venue for the opera house. In fact, three locations were considered before it was decided to build on a tract of land owned by Columbia University, bounded by Fifth and Sixth avenues between 48th and 51st streets. This, of course, is the site now occupied by Rockefeller Center.

The matchmaker in what unfortunately turned out to be a failed alliance was John Tonnele, a patrician New Yorker and real estate adviser to Columbia University, who traced his family roots back to the city's earliest settlers. The inspiration to join up the Met's search for a new home with the university's need for additional income reputedly came to Tonnele upon waking one morning, when he turned to his wife to announce that he had found the solution to Columbia's money problems. The university's status as a centre of intellectual excellence was indisputable, but in the managing of its property portfolio it was found woefully wanting. Columbia had taken a hit on some imprudent property sales and also needed to attract sound commercial tenants for the remaining leases, which were shortly due to expire.

Tonnele's idea was for the Met to move into Columbia's uptown Sixth Avenue property holdings, on the expectation that the presence of a world-class opera house in the neighbourhood would act as a magnet for prestige-seeking corporate customers. Architect Morris, the imposingly tall grandee who was by coincidence a graduate of Columbia's School of Architecture, was put on the case. After conducting a feasibility study, he reported back that all he needed was $2.5 million to pay for construction costs. Morris could count on the enthusiastic backing of Robert Fulton Cutting, president of the Metropolitan Opera and Real Estate Company. But with all the goodwill in the world, there was no question of Columbia coming up with that amount of cash. Cutting entertained no doubts that the only realistic solution was to go out and find a group of well-heeled investors. On 21 May 1928, he hosted a dinner party for some of the richest men in New York at the Metropolitan Club's Fifth Avenue banqueting hall. The guest list resonated with the illustrious surnames of opera-box holders such as Chrysler, Baruch, Guggenheim, Warburg, Lehman and Whitney. Otto Kahn was also in attendance, since it seemed only natural for at least one financier with a genuine passion for opera to be present at an event that was to decide the Met's future.

ROCKEFELLER TO THE RESCUE

The one person conspicuous by his absence at the dinner table that evening was the doyen of Manhattan's mega wealthy. John D. Rockefeller Jr knew full well that what awaited his fellow plutocrats at the Metropolitan Club was a pitch for money. He was quite accustomed to envoys of worthy causes knocking at the door of his nine-storey 52nd Street mansion off Fifth Avenue, begging bowl in hand. Not wishing to spend the evening listening to a tiresome hard sell, he deputised his representative Ivy Ledbetter Lee to attend on his behalf and brief him on the merits of the Met's proposed relocation.[2] When the dinner party broke up in the late hours, Lee walked away from the table a confirmed convert to the idea's commercial merits, but neither he nor anyone could have perceived the coming disaster that would oblige the Met to scupper its plans.

Rockefeller quickly recognised the scheme's commercial potential. His thoughts, however, swept across a far broader horizon than the mere relocation of an opera house. What he foresaw was the Met as a great cultural icon, one that would act as a magnet for corporations seeking a home in the heart of Manhattan.

> The plan commended itself to me as a highly important civic improvement and I agreed to participate in it. Materially changed and greatly enlarged in scope, the project finally took the form of my personally acquiring from Columbia [...] the substantial three blocks which it owned.[3]

On 6 December 1928, Rockefeller set up the Metropolitan Square Corporation, as the area was initially called, to serve as the vehicle for his enterprise. He did not doubt for a moment that the plots unoccupied by the Met could be sublet to corporate customers, who in turn would take on the financing of their own building programmes. He struck a deal with Columbia on a $3.3 million annual leasing fee for an initial 21-year renewable period. He then wasted no time in commencing demolition work to clear the three-block area of its unsightly tenements. It was expected that Metropolitan Square would be ready for occupancy within four years, but it was not long before two closely linked events threatened to bring down the curtain on Rockefeller's venture. Indeed, it can be said that one – the Great Depression's sledgehammer effect on the entire country's business plans – was the direct cause of the other, which was the Met's inability to dispose of its existing property. This had been the precondition for the move. In early December 1929, the Met's directors regretfully announced they would not be moving uptown to Metropolitan Square.

It was a classic Catch-22 situation: construction of the proposed new opera house could not be undertaken without external funding, but securing a mortgage was out of the question until the Met had disposed of its old premises. Rockefeller was not prepared to put up the cash. He had already paid a fortune, even within the parameters of that mighty family's means, to acquire the leases on a large uptown plot from Columbia. Rockefeller himself later acknowledged that the cold and calamitous winter of 1929 had confronted him with a choice: abandon Metropolitan Square and cut his losses, or carry on with plans for a much greater and more far-sighted project, in the knowledge that he alone would have to finance and build it. He opted for the second, a decision that involved redeveloping the entire site in order to attract tenants. At the time, Rockefeller was collecting less than a tenth from existing buildings of what he was obliged to pay Columbia in rental fees.

The son of the founder of the Rockefeller dynasty was a philanthropist of enormous means. But he was also a man of sweeping vision, which he employed to initiate a massive construction programme in New York. Through his efforts he succeeded in alleviating the staggering unemployment in the building industry. While he created jobs for thousands of workers, he also endowed the city with a complex that would serve the needs of the general public and constitute a permanent gift for future generations.

Reports on the construction and development costs of what was to become 6 million square feet of rentable space varied wildly, with some sources putting the total outlay at as much as $350 million. The *New York Times* was closest to the mark, with an estimate of $100 million, or about $1.7 billion in today's terms. Rockefeller dipped into the family fortune to cover his ongoing expenses through the sale of oil-company stocks, supported by a line of credit from the Metropolitan Life Insurance Company. He was now ready to undertake what was then the country's largest ever privately financed building project.

Rockefeller had chosen the property developers Todd, Robertson, Todd for the original Metropolitan Square programme. The company's executive director, John R. Todd, exercised the greatest influence on the fledgling Rockefeller Center as the development's principal builder and managing agent. Todd was not dismayed in the slightest by the Met's departure from the scheme – on the contrary, he rejoiced at the opera house's decision. Having divested itself of unprofitable cultural frills, he reasoned, the venture had now achieved a unity of commercial purpose. Todd voiced the opinion that an opera house on the site, far from acting as a 'magnet' for attracting corporate tenants, as Rockefeller had imagined, would have represented 'a dead spot, and greatly reduced shopping values in all property facing it'.

On 17 May 1930, Rockefeller looked on, with fingers crossed, as the first of the wrecking balls began pummelling to dust the aged tenements that blighted Fifth Avenue. Two months later, eight bulldozers, 100 lorries and some 300 demolition workers began excavation work on the greater part of a three-block area, hauling away more than one and a quarter million tons of debris. Soon, more than 75,000 construction workers were clambering about the site, putting up the first of the 14 buildings between 48th and 51st streets. At least twice that number of builders worked off-site, while the total employed by suppliers and manufacturers of construction materials numbered in the tens of thousands. In total, some 225,000 workers were on the job during the construction process, a godsend for a city experiencing the worst unemployment crisis of its history.

By June 1930, a deal had been struck to build a development of office buildings and theatres on a 550,000-square-foot site, initially to be called 'Radio City'. The name 'Rockefeller Center' had been suggested by Ivy Lee, as he believed it would act as an incentive to draw in business. Rockefeller himself, however, the man who risked his all to make the project a reality and who wanted to call the entire development Radio City, was at first strongly opposed to using his family name as a crowd-puller. But Lee was able to persuade his boss of the acumen of attaching the family name to the complex, and thus Metropolitan Square became Rockefeller Center.

Once Rockefeller decided to take the plunge, there was to be no scrimping on cost. To ensure the finished product matched the highest standards of design, three firms of architects were recruited to develop the complex. This triumvirate was known collectively as Associated Architects and comprised Hood & Fouilhoux, Reinhard & Hofmeister and Corbett, Harrison & MacMurray, all revered names in New York's architectural circles. Their brief was to work together to draw up designs and plans for buildings that would attract tenants, who in turn would provide rental income. Each architect brought an impressive list of achievements to the task, in particular Raymond Hood. In 1922, Hood had won the *Chicago Tribune*'s competition to design the paper's headquarters, which he did in Gothic Revival style. It is said that Rockefeller, who travelled to Chicago because of the family's connection with Rockefeller University, saw Hood's tower and believed that Rockefeller Center would likewise be designed along Gothic Revival lines. However, Hood's American Radiator Company and Daily News buildings, completed in 1929 and 1930 respectively, shortly before he embarked on the Rockefeller Center project, demonstrated the architect's stylistic transition away from neo-Gothic and towards art deco and modernism. In fact, Hood was a firm believer in the axiom that form follows function. He saw this embodied in Radio City Music Hall, a creation of Edward Durell Stone, another member of the Associated Architects group brought together to work on Rockefeller Center. When confronted with arches on a building's facade (a characteristically Gothic feature), Hood's thick dark eyebrows were likely to rise in indignation at what he considered a feature whose only effect was to darken the windows they enclosed. Others might run up long pilasters for ornamentation: not so Hood, who would reject such a contrivance if it meant obscuring a row of windows that supplied light and air. Rockefeller was eventually won over to the art deco design, particularly after he returned from Egypt, where he had marvelled at the hieroglyphics from which art deco in part takes its inspiration.

Hood threw himself into his mission body and soul, creating a Rockefeller Center that responded to a spirit of daring innovation, championing comfort and convenience over appearance and effect. In doing so, his efforts produced a work of supreme beauty that embodied an era that had left behind the extravagance of the Roaring Twenties, in a style more deferential to the austerity of New York's Depression years. The project got under way with Radio City Music Hall, and it was fitting for a city that revels in superlatives to host what would be the world's largest indoor theatre. The massive auditorium would go on to boast the 'Mighty Wurlitzer' organ, with pipes housed in 11 separate rooms, along with impresario Samuel 'Roxy' Rothafel's legendary Rockettes, the high-kicking dance troupe that has been performing on the same stage since its opening on 27 December 1932.[4]

What Radio City Music Hall lacked in highbrow entertainment it more than made up for in sheer volume. The hall could seat more than 6,000 spectators, fully 1,000 more than had been planned for the Metropolitan Opera. It was, moreover, a logical business proposition: in those desperate times people with disposable income, however small, were more likely to dip into their pockets to be cheered by a line of glamorous chorus girls or vaudeville entertainer Ray Bolger than to sit through nearly three tragic hours of Mussorgsky's *Boris Godunov*.

John R. Todd went in search of big-name tenants in the corporate world, those who, he reasoned, would take an interest in the new office space development. In December 1929, the first potential tenant he approached was the New York firm General Electric (GE). The formal talks that began two months later were aimed at opening the doors to a handful of corporate clients clustered under the GE umbrella, names such as RCA and its affiliates NBC and the Radio-Keith-Orpheum (RKO) chain of theatres.[5] The negotiations moved apace, facilitated by a close personal relationship between Rockefeller and GE's chairman Owen Young, who was likewise the founder of RCA.

Construction was well under way when RCA moved into 30 Rockefeller Center, with 'Roxy' appointed general manager of Radio City Music Hall. He and several of the architects involved in the project boarded a liner to Europe, to draw inspiration from the continent's latest innovations in theatrical design. They were most impressed by the impact of the 1925 Exposition Internationale des Arts Décoratifs et Industriels Modernes in Paris.[6] This was a brave attempt, after the calamities of the First World War, to convince the world that the City of Light still towered above all others, at least in the design arts. The exhibition heralded the advent of a movement that much later came to be known as art deco, the style whose very essence was reflected by Rockefeller Center's original 14 buildings.[7] Among the many overseas visitors to attend the Paris event six years previously was Donald Deskey, a young, moustachioed and stylishly attired American industrial designer, who in 1932 was to win the design competition for Radio City Music Hall's interiors. Deskey had embarked on a lucrative career in advertising after taking a degree in architecture from the University of California. The year 1925 found him in Paris, where he had taken up residence to study painting.

One day, he and his wife bought tickets to the exhibition, a visit that left him so captivated by what he saw that he decided to return to New York and become a designer. Edward Durell Stone was the architect largely responsible for the music hall's interior design, but it was the industrial designer Deskey whom Roxy retained for the decoration of more than 30 areas, and his hand is everywhere in evidence in the building's interior, including lobbies, smoking and powder rooms, foyers, lounges and even a private suite for his employer.[8] The high-ceiling apartment he created for Roxy atop the Radio City Music Hall is the only interior remaining of the dozens he designed throughout his career for such prominent clients as Adam Gimbel, Abby Aldrich Rockefeller and Helena Rubinstein. Elsewhere, the theatre's essence is portrayed in bronze plaques depicting theatrical entertainment – acrobats, clowns and musicians, as well as more exotic acts like snake charmers. From walls and ceilings, to the mirrors of the ladies' lounge, Radio City Music Hall stands out as a swanky product of Deskey's imagination. The Deskey manner, notwithstanding the stunning contributions of craftsmen like Hood and Stone, was imprinted on the entire Rockefeller Center complex. This 'machine-age temple', as Le Corbusier described it, arose from the rubble of the tenements, a transformation that symbolised the jettisoning of an age of cluttered and ponderous architecture.[9]

If one were to describe in general terms the two designers' individual contributions to Radio City Music Hall, one would attribute the building's exterior to Stone, while the spectacular interior vividly reflects Deskey's love affair with the modern style, a passion he had acquired at the 1925 Paris exhibition. Deskey enjoyed the patronage of Rockefeller's wife, Abby Aldrich Rockefeller, who had employed the young designer to apply his skills to part of the family's New York townhouse. As a philanthropist and patron of the arts, Abby later became instrumental in securing Deskey a commission to create interior designs for MoMA, of which she was one of the three founders. His work earned him an enthusiastic following and his prominence brought considerable commercial success, to the point that he was able to maintain homes in Scotland, Jamaica and Florida, as well as Manhattan.

Radio City Music Hall was the first of the nine original structures making up the complex, whose buildings would contain 28,000 windows and 125,000 tons of structural steel, as well as more office space than the Empire State Building. Less fanfare was lavished on the music hall's short-lived sister entertainment venue, the RKO Roxy Theatre, named after the man put in charge of both this institution and Radio City Music Hall, Samuel 'Roxy' Rothafel. The ill-starred RKO film studio had been set up by RCA chief David Sarnoff in 1929 – in the midst of the stock market storm – through a merger between two independent entertainment companies. It was hardly a triumph of foresight, for even as work began on the complex in May 1930, the cinema industry was finding itself in serious financial trouble and RKO was struggling to stay afloat in the face of rapidly declining profits. The move to 'Radio City' at first seemed to promise a reversal of fortune, but it turned out to be merely a brief respite before the curtain came down, quite literally, on the venture. The RKO Roxy Theatre was built on the same 49th Street site as Radio City Music Hall, and offered films to a public its promoters assumed would be anxious to escape the calamitous Depression. But a few days after opening in December 1932 with the David O. Selznick-produced comedy-drama *The Animal Kingdom*, starring Leslie Howard and Ann Harding, the theatre was forced to shut its doors. It was rightly deemed a needless duplication of entertainment facilities. Shortly after Radio City Music Hall's opening in January 1933, RKO itself went into receivership.

On 24 December 1931 serendipity stepped in with an unscripted event, one that has been transformed over the years into one of New York's most cherished Christmas traditions, the lighting of the giant Rockefeller Plaza tree. On that day in 1931, a group of construction workers set up a small fir on the site that was to house the British Empire Building and La Maison Française. The builders decorated the humble tree with tinsel, garlands of coloured paper and odds and ends collected from the site. They then proceeded to form a queue in front of a company clerk, who handed each man in turn his weekly wage. Within five years this had become an annual institution. Joined by an audience of tens of thousands of onlookers, the tree-lighting ceremony was the occasion for a blaze of thousands of fairy lights, choral singing and organ music, a musical extravaganza broadcast by Rockefeller Center tenant NBC across the nation.[10]

The spirit of 'Radio City' is embodied in its very name. It represents the triumph of America's machine-made expressions of entertainment: the radio and fledgling television industry. The music hall was the first of the nine original Radio City structures to be completed and its interior is a celebration of that age of mechanical progress. The sleek art deco style which the music hall's designers drew from the 1925 Paris exhibition is skilfully embedded in every bit of decoration. Not only was Rockefeller Center the most ambitious private development ever undertaken in America, it also became the proving ground for daring advances in decorative materials. This is evident at the 50th Street east entrance, over which three stylised plaques catch the eye, depicting dance, song and drama. They are executed in innovative materials that reflect the boldness of new trends in design, including carbon steel, copper, chrome–nickel alloy and aluminium. These are the work of Hildreth Meière, a decorative artist of mosaics and murals who had been awarded more than 100 commissions in the United States. A native New Yorker, Meière served in the US Navy in the First World War and is acclaimed as one of the greatest masters of art deco design. She was enthusiastically commissioned to apply her expertise to the new medium of mixed metal and enamel, a feat she accomplished in these three roundels, each 18 feet in diameter.

The murals and sculptures adorning not only Radio City Music Hall but the entire Rockefeller Center complex were carried out by a team of art deco artists that included, among others, Meière, Rene Paul Chambellan, Barry Faulkner, Ezra Winter and Lee Lawrie, along with top-name sculptors specialising in the same style and materials. A committee of museum and cultural professionals hired some 30 artists, who executed more than 100 pieces based on the theme 'the progress of man and new frontiers'.

The buildings of Rockefeller Center conform to the art deco dictates of sweeping vertical lines and streamlined facades, largely devoid of baroque ornamentation. They mirror the aesthetics of the machine age, manifested in those other great monuments of the early Depression years, the Chrysler and Empire State buildings. The terraced crown of the Chrysler Building, illuminated in the night sky, is a spectacle almost matchless in modernist beauty. The top 16 storeys of the Empire State Building are unarguably a striking triumph of art deco splendour, likewise the spire, the lifts and the stainless-steel canopies of the 33rd and 34th Street entrances. While the interiors of these skyscrapers are unarguably splendid, one could make the case that for the most part, the glory of these lies primarily in their external features. In contrast, Rockefeller Center offers the added allure, within and throughout, of being a showcase of unique interior magnificence.

This view is supported by a noted art deco historian, who describes his first glimpse inside Radio City Music Hall: 'It is about its great indoors, and neither the platonic urbanity of surrounding Rockefeller Center nor its own exterior features suggest what lies within.'[11] The interior comprises a magnificent sequence of intimate and grand spaces. This is one of the greatest triumphs of modernism to appear in the period between the world wars. The building transmits energy, in its sweeping spaces, splendid furnishings and finishes. The collection of artworks radiates the theme of Rockefeller Center, which is humanity's progress in art, science and industry.

The agreement struck between Rockefeller and RCA president David Sarnoff on what was to become Rockefeller Center's focal point and tallest structure, the 70-storey RCA Building, brought with it the studios of NBC, no fewer than 35 of them, making the broadcaster the complex's largest tenant. Le Corbusier said of the RCA Building and its NBC studios: 'The temple is solemn, surfaced with somber marble, shining with clear mirrors mounted in stainless steel frames. Silence.'[12] The names of Lee Lawrie and Josep Maria Sert are closely associated with the artwork adorning the RCA Building, now the GE Building and also known as 30 Rockefeller Plaza (or '30 Rock'). Lee was a prominent architectural sculptor, whose monumental 45-foot, seven-ton bronze statue of Atlas stands in the Fifth Avenue forecourt facing St Patrick's Cathedral. His 22-foot, limestone and glass sculpture *Wisdom*, which rises over the entrance, its titular figure glaring down behind a flowing beard, is a statement of raw power above the words of Isaiah 33:6: 'Wisdom and knowledge shall be the stability of thy times.' The depiction of *Sound and Light* in flight, executed in the same materials and placed on either side of *Wisdom*, shouts the building's *raison d'être*, the advent and growth of radio and television. *Prometheus* is perhaps the best-known sculpture in Rockefeller Center, however. It also has the distinction of being the most photographed monumental sculpture in New York City. Created by famed

American sculptor Paul Manship, for whom mythological subjects and events held a great fascination, it has become the main attraction of the Lower Plaza.

Lawrie could lay claim to being Rockefeller Center's most prolific artist but it was Sert, the designer of murals at the nearby Waldorf-Astoria, who contributed the bulk of the RCA Building's great works of art. Sert was brought in after Henri Matisse and Pablo Picasso declined invitations to paint murals for the walls facing the main entrance. Sert was a much-sought-after Catalan muralist who moved in all the right circles, being a friend of Salvador Dalí and a darling of fashionable Barcelona and Paris society. He was the creator of eight murals in the RCA Building, many of which are vast in size, such as the 5,000-square foot depiction of Titans, each symbolising the passage of time, which Sert painted on the ceiling of the main lobby, which also holds side panels by the British artist Frank Brangwyn.

Sert stepped in as the white knight after a rancorous incident over a mural by the Mexican muralist Diego Rivera, an extraordinarily complex and controversial character. Rivera was an atheist descended from a Jewish family who had been forced to convert to Catholicism. He became a member of the Mexican Communist Party, from which he was expelled in 1929 for alleged anti-Soviet activities. He was also host to Leon Trotsky during the Marxist revolutionary's exile in Mexico. Rivera's work was acclaimed worldwide and enjoyed enormous success in the United States. In March 1933 he began work on his mural, *Man at the Crossroads*, commissioned by John D. Rockefeller Jr's son Nelson for the walls of the RCA Building's main foyer. Everything was going swimmingly, until a month later when it was shockingly revealed that Rivera had added a portrait of Lenin to his mural.

The New York press had a field day with what it deemed a trick deeply offensive to American values – and by none other than a Mexican socialist. 'Rivera paints scenes of communist activities and John D. Jr pays the bill' screamed the headline of the *New York World-Telegram*: 'The dominant colour [of the mural] is red: a red wimple, a red flag, red waves of a victorious force.'[13]

Ten days later Rivera opened a telegram signed by Nelson A. Rockefeller, asking the artist to delete the portrait of Lenin from the mural, which he sheepishly explained might be offensive to some people. Rivera sent Rockefeller a snappy reply to the effect that rather than commit an affront to the hero of the Soviet Revolution, he'd sooner have the mural destroyed. Rockefeller was relieved: Rivera would have his wish granted. A squad of uniformed guards, backed by mounted police outside to prevent what was feared could turn into a scene of violence, marched in to hand Rivera a cheque for $21,000, along with instructions to vacate the premises. The mural remained covered for nearly a year while art experts struggled to find a way for the fresco to be removed intact, but no technique for removing it in one piece proved workable. And so, at midnight on 9 February 1934, the mural was sledgehammered to pieces and the chunks of plaster carted off in 50-gallon oil drums.

Diego Rivera's dismissal and the pulverising of his mural touched off an unprecedented fracas in the international art world. A group of nearly 50 leading American artists and writers – John Sloan, Hugh Ferriss and Lewis Mumford among them – signed a petition to John D. Rockefeller Jr condemning the action. A group of New York artists due to exhibit their works at Rockefeller Center withdrew from the show, while Leon Kroll, president of the American Society of Painters, Sculptors and Engravers, pronounced himself 'greatly distressed at the destruction of the Rivera mural'. On the other side of the fence, Henri Matisse took advantage of the row to denounce Rivera's work as 'equivocal' and 'propagandistic', declaring that 'art should be above politics and the realities of a small era in history'. Henry Watrous, president of the National Academy of Design, dismissed the anti-Rockefeller outrage as 'poppycock', since Rockefeller 'had the painting destroyed as he had a perfect right to do'.

That was when the trustworthy Josep Maria Sert was drafted in, as part of a damage-limitation exercise, to paint a far larger mural based on an allegorical scene of modern America under construction. There is a touch of irony in Sert's artistic creation. One cannot but smile at the hint of Stalinist airbrushing in the Spaniard's rendering of the mural, in which Lenin was replaced by Abraham Lincoln, while the title *Man at the Crossroads* was changed to *American Progress*.

This was not the first time Rockefeller Center had been hit by political controversy. A row far more incendiary in nature had in fact broken out in June 1932, when it was revealed that Rockefeller Center's executive manager,

Hugh Robertson, had been in touch with agents in Berlin to seek out investors for a German building to be erected in Fifth Avenue, to be named Deutsches Haus. This took place six months before Adolf Hitler grabbed power as German chancellor. The Berlin talks came perilously close to fruition. As late as October 1934 Robertson was still lobbying to open the building to German commercial tenants, but business as well as humanitarian sense prevailed when Rockefeller put the brakes on striking any deals with the Nazis. The vacant premises were christened International Building North and soon became a centre of wartime intrigue.[14] William Stephenson, the Canadian-born spymaster and senior representative of British intelligence for the entire western hemisphere during the Second World War, ran his operations from the building.[15]

Robertson persisted in cavorting with America's future enemies by travelling to Rome to display a model of the proposed Italian Building to Benito Mussolini, who had on numerous occasions expressed his contempt for America and its democratic system. This time the undertaking was a Rockefeller initiative, intended to drum up enthusiasm for a building that he envisaged as the Palazzo d'Italia. The building was completed in 1935, with walls of Travertine limestone and floors paved with Venetian terrazzo squares. But when America became a belligerent after the Japanese attack on Pearl Harbor in December 1941, the federal government seized the offices of the complex's remaining German, Italian and Japanese interests. The Italian Fascist government's Palazzo d'Italia suffered the ignominious fate of having the royal coat of arms over the entrance, as well as Italian American sculptor Attilio Piccirilli's crypto-fascist labourer figure, boarded up with planks.

Two other low-rise structures were put up in Fifth Avenue, flanking the Channel Gardens, a series of small pools and plant installations decorated with sculptures by Rene Paul Chambellan. These were the aforementioned British Empire Building and La Maison Française. The former was to represent the glory of Britain and her colonial possessions. During the war it became a safe haven for a multitude of British business interests. La Maison Française was completed in 1934, a year after its neighbour. The spirit of the building was emblazoned in a bronze plaque displayed above the main entrance, the work of the French sculptor Alfred Janniot, symbolising the friendship between

France and America. The facade of the British Empire Building also bears a bas-relief, an 18-foot bronze panel embellished with nine gilded allegorical figures, each representing an industry found in Britain's colonies.

The inauguration of La Maison Française put the finishing touches on Rockefeller Center's first stage of development. But the project's promoter and guiding spirit, John D. Rockefeller Jr, along with his business associates, were resolved to press briskly on with their ambitious plans for expansion. The completion of the International Building in 1935 set in motion the second phase of construction. On 9 December 1936 work began on the Rockefeller Plaza skating pond, which opened to a cheering throng of ice skaters on Christmas Day. In 1938 the Associated Press took the tower north of the Plaza and could boast of having the largest of 15 air-conditioning units made by the Carrier Corporation for Rockefeller Center, 'doing the same job as melting eight hundred tons of ice daily'![16] The Japanese American sculptor Isamu Noguchi's stainless-steel art deco plaque *News* soars above the entrance, with a depiction of five journalists engaged in various reporting activities. The last of the original 14 structures, the Eastern Airlines Building, with its fantastic murals of aeroplanes held aloft by gilded, heroic-looking women and *The History of Transportation* by Dean Cornwell, found its first tenants in 1939.

It was done, but on the day of the dedication ceremony in 1939, a decade after the Great Crash, a dark cloud of uncertainty still hung over New York's office rental market. Widespread scepticism notwithstanding, some market pundits pointed to signs that business was beginning to perk up, albeit slowly. The leading property firm William A. White & Sons announced that, in terms of square footage, the amount of occupied office space in New York was 10 per cent higher than at the onset of the Depression in 1929. By the following year Rockefeller Center had managed to lease nearly 90 per cent of its office space and, in 1941, the business was squarely in the black.

So in the end the great dream had come true. Three square city blocks of almost fully rented office space, conceived for commercial gain but also for the millions who each year flock to New York's most visited attraction to work, drink, dine, shop, visit the post office, be entertained, ice skate, sing Christmas carols, or simply delight in the multifarious centre's collection of art deco masterpieces. The world's first landscaped skyscraper complex, created for commerce, conceived in art deco genius with the machine age and new building materials in mind. It was a true success story, as foretold in the 1937 film *Shall We Dance*. The movie itself became one of the lasting icons of the 1930s, starring larger-than-life personalities Fred Astaire and Ginger Rogers, gliding across the screen to the tune 'They All Laughed', music and lyrics courtesy of the immortal George and Ira Gershwin. As the song says: 'Ha, ha, ha, who's got the last laugh now?'

John D. Rockefeller Jr, of course.

12

VILLAGE LIFE

P eriods of political and social turmoil in a country's history have traditionally given rise to an outpouring of creativity, most of it in literary form. Fyodor Dostoevsky's great novels come to mind, many of which were published during Russia's conquest of the khanates of Central Asia and in the wake of the Russo-Turkish War of 1877–8. Johann Wolfgang von Goethe produced some of his most outstanding works at the time of the rise of German nationalism and a wave of anti-monarchist upheavals. Victor Hugo's *Les Misérables* is rooted in the disastrous events of the 1848 revolutions and the downfall of the Orléans monarchy. Miguel de Cervantes' knight errant Don Quixote made his debut when the catastrophe of the Invincible Armada was still fresh in people's minds and Spain and its empire were starting to fall to pieces. William Shakespeare made his name just as England emerged victorious over the Spanish and the country embarked on its imperial adventure with the formation of the East India Company. The eminent English novelists of the nineteenth century – Thomas Hardy, Jane Austen, Charles Dickens, Charlotte Brontë, William Thackeray – were contemporaries, or in the case of Austen a near contemporary, of the unbridled self-confidence that personified the Victorian age and some of its most notable events: the Industrial Revolution, the defeat of Russia in the Crimean War and the Boers in southern Africa and the Great Exhibition of 1851.

America's Great Depression, a socio-economic catastrophe of unprecedented proportions for that country, inspired and served as the backdrop to the works of John Steinbeck, Sinclair Lewis, John Dos Passos and Henry Miller, among other celebrated writers. New York was America's cultural powerhouse in that turbulent decade. The city therefore became the inevitable spawning ground for literature, art and learning, fostering innovative and in many instances experimental movements, which would shape American trends for decades to come.

During the 1930s, a creative effervescence took hold in Manhattan, literally from top to bottom. At the southern reaches of the island, where ancient cobbled streets and leafy squares defined the bohemian character of Greenwich Village, one could hardly set foot in any of the lively watering holes and coffee houses without spotting local artists like Edward Hopper, Willem de Kooning, Jackson Pollock or Franz Kline propping up the bar – perhaps at the White Horse Tavern, or Caffè Reggio, the first place in America to serve cappuccino. It is worth noting that none of these artists was a native of New York City; De Kooning was not even American-born. One exception was New Yorker Jo Davidson, who by the 1930s had secured his reputation as a giant among sculptors. Among world celebrities who sat at his Village studio were Albert Einstein, Arthur Conan Doyle, Charlie Chaplin and Joseph Conrad.

The 'Village', as it is known to New Yorkers, was the natural magnet for aspiring talent from other parts of the country. The neighbourhood had been home to a long line of gifted artists, from Edgar Allan Poe and Walt Whitman to Henry James and Mark Twain. The British poet laureate John Masefield kept body and soul together in the late 1890s by scrubbing the floors of a Village saloon.

As far as any self-respecting Villager was concerned, it was an indisputable fact that every cultural amenity a person could desire – except for the great museums, theatres and opera of Manhattan's northerly reaches – lay within the confines of an area bounded by Bleecker and 14th Street, by Second Avenue and Greenwich Street. No other residential section of New York could hold a candle to the cultural vibrancy of Greenwich Village. Those who lived outside this privileged enclave scarcely existed. Wall Street might just as well have been in Illinois, and Madison Avenue a part of Ohio.[1]

The Village's claim to be America's repository of avant-garde art and social enlightenment was put forward with habitual eccentricity one bitterly cold morning in January 1917. Washington Square Arch, erected in the early 1890s to commemorate the centennial of George Washington's inauguration as the first US president in 1789, became the symbol of Village bohemianism. The painters John Sloan and Marcel Duchamp, along with friends, climbed to the top of the arch to proclaim that Greenwich Village had seceded from the Union and would thenceforth be the Free and Independent Republic of Washington Square.

In the 1930s, the Village became a powerful symbol of the potential for cultural rebirth, a community that set its sights beyond the desolation of the Depression, keeping alive and cultivating the arts in all their manifestations, in the best of the 'man shall not live by bread alone' spirit. Many Village residents, as well as those who came to partake of its nonconformist culture, became leading activists in the social-reform movement. Barney Josephson, the son of a Jewish Latvian immigrant, was a jazz fan and frequent visitor to the Cotton Club. Much as he enjoyed the music, Josephson was troubled by the club's racial-segregation policy. Determined to put right this injustice, in 1938 he opened Café Society in the heart of the Village, a dark and cosy basement meeting place. This became America's first racially integrated nightclub, where top performers like Billie Holiday and jazz pianist Teddy Wilson lost no time in showing Josephson their support and gratitude, both putting in regular appearances at the Sheridan Square venue.

NEW SCHOOL, NEW LIFE

Always in the vanguard of progressive thought, at the time of Hitler's ascendancy the Village became a beacon of salvation for persecuted German academics, guiding them to a safe harbour of promise. The New School for Social Research was created after the First World War as a place of learning for students seeking an alternative to the city's less democratic universities. Given the institution's remit, the Village was always going to be the place for it to set up shop. In 1919 the New School opened its doors in West 23rd Street. When its original home was later demolished to make way for a residential development, the institution moved to permanent headquarters in West 12th Street, a brick-fronted building executed in the International Style by Austrian-born architect Joseph Urban. By the early 1930s, the New School had consolidated its reputation as a centre of academic excellence, under the guidance of its director Alvin Johnson, associate editor of the *New Republic*, whose ambition was to promote scholarly research of a high academic standard.[2]

The dismissal of Jewish faculty staff from German universities presented Johnson with the opportunity to see his hopes realised. The *New York Times* broke the story of his plans in May 1933 under the headline 'Graduate school to employ 15 professors ousted from Germany is being planned'. The paper reported that Johnson's idea was to create a 'University in Exile', with the backing of a diverse group of notables, which included former Supreme Court chief justice Oliver Wendell Holmes, founder of the American Civil Liberties Union Felix Frankfurter, philosopher John Dewey and newspaper editor Herbert Bayard Swope.[3]

With the support of the Rockefeller Foundation and a few other wealthy patrons, Johnson was able to get his scheme off the ground. By 1934, he had raised enough funds to bring a dozen highly regarded German Jewish academics to New York. In the ensuing decade, more than 1,000 European intellectuals settled in the United States and, of these, nearly 200 were given employment at the New School. A number of those scholars who fled Germany had intuited what was in store when the Nazi regime issued its infamous Gesetz zur Wiederherstellung des Berufsbeamtentums (Law for the Restoration of the Professional Civil Service) in April 1933. Under this proclamation, Jews living in the Third Reich were summarily dismissed from their jobs in the civil service and the academic world.

In 1932, Adolph Lowe, an economist and adviser to the Weimar Republic, had been put in charge of the Frankfurt Institute for Social Research. Sensing the imminent peril posed by the Nazis' rise to power, he and his wife wisely decided to keep suitcases packed in preparation for a hasty departure from Germany. The couple got out by the skin of their teeth in 1933, on an early-morning train to Geneva, scant hours before the order requiring Jews to hand in their passports came into effect. After initially settling in Britain, Lowe later accepted Johnson's invitation to join the New School faculty, where he taught for nearly four decades. Lowe died in 1995 at the age of 102, the last surviving member of the University in Exile.

Johnson had fulfilled his dream and at the time of his retirement, after more than two decades at the helm, the New School had consolidated its reputation as a world-class centre for graduate studies in political and social sciences. Johnson's credentials as one of the most distinguished scholars of the 1930s working in New York were further supported by his contribution to the *Encyclopaedia of the Social Sciences*, a groundbreaking 15-volume reference work first published in 1930, which became the standard source of scholarly research for the study of human affairs.

New York's burst of intellectual activity during the Depression years was not confined to the academic world or, for that matter, to the garrets and coffee houses of Greenwich Village. The New York literary panorama had taken a severe battering in the aftermath of the 1929 Crash. Novelists, social commentators and poets alike reacted angrily to the economic calamity, which for many bore the hallmark of a systemic failure of the capitalist system. Radicalism was in the air; workers infatuated with the Soviet Union's panacea of socialist revolution staged noisy marches along Fifth Avenue, while writers proclaimed their call for justice and equality in the pages of leftist journals, which began to appear in the 1930s.

The first literary reaction to the Depression came mostly from the pens of CPUSA militants and sympathisers. In the early 1930s Ukrainian-born Philip Rahv and New Yorker William Phillips co-founded the influential journal *Partisan Review*. Many publications of this kind, notably the Marxist magazine *The Masses*, the forerunner of *The New Masses*, launched in 1926, had been forced to cease publication due to their opposition to American involvement in the First World War. The intellectuals behind the revival of leftist ideas in the 1930s were committed radical firebrands, who launched their attacks on the established order in street rallies, on the pulpit and in their publications. But as the decade progressed, editors and writers alike found themselves experiencing painful ideological vicissitudes once Stalinism began to reveal its true totalitarian face.

The circle of socialist thinkers and writers of the early 1930s, popularly styled the 'New York Intellectuals', came into being largely through the efforts of Rahv and Phillips. Both men were disenchanted with *The New Masses*, the established New York-based journal of leftist thought, which in their view had sacrificed literature to politics. In 1933 they came up with the idea of a quarterly publication that would exalt the principles of 'proletarian literature'. There was no disguising the fact this was destined to become a highly polished mouthpiece for Soviet propaganda, though its principles were couched in more decorous terms.

The two founders brought on board a number of outstanding personalities from the New York literary world. Mary McCarthy, who for a time was Rahv's lover, was a highly successful novelist and left-wing political activist. After repudiating her Catholic upbringing she joined the clique of fellow travellers, until finally breaking with Moscow over the show trials of 1936 and 1938, which led to the execution of thousands of Stalin's opponents. Frederick Wilcox Dupee, a literary critic who was also to turn his back on radical Marxism, became another prominent name on the editorial board. Likewise the writer and editor Dwight Macdonald, who had been an early supporter of Trotsky. Macdonald later rejected his political idol, as well as Stalin, to espouse the politics of democratic socialism. Under the leadership of these and other idealists, *Partisan Review* became the rallying point for America's intellectuals of the Left.

To raise money for the new magazine, Rahv and Williams invited the British Marxist John Strachey to New York to give a talk on the spellbinding subject of 'Literature and dialectical materialism'. The suave, Oxford-educated Strachey, who had drifted from Oswald Mosley's fascist Blackshirts to communism, enjoyed an enormous following among New York radicals. Such was his reputation that the lecture raised the sum of $800, enough to launch the magazine and keep it going for a year.

The break of many of its editors and contributors with the CPUSA in 1936 spelled the demise of *Partisan Review*, at least until its reappearance the following year as an anti-Soviet publication. Rahv and Phillips shared the uneasiness felt by many of the New York Intellectuals group. The journal steadily adopted a moderate social democratic editorial line, and during the Cold War it was widely believed to have accepted funding from the CIA as part of that organisation's effort to influence intellectual opinion. When *Partisan Review* folded in 2003, New Yorkers had long since turned to mainstream political and literary publications like the *Atlantic Monthly*, the *New Yorker* and the *New York Review of Books*. Nevertheless, the defunct journal could take satisfaction in having showcased original works by some of the great literary figures of its day, names like T. S. Eliot, George Orwell and Saul Bellow.

Not all the writers who made their name in the 1930s were from New York, but a majority of them were drawn to the city. Albert Halper, a native of Chicago, moved to New York in the early 1930s, where he became a regular contributor to *Commentary*, *Dial* and other prominent literary magazines. His 1933 novel *Union Square*, a politically charged work about the lives of the working class during the Depression, was a runaway best-seller. Hungarian-born Edward Newhouse made his home in New York, where he, too, wrote novels based on the lives of the proletariat. Granville Hicks was originally a New Englander who in New York became an influential Marxist literary critic, editor of *The New Masses* and CPUSA member until his stormy resignation in 1939. Grace Lumpkin left her Georgia home for New York to become a staff writer for the highly successful pacifist weekly *The World Tomorrow*, where she produced early feminist literature. After a period of flirtation with the CPUSA, she returned to her Christian roots and became an active opponent of the USSR. Brooklynite social philosopher Sidney Hook was in his early days an enthusiastic supporter of the Soviet Union and in 1932 backed the American communist William Z. Foster's quixotic bid for the presidency of the United States. One year later Hook broke with Moscow, whose policies he held responsible for the triumph of Nazism in Germany. Hook was a prominent member of the New York Intellectuals circle, publishing hundreds of articles and over 20 books on Marxism and social democracy in a literary career that spanned more than 60 years.

HARLEM'S GOT TALENT

The city's flourishing literary life was not confined to the editorial offices of university-educated, middle-class radicals. Some eight miles to the north of Greenwich Village, inspired by the outcry of black anger against a society that refused to reject its racial prejudices, a group of novelists, poets and play-wrights was breathing fresh life into the Harlem Renaissance. New York, as the nation's creative capital, where the great social and literary battles of the day were waged, became the breeding ground for a generation of prominent black writers and intellectuals. It is commonly held that Harlem's foremost literary figures reached their maximum level of expression in the 1920s, under the influence of Wallace Thurman, Claude McKay and a handful of other seminal black literary figures. The movement was at its creative peak in those fervent years, it is avowed, while the demise came with the onset of the Depression. That was when the lights of Harlem's literary achievements went dim. There is some truth in this hypothesis, though what really took place in those pivotal years was more a shift in focus than the end of a movement. Moreover, the Depression acted as a catalyst for creativity by forcing many moneyless artists who had travelled to Europe seeking literary inspiration to return to America. This 'homecoming' brought them together in a critical mass that surpassed in numbers and talent any black cultural movement of the past.

> Black authors of the thirties, like their compatriots, faced reality more squarely. For the older lightheartedness they substituted sober self-searching; for the bravado of false Africanism and bohemianism they substituted attempts to understand Negro life in its workaday aspects in the here and now.[4]

The literati of the Harlem Renaissance, though more concerned with the plight of black America than with that of the international proletariat, had one thing in common with their white confrères of the Village and the New York Intellectuals: very few of the leading names of Harlem were from New York. Jessie Fauset, a disciple of the redoubtable historian and civil rights crusader

W. E. B. Du Bois, was born in New Jersey. She made the pilgrimage across the Hudson River in the late 1920s to pursue a career as a literary editor, a supporter of up-and-coming black writers and a novelist in her own right. One of the most widely acclaimed painters to emerge from this movement was Aaron Douglas, who hailed from Kansas. Douglas, distinguished by his ubiquitous pipe and avuncular smile, took his talent to New York in the mid-1920s, where he produced illustrations for the *Crisis* and *Opportunity*, the two most important magazines associated with the Harlem Renaissance. Influenced by art deco, the flat profile designs of ancient Egypt and what he called the abstract qualities of spirituals, Douglas created his own style of geometrical figural representation in dealing with 'Negro' subject matter. In the 1930s he painted murals that today adorn the walls of Fisk University in Tennessee, whose student body was historically black, and the New York Public Library. Charles S. Johnson came up from Virginia to distinguish himself as a sociologist and the 'entrepreneur' of the Harlem Renaissance, in whose name he sponsored literary prizes for aspiring young writers. He also served as Fisk's first black president and worked tirelessly to advance the cause of civil rights.

According to Langston Hughes: 'Harlem was like a great magnet for the Negro intellectual, pulling him from everywhere [...] Only a few of the New Negroes lived in the Village, Harlem being their real stamping ground.'[5] Hughes, the most celebrated black novelist, poet and playwright of his generation, points out that New York exercised an irresistible attraction for these black writers from the American hinterland. It was the magazine *The Messenger* – edited by Wallace Thurman, who held court in his 137th Street apartment, known as 'Niggerati Manor', the meeting place of black avant-garde writers and visual artists – that took Hughes's first short stories, for a fee of $10 each, despite Thurman telling Hughes that he regarded their literary quality as 'very bad'. Thurman always affected a scornful posture towards the idealistic black writers of his day. In 1932 he published a minor classic of the Harlem Renaissance, *Infants of the Spring*, a satire on life in Niggerati Manor.

Langston Hughes was the offspring of a family of humble, but by no means impoverished means. He left his Missouri home after finishing school, where in his teens he was hailed as a poet of great promise. In the 1920s, after a sojourn in England and France, like many others Hughes returned to

America to take up residence in Harlem, where he remained for the rest of his life. His move to New York was encouraged by Fauset, who as editor of the *Crisis* had spotted his talent in a poem he wrote at the age of 19, which spoke of the plight of America's black communities.

Hughes enrolled at Columbia University but later abandoned his studies, denouncing the university as a haven of racism. In 1930, the success of his first novel, *Not Without Laughter*, launched him on a prolific and buoyant career in fiction, poetry and the theatre. The semi-autobiographical story is set in Kansas, for the majority of New Yorkers a place as remote as the moon, but at the same time as American as the Fourth of July or Norman Rockwell. It was an appropriate setting within which to narrate the life of a small-town African American youth, Sandy Rogers, growing up within two generations of slavery and at a time when the Ku Klux Klan was at its peak in membership and political clout in the south and Midwest. Hughes was also recognised as the leading black playwright of the 1930s, a reputation that rested largely on his 1935 production *Mulatto*, the most successful of all the plays staged during the Harlem Renaissance. The plot is set in the Deep South, this time pointing the finger at a white plantation owner who refuses to acknowledge his children by a black woman.

The Harlem Renaissance yielded a flowering of black artistic and cultural life, the likes of which had never been seen in America. By the late 1930s, however, the movement's dynamism had begun to wane. It was not until well after the Second World War and the emergence of the civil rights movement that newcomers of the calibre of Hughes, Claude McKay or James Weldon Johnson began to appear. Thanks to the artists, intellectuals and social crusaders who set Harlem abuzz in those earlier years, members of America's black communities found a voice to express the hardships they faced under a system of racial segregation, in a country they would soon be called upon to defend with their lives. The Harlem Renaissance set the groundwork for a social awakening that after years of campaigning and civil strife brought equal rights for African Americans, an achievement that Hughes and many of his Harlem colleagues would fortunately live to see become a reality.

*

It is nothing short of astonishing that the art world of New York managed not only to defy the Great Depression but to continue to thrive in the 1930s. It was as if the energy of the city's phenomenal growth in previous decades had developed an unstoppable momentum of its own. Greenwich Village and Harlem, at opposite ends of Manhattan and worlds apart in social profile, were standard bearers of artistic expression during this period. These two neighbourhoods gave the world writers and activists whose voices echoed across the nation the anguish of those troubled days. At the same time, another movement was in progress, building the reputation of New York as the home of some of the world's greatest museums. Two major initiatives of that decade, the Whitney Museum of American Art and the Frick Collection, trace their origins to the beginning of the twentieth century.

Gertrude Vanderbilt Whitney, a daughter of the wealthy New York Vanderbilt family, was an avid art patron, collector and sculptor. In 1907 she established a studio in Greenwich Village and a year later opened two galleries in her 8th Street apartment, which she used to exhibit works by contemporary American artists. Within six years this had expanded into the three-gallery Whitney Studio Club, where for nearly three decades young artists had the opportunity to meet some of the leading talent in the US art world. The club proved so successful that in 1931 she recognised the need to establish a proper museum and, in that year, the Whitney Museum of American Art opened to the public. The inauguration was attended by 5,000 guests. President Herbert Hoover, ever on hand to preside over inaugural ceremonies from his Washington office, sent Whitney a letter expressing his conviction that the museum 'should quicken our sense of beauty and increase America's pride in her own culture'.

The museum's founder and patron wanted her project to embody the principles of the earlier Whitney Studio Club, namely the unacknowledged contribution of living American artists to the nation's cultural heritage. This came at a time when dealers and established museums steeped in orthodoxy had turned their backs on what was being produced by contemporary artists, a hurdle the Whitney and other museums of the era were determined to overcome. Within six years of its opening, the Whitney had put together a collection of more than 800 paintings, 100 pieces of sculpture and 1,000 drawings, etchings and other lithographic works. The number of exhibits has today risen to more than 21,000. They are now housed in the Whitney's new permanent building, finally back in its West Village home after two successive moves to uptown premises had proved inadequate to cope with the great array of displays as well as the crowds that flocked to view them.

Around the time that Whitney opened her Greenwich Village galleries, the Pittsburgh industrialist Henry Clay Frick came to settle in New York, where in 1906, for $2.55 million he acquired the Fifth Avenue Renaissance Revival-style Lenox Library building. The lavishly bearded, portly kingpin of the coke, steel and property markets was soon to be welcomed into New York society as an honoured patron of the arts. That said, Frick left few friends behind in Pittsburgh, especially among his former employees, to whom he was renowned as a ruthless union-buster. In the course of a protracted lockout of steel workers in 1892, the Latvian-born anarchist Alexander Berkman decided to take action in the name of working-class justice. He burst into Frick's office, brandishing a pistol and a sharpened steel file. In the desperate scuffle that ensued, Berkman managed to put two bullets into Frick's neck and stab him four times before he was wrestled to the ground by office workers. Berkman served a 22-year prison sentence, while the stalwart Frick was back at work within a week.

Frick also purchased an area of land adjoining the library, which faced Central Park between 70th and 71st streets, intending to demolish the former and build a mansion for himself. The *New York Times* assured its readers that 'of course' Mr Frick would not live in Fifth Avenue any great part of the year: 'Nobody would, who didn't have to, for while there are in the city several streets less pleasant for constant residence, it has no particular charms in these days when appreciation of rural joys is so nearly general.'[6] There was speculation in society circles that Frick's property investment was intended to outdo the grandeur of his former employer Andrew Carnegie, another Fifth Avenue resident, whose 64-room mansion stood a quarter mile up the road.[7] It was often a strained relationship between the two tycoons, who had met in New York on Frick's honeymoon. Carnegie later appointed Frick chairman of the Carnegie Steel Company, only to treat his every initiative and suggestion with supreme disregard. Fed up with the thankless corporate life of Pittsburgh and its deadly coal smog (for which he was largely responsible), at the age of 56 Frick followed in Carnegie's footsteps and went to spend his retirement in New York.

Frick sensed the calling of a benefactor stirring in his very deep pockets, more so after learning of Sir Richard Wallace's decision to bequeath his regal London home to the British Museum. The mansion was gifted on the agreement that it would become a museum, today known as the Wallace Collection. Frick was seized with the desire to create a private collection of his own, as outstanding as the one he had visited in London, and had already used his fortune to acquire works of art that would form the basis of his collection. He proceeded to demolish the Lenox Library in 1912 and replace it with an even grander house in the Louis XVI manner, designed by the New York firm of Beaux Arts architects Carrère and Hastings.

Frick travelled extensively, purchasing works by the great fourteenth to nineteenth-century artists of Europe. No longer did he permit himself the luxury of paintings bought merely because of emotional appeal to the collector. He disciplined his taste, directing his interest solely to those painters who stood in the recognised top rank. In his will, Frick stipulated that his entire collection be put on view in the museum, financed by a $15 million endowment. The museum's permanent collection includes paintings from Frick's most active period of acquisitions, the years between 1900 and 1919. He was an avid purchaser of works by immortals such as Velázquez, Constable, El Greco, Goya, Rembrandt and Titian, as well as major works of sculpture, eighteenth-century French furniture and porcelain, works on paper by Old Masters, Limoges enamel and other exhibits of remarkable quality. Before his death in 1919 – the same year Carnegie died and 16 years before the gallery's 1935 opening – Frick left instructions for his entire collection to be housed in the museum, financed by the endowment.

On 16 December 1935, free tickets were handed out to 750 guests attending the Frick Collection's inaugural reception. Digging into their pockets for the entrance fee would not have been much of a burden for a handful of the guests – the Astor, Vanderbilt, Carnegie, Mellon, Warburg and Rockefeller families were out in splendour that morning at 1 East 70th Street. However, for the average New York art lover in 1935, the chance 'to enjoy $40 million worth of art in the quiet atmosphere of a rich man's home', as one magazine blithely put it, produced a sense of both awe and pride that Gotham had given the nation such an outstanding art museum.[8]

A variety of smaller museums were added to New York's cultural panorama during the Great Depression. The Abigail Adams Smith Museum (now the Mount Vernon Hotel Museum), located near the East River in 61st Street, is one of Manhattan's few surviving eighteenth-century buildings. In its more than 200-year history it has gone through a number of incarnations. It was first built as a carriage house and stable and was in 1826 converted into a hotel, 'free from the noise and dust of the public roads', about four miles north of New York, which at the time extended only to 14th Street. The building was purchased in 1924 by the Colonial Dames of America, a New York organisation for women whose forebears lived in America in the years of British rule. These formidable dowagers turned the house into a museum in 1939. Its displays tell the story of the completion of the Erie Canal in 1825 and how this event sparked a period of tremendous growth in the city's commercial life. They named it the 'Abigail Adams Smith Museum' after the daughter of the second president of the United States, who with her husband had briefly owned the house in 1795.

The opening of the Cloisters in 1938, built on a hill in Washington Heights, furnished New Yorkers with a remarkable collection of some 5,000 Gothic and Renaissance artefacts. It is a branch of the Metropolitan Museum of Art and serves to exhibit the museum's extensive collection of art, architecture and artefacts from medieval Europe. Outstanding among the exhibits are rare Flemish tapestries, manuscripts and illuminated books. The highlight is in the architecture of the complex, for the museum incorporates parts of five French abbeys, which were shipped to New York and reassembled along with other buildings in the medieval style. The delightful cloistered herb gardens were planted according to descriptions found in early manuscripts. These restful grounds acted as a magnet for families as well as art lovers, who in fine weather made the long subway journey uptown to enjoy an outdoor lunch overlooking the Hudson River, a tradition that continues today.

Another museum founded in the 1930s gave New Yorkers the chance to escape their Depression-era city by travelling through the vastness of outer space. The Hayden Planetarium, part of the American Museum of Natural History, attracted more than 120,000 visitors in the first month after its opening in September 1935. Stargazers seated under its giant dome thrilled to realistic images of the cosmos shown through the Mark II Zeiss projector, while listening to acclaimed astronomers like Sir Fred Hoyle explain his controversial views on the mysteries of space. The three meteorites lodged permanently on the ground floor were the planetarium's most popular display, weighing a total of 54 tons. This $10 million exhibit had to be transported from the museum's main building in Central Park West on specially fitted iron tracks. The planetarium is now part of the museum's Rose Center for Earth and Space.

Equidistant between the West and East Village, the distinctive, nineteenth-century Seabury Tredwell family home in 1936 became the Merchant's House Museum. The Tredwells, who occupied the house for nearly a century, belonged to New York's merchant class. The museum is now owned by the city and contains a collection of more than 3,000 of the family's items, from furniture and clothing to early photography and books, all of which give a unique glimpse into genteel New York family life in the nineteenth century. It is whispered that the ghosts of departed Tredwells resent this usurping of their family possessions. To this day, visitors enter the museum with some trepidation, as it is rife with legends of inexplicable sounds, smells and sightings. This author had the privilege of once spending a night on the premises and can attest that it was an unsettling experience.

The Guggenheim, named after its patron, Solomon R. Guggenheim, the art collector and founder of the Yukon Gold Company, is identified with the boldly designed cylindrical Frank Lloyd Wright building of Fifth Avenue and 89th Street, which opened in 1959 as the museum's permanent headquarters. The original museum, however, was established in East 54th Street by the Guggenheim Foundation in 1939. It was called the Museum of Non-Objective Painting, whose director was the French American abstract artist Baroness Hilla von Rebay. Guggenheim brought in 350 paintings that hung in his apartments at the Hotel Plaza, along with another set of his 'non-objective', or abstract, works – by Chagall, Picasso, Modigliani, Klee,

Kandinsky and others – which von Rebay had amassed for her employer between 1929 and 1937. It was also von Rebay who persuaded Guggenheim to commission the new building from Frank Lloyd Wright.

The Museum of Modern Art was a pre-Depression creation – but only just. Seemingly in contempt of the economic collapse, MoMA, as it is popularly known, opened its doors to the public nine days after the Stock Market Crash. Though this was not strictly speaking an event of the 1930s, these years marked the museum's heyday, to the point that in 1939 it moved from its temporary Fifth Avenue headquarters to its current address at 11 West 53rd Street to accommodate a larger collection and a growing number of visitors. MoMA was inaugurated in 1929 with an exhibition of outstanding artists, such as Van Gogh, Gauguin, Cézanne and Seurat. As its fame and popularity grew, the museum moved into three more temporary locations before arriving at its present headquarters, almost adjacent to Rockefeller Center. The name figures prominently in the museum's history and evolution, for it was John D. Rockefeller Jr's wife Abby Aldrich, with her friends Lillie P. Bliss and Mary Quinn Sullivan, who made MoMA a reality.

The museum expanded its collections in a variety of ways in its first decade of life. It gained the reputation of an originator, a pioneer of unusual exhibitions. It was famed for its openly experimental exhibitions and throughout most of the 1930s the museum kept a close working relationship with government art programmes through the Works Progress Administration (WPA).[9]

MoMA was from its inception an unorthodox institution. It treated pre-Columbian tribal art as art rather than anthropology. American artists who were left destitute by the Depression were given an opportunity to display their works under WPA sponsorship. MoMA also marked a sweeping departure from the accepted museum curatorship of its day, featuring during the 1930s a host of distinctive, not to say controversial, exhibitions. The first showing of African sculpture took place in 1935, displaying works which previously would have been relegated to museums of anthropology and archaeology. Two years later, more than one critic was left outraged over an exhibition of Dadaism and surrealism that included works by children and the 'insane', an initiative the museum's director Alfred H. Barr Jr justified as part of the 'imaginary world' in which these artists lived. Then, in August

1939, MoMA put on a show of paintings formerly owned by German museums, and which had been condemned by the Nazis as 'degenerate'. Barr commented:

> By their exclusion from German Museums, these exiled works of art have joined the glorious company of paintings by van Gogh, Gauguin and other masters of modern art which have been banished from Germany to the enrichment of collections in other countries.[10]

As we have seen, New York City's cultural life between the cataclysmic events of the Stock Market Crash and the Second World War was enhanced by the opening of museums to suit the tastes of all art lovers, as well as by the novels and poetry of the Harlem Renaissance and the social protest magazines and books by the New York Intellectuals. This was achieved thanks to the support of grandees of commerce and finance like Frick, the Rockefellers and Guggenheim, who led the fashion of philanthropy and patronage of the arts. It was enriched further by mainstream magazines like the New York-based *Newsweek*, which was founded in 1933. There was something for everyone, with virtually nothing left uncovered in the worlds of narrative and artistic expression.

Well, almost nothing.

A long time ago in a galaxy far, far away – called the Bronx – a teenage son of East European Jewish immigrants dreamed of becoming an illustrator. In the early 1930s Bob Kane (born Robert Kahn) had no idea where his ambition would lead him, so he spent many hours experimenting at the drawing board, which was his natural means of artistic expression. He had his eye on the rapidly expanding business of producing the newspaper comic book format as a separate publication.

The American comic book was invented in New York City in the 1930s, which quickly became the hub of the burgeoning industry, boasting six comic book publishers by 1936. Crucial to the success of the new form was the invention of the superhero. In 1933, while still at high school in Ohio, writer Jerry Siegel and artist Joe Shuster achieved this in the form of

Superman, who five years later moved to New York, where he was sold to Detective Comics, Inc. (known today as DC Comics) and appeared for the first time in the inaugral issue of *Action Comics* in 1938. Superman's success put the company's editors on the lookout for more heroes of this kind, whose overnight popularity satisfied the need for an escape into fantasy from the seemingly never-ending Depression. Kane's inspiration came to him one day when he placed a sheet of tracing paper over a drawing of Superman and superimposed several variations of his costume: 'Pulling ideas from Leonardo da Vinci's sketches of a flying machine [...] Kane showed his drawings to his collaborator Bill Finger, who proposed changing the bird-like wings to more of a cloak and adding pointy ears.'[11] Thus was born the Dark Knight, who made his comic book debut in May 1939, in *Detective Comics* (No. 27).

What endeared this strange figure of the night, this pulp noir hero, to the citizens of Gotham was the fact that unlike Superman, he was not a superhero at all, but a flesh-and-blood crime-fighter, a son who sets out to avenge the murder of his parents. This crusader against evil relied on his wits, his fists and, when all else failed, the Wayne family fortune, all of which made him so glamorous a figure to his readership. For millions of fans, Batman is the self-appointed seeker of justice, a real person endowed with human strengths and weaknesses, but who in the end always triumphs over evil. From his perch on Gotham's rooftops, arms defiantly akimbo, he offered a symbol of hope to the city's struggling, ground-down citizens.

13

HUDDLED MASSES YEARNING TO BREATHE FREE

There is a plaque on the wall of New York's Center for Jewish History that quotes a remark by Sultan Bayezid II, who ruled over the Ottoman Empire from 1481 to 1512. It reads: 'You call Ferdinand [of Spain] a wise king, he, who by expelling the Jews has impoverished his country and enriched mine.' Does history repeat itself? Consider Spain's expulsion of the Jews in 1492 and the ensuing Sephardic Diaspora throughout the sultan's realms. Then compare those events with what took place in Germany 450 years later: the Nazi persecution that forced tens of thousands of Jews to flee. This was unleashed in the identical spirit of Ferdinand's Edict of Expulsion, in what would today be called a wave of ethnic cleansing. Thousands of those who escaped Germany and the Nazi-ruled countries of Europe found refuge in New York City. Many brought with them their skills as academics, scientists, physicians or artists. Others were poor and arrived with little more than the clothes they stood up in, along with a deep sense of relief at their deliverance from brutal Nazi persecution and the concentration camps. But there cannot be any doubt as to who reaped the benefits of this twentieth-century expulsion, a disaster that left Germany and many of the countries of Eastern Europe in a state of cultural and intellectual impoverishment, as well as physical devastation.

The writing leaped menacingly off the wall in early February 1933, following President Paul von Hindenburg's appointment of Adolf Hitler as chancellor of Germany on 30 January of that year. The news that the Nazi leader had grabbed power, in what was a *coup d'état* in all but name, was received with predictable dismay by the more than half a million Jews living in Germany at the time, who could not ignore the anti-Semitic ranting of the future Führer and his henchmen. At the outset, the reaction was in most cases one of disquiet rather than alarm. The eminent Berlin physician Theodor Friedrichs was almost dismissive of the threat posed by the Nazi regime:

> I was slow to recognise the changes that the year 1933 would bring to all our lives. In the beginning I saw no difference in my practice. The southeast of Berlin was Social Democratic or Communist in its leanings and, if anything, the number of my patients increased.[1]

It was not long before Friedrichs and his family found themselves among the estimated 37,000 Jews who fled Germany in that year. They escaped by a less-travelled route: first to Shanghai, and eventually to New York.

Any lingering doubts regarding the Nazi regime's intentions were brutally dispelled when the new chancellor sent his Brownshirt thugs to tyrannise his communist and social-democrat adversaries. The Reichstag fire of 27 February 1933, responsibility for which remains a historical enigma, gave Hitler the justification he was looking for to suspend all civil liberties. He initiated a crackdown, first against the anti-Nazi press, and then against any Jewish-owned enterprise or political opponent, all of which ranked as priority targets.

It was around this time that Max Reiner, a prominent journalist at the *Vossische Zeitung*, one of the Berlin newspapers owned by the German Jewish Ullstein publishing family, detected a mood of apprehension among his office colleagues. A boycott of Jewish shops and businesses had gone into effect in April 1933, leaving many families humiliated and deprived of a means of support. Reiner had not yet appreciated the full impact of the Nazi persecution of Germany's Jewish population, most of whom considered themselves German first and foremost, in the same way that German Protestants or

Catholics identified more closely with their nationality than with their religion. One day a friend took him to a Jewish cemetery in Berlin, where Reiner was shown many new double graves. These were the graves of couples who had committed suicide together.

By the autumn of 1933, the Nazis had purged all Jews from the national media. The journalist Hans Sahl was among those who fled Berlin for Czechoslovakia, which Hitler had yet to annex. Sahl eventually made the crossing to New York, where he became a prominent figure in Germany's community in exile. Leaving their homeland was often the ultimate humiliation for those German Jews prosperous enough to have secured an exit permit. Refugees arriving at the Czech crossing point were beaten and robbed of their possessions by mobs, and then compelled to crawl on their hands and knees from the German to the Czechoslovak side of the border, promising never to return to Germany. But Sahl reneged on his word: he went back to the country of his birth in 1989, dying there four years later at the age of 90, leaving behind a brilliant career as a poet, critic and novelist in New York. During his years of exile he had also achieved notoriety for his German translations of the works of Tennessee Williams, Arthur Miller and Thornton Wilder.

In the 1930s, New York reigned supreme among American cities in every manifestation of culture and Gotham was therefore the natural lodestone for refugee artists and intellectuals, journalists included, who found themselves on the run from the Nazi witch-hunt. One such was Lil Picard, the flamboyant daughter of a Jewish wine merchant, whose name is held in reverence by New York's artistic community. Before emigrating to New York, Picard worked as a cabaret performer and fashion editor on several German magazines, including *Der Spiegel*. She struck up a close friendship with members of the Berlin Dada group, a school associated with nihilism and opposition to conventional standards. Dadaism was despised by the Nazis, who perceived it as a symbol of cultural decadence and an insult to the principles of National Socialism. The movement's most prominent German exponents, Richard Huelsenbeck and George Grosz, both emigrated to New York in the early days of the Hitler dictatorship. Huelsenbeck, a psychoanalyst by training, was on the Nazi blacklist and, after several arrests and interrogations, forbidden to publish any of his writings. In 1936 he managed by the skin of his teeth to obtain an immigration visa to the United States, where he practised medicine and psychoanalysis in New York. The popular caricaturist Grosz made his move with foresight: sensing what was in the air, he left Germany in 1932, before Hitler came to power, and accepted an invitation to teach at the Art Students League of New York.

Lil Picard rose to glittering stardom in Manhattan's counter-culture movement. Having first worked as a hat designer, she later opened a millinery boutique at Bloomingdale's department store. In the post-Second World War years Picard's irreverent poetry, feminist reliefs and her tablets and provocative articles in anti-Establishment publications like the *Village Voice* and *SoHo Weekly News* boosted her to celebrity status in Manhattan's underground and experimental arts circles. She was acclaimed as 'the mother of the hippies', 'the muse of the American avant-garde', and even 'the Gertrude Stein of the New York art scene'. At the time of her death in 1996, at the age of 94, Picard's huge influence on the New York art world over more than half a century was an acknowledged fact.

The German journalist Kurt Bachrach-Baker at first attempted to carry on writing in Berlin under various pseudonyms, but when this became too risky he applied for and was granted a US visa. He sailed into New York Harbor in 1937, leaving behind his parents, who perished in the Holocaust. Like many German exiles, Bachrach-Baker found his reconciliation with the land of his birth after the war, though for the rest of his life he remained in the United States, where he worked as New York correspondent for *Der Spiegel*.

Henry Marx was a regular contributor to several German newspapers. When the Gestapo took an interest in him as a Jewish journalist with an offensive surname, Marx was interrogated and charged with publishing anti-regime articles. This earned him a spell in a concentration camp. The full wrath of the Third Reich had yet to be unleashed against the Jews and so, living under the fragile remnants of rule of law, Marx was released after serving his term. He knew his luck was bound to run out and therefore immediately arranged to obtain exit papers and book his passage to America. He landed in Manhattan around the same time as Bachrach-Baker, and embarked on a new life as editor-in-chief of the German Jewish newspaper *Aufbau* and the founder of New York's Deutsches Theater.

The renowned sociologist Erich Fromm, the celebrated philosopher Herbert Marcuse, the composer Kurt Weill, the Austrian conductor Erich Leinsdorf – all Jewish refugees who settled in New York and were instrumental in upholding the city's pre-eminence as the country's cultural and intellectual capital. But in fact Jews and left-leaning thinkers of all religious persuasions made up a minority, in fact less than a quarter, of the Germans who fled to the United States in the early 1930s, though their names attracted the greatest public attention. The majority of émigrés were ordinary businessmen and their families, along with other middle-class Germans and later those Austrians who possessed the means to buy their way out of the Third Reich.

Until the late 1930s Jews without a political past, meaning those who had not openly spoken out against the Nazis, were allowed to emigrate, although this meant accepting homeless status and abandoning their material possessions. But after 1938 the situation grew increasingly precarious for German and Austrian Jews. Dachau and Buchenwald concentration camps were in operation, and by that year deportations en masse were under way. The *Anschluss* of March 1938 extended Germany's anti-Semitic laws to newly annexed Austria. Legislation was enacted in both countries requiring Jewish physicians to treat only Jewish patients and Jewish lawyers to represent only Jewish clients. In October, passports of Jews were stamped in red with the letter 'J'.

The tipping point came on 7 November 1938. That morning Herschel Grynszpan, a 17-year-old Polish Jewish student in Paris, whose parents had been expelled from Germany, took it upon himself to assassinate the German ambassador to France. By accident he instead gunned down a relatively minor official, the third secretary of the German embassy. The shooting was just what propaganda minister Joseph Goebbels needed to bring his incendiary campaign against the Jews to boiling point. Two days later a wave of anti-Semitic rioting and looting known as *Kristallnacht* swept through the streets of Germany and Austria. More than 1,000 synagogues were put to the torch; 7,000 Jewish businesses were trashed and looted and many Jewish schools, cemeteries and homes were destroyed. Nearly 100 Jews were killed on that night alone and thousands more were subjected to wanton and sadistic beatings in the streets. The serious business of ethnic cleansing began on 12 November, with the arrest of more than 30,000 Jewish men, who were deported to concentration camps. As many as 1,000 Jews were murdered in the camps in the next six months.

Clearly no time was to be lost. Anyone hoping to escape the rampaging mobs and the Gestapo would have to arrange their exit papers without delay. According to a contemporary report by the American Jewish Committee:

> Only those people who experienced events in Germany up to the very last minute can visualize the life in these ruined Jewish communities. Every day brings new fears and terror. Threats, like a ghost, emerging from the speeches of Party leaders and newspapers in the evening, assume bloody reality in the morning. This methodical persecution continually preys on their minds in such a way that the actual event at times is considered less severe than the threat. A system has been evolved which perpetuates panic.[2]

By 1939 nearly half the Jews living in Germany had emigrated. More than 100,000 of them, accounting for a fifth of the country's pre-war Jewish population, went to the United States.[3] It is not difficult to imagine the elation experienced by these exiles, many of whom spent weeks in steerage during the Atlantic crossing, on reaching the safety of New York Harbor. Jacques Lipchitz, the cubist sculptor who in Paris had worked with Pablo Picasso, Juan Gris and Amedeo Modigliani, left a brief but poignant testimony of the day his ship docked in New York: 'I can't explain what kind of feeling I had. It was like I came from life to death.'[4] In the years Lipchitz lived and worked in New York, he rose in prominence to become a leading exponent of the city's artistic community. His sculptures were exhibited at the Metropolitan Museum of Art and MoMA, as well as in galleries across the country.

AMERICA'S HEAD IN THE SAND

Securing an exit permit from the Nazi authorities to sail to America was only part of the problem. Political refugees scrambling to get out of Germany

were seeking entry to a country that had begun to suffer from an outbreak of
xenophobia of almost epidemic proportions. The widespread hostility towards
foreigners was triggered by the influx of hundreds of thousands of new settlers,
beginning in the nineteenth century. The surge of migration experienced by
the United States between 1820, when records started, to the early 1840s, is
without parallel in modern times. In little more than two decades the stream
built up into a flood, with the annual number of immigrants soaring from a
little more than 8,000 to nearly 105,000 in this period. The Irish famine of
1845 and the abortive German revolution of 1848 were singular upheavals
that gave rise to further great population shifts from Europe. By the 1890s,
some 276,000 people were being admitted annually, placing a severe strain
on the job market, not to mention the tolerance of those who had preceded
the new immigrants. This was grist for the propaganda mills of anti-foreigner
politicians, who in 1930 could rightly point out that in no European country
did foreigners account for more than 10 per cent of the population, as was
the case in the United States.

The threats to social order came from the far Right, as well as from leftist
agitators who took part in the Harlem riot of 1935. La Guardia was several
years into his first term of office when he had to confront the spectacle of
hundreds of pro-Hitler militants of the 'German American Bund' marching
up Manhattan's East 86th Street, the heartland of the city's German immigrant community, in October 1938. On 20 February 1939, on the eve of war,
American Nazis gathered their followers for a mass rally in Madison Square
Garden. On that day the turnout was 20,000 strong: Hitler admirers with
their arms outstretched in the Nazi salute filled the hall above its capacity. The
rally attracted nationwide attention. Even before it was held, many groups
and individuals urged La Guardia and the management of Madison Square
Garden to prohibit the meeting. The majority, however, including Jewish
leaders, reasoned that a ban on the meeting was a violation of civil liberties
and would do more harm than good to the cause of democracy.

The German American Bund was not, strictly speaking, a direct by-product
of the Depression, though it was founded in the aftermath of the worldwide
economic collapse that brought chaos to Germany and helped to catapult
Hitler to the zenith of power. This was a movement of American racists,

anti-Semites and non-interventionists expressing their hatred of Roosevelt's supposedly communist-inspired New Deal. Its leader, Fritz Kuhn, in his speech at the New York rally, went so far as to refer to the president as 'Franklin D. Rosenfeld'. Apart from sporadic street clashes in New York and elsewhere between Bund thugs and Jewish protestors, this was essentially a problem for the federal government to deal with, which it did by outlawing the organisation as soon as the United States entered the Second World War in December 1941.

The widespread American antipathy towards outsiders was enshrined in a 1917 law, enthusiastically adopted by Congress, which set down 'medical' guidelines for excluding immigrants in language that almost beggars belief. The list included persons who were 'mentally defective', 'idiots', 'imbeciles', 'persons of constitutional psychopathic inferiority' and 'persons afflicted with a loathsome or dangerous contagious disease'. In short, this was the sort of language that could have been lifted straight from a Nazi manifesto. This was a clear, if objectionable expression of America's resolve to deter a repetition of the massive immigration of the nineteenth century. The spirit, if not exactly the letter of this law prevailed in later legislation.

The US Immigration Act of 1924 imposed stricter quotas than previously had been in place on the numbers of foreigners coming to settle in the country. Five years later, Congress brought in a further tightening up of the law by limiting to 153,744 the annual number of immigrants. Moreover, quotas were assigned by country, so that Germany and Austria combined were restricted to 27,370 per year, regardless of the circumstances of the individuals concerned.

Where were these people to go to escape Nazi tyranny? New York City, with its large, well-established Jewish community and aid agencies, was the natural destination of preference for Jewish refugees. A glimmer of hope appeared in July 1938, when President Roosevelt convened the Évian Conference in France, a meeting of 32 countries and 63 private organisations, to address the quota barriers. The meeting broke up eight days later in total failure when the major Western countries, most notably the United States, refused to relax their quotas by any meaningful degree. Hitler himself had supported the aims of the conference, to which he sent a message expressing his delight at the prospect of seeing his country rid of its entire Jewish population. The Führer went so far as to propose the creation of a Jewish state in Uganda or Madagascar, with the hope they would all die of disease in these inhospitable places.

Four months after the disastrous Évian Conference, the US secretary of the interior, Harold L. Ickes, came up with a slightly less far-fetched proposal for the resettlement of Jewish refugees. Unlike Hitler, Ickes spoke without malice when he suggested skirting the immigration quotas by offering Alaska as a Jewish homeland. Ickes had that summer toured the territory, which the United States had purchased from Tsarist Russia for $7 million in 1867. He saw that attempts to attract settlers to Alaska had not met with an enthusiastic response. This caused concern about the territory's strategic position, with Japan's mounting aggression against China and the likelihood of war in Europe. The idea never got off the ground. The proposal came in for criticism by the American Jewish Congress, whose leaders feared it would be interpreted as a Zionist takeover of US territory. Roosevelt, in secret talks with Ickes, sealed the fate of his close collaborator's scheme, explaining that the plan would necessitate exceeding the number of Jewish immigrants he was prepared to allow into the country.

Isolationist fervour was whipped up by powerful bigots like Democratic senator Robert Reynolds of North Carolina. Reynolds spoke as an unabashed apologist for the Nazis, and when the news broke in 1939 of the proposed refugee bill for Alaska, the senator attacked it as the 'opening wedge' to bring in hundreds of thousands more aliens.

By the summer of 1939, it was obvious that the countdown to war had begun. Hostilities were imminent but the storm was gathering far across the sea. Even the people of New York, who are culturally and geographically closer to the Old World than those of any other major US city, found it difficult to believe that their country would be dragged into another European conflict. Be that as it may, on 4 July 1939, America's Independence Day, the thoughts of most New Yorkers were fixed squarely on baseball, and in particular on Lou Gehrig, one of the New York Yankees' greatest hitters of all time. More than 62,000 fans were crammed into Yankee Stadium in the Bronx on that momentous afternoon, for the immortal Lou Gehrig stood in the middle of the field to take a standing ovation alongside the Yankees' outfielder, Babe

Ruth. A third New York hero figure exchanging embraces with Gehrig and Ruth in Yankee Stadium that sweltering July afternoon was Mayor Fiorello La Guardia. Ruth was still on top form – not so Gehrig, whose game that season had suffered an abrupt decline. He had been sent to the Mayo Clinic, where he was diagnosed with the rare neurodegenerative disease that now bears his name, and that two years later was to send him to his grave.

Two months after Gehrig and Ruth's joint appearance at Yankee Stadium, Hitler's panzers rolled into Poland and for the second time in less than a generation Britain and France were at war with Germany. In New York, throngs gathered in Times Square the night after the Germans launched their offensive to follow the bulletins flashing across the electronic panel on the New York Times Building. The mood in the crowd ran from one of curiosity to deep concern. But all stood in silence, lining the kerbside from 39th to 47th streets, to catch a glimpse of the news bulletins as they were updated. The NYPD information booth in the centre of Times Square was besieged by panicked foreign tourists desperate to locate their respective consulates. Alongside these anxious visitors, many others were simply asking directions to the World's Fair, the theatres or Coney Island. Gotham has a knack for taking calamity in its stride.

La Guardia was less apathetic than the news-hungry onlookers in Times Square. As reports piled in about the Wehrmacht's rapid advances in Poland, the mayor summoned the heads of six key departments to City Hall for a strategy meeting on how to defend New York City in the event of enemy attack. Europe was thousands of miles away, yet in contrast with the Great War, which La Guardia had experienced first-hand, the prospect of aerial bombardment from across the sea was in 1939 by no means unthinkable. The celebrated aviator Charles Lindbergh had made the non-stop Atlantic crossing in his single-engine monoplane, the *Spirit of St Louis*, in 1927. Who could say for certain whether the Luftwaffe was not already rolling out long-range bombers that could do the same? Even if their planes lacked this capability, the threat of German aircraft carriers delivering airborne devastation to any corner of the globe seemed very much within the realm of reality.

In two hours of meetings with the commissioners of the police, the fire brigade, the docks, transport, water and gas supply and health, La Guardia and his department heads mapped out a disaster-contingency plan for the city. The immediate aim, in the event of the United States being drawn into the war, would be to detect and safeguard against sabotage by enemy agents. Police commissioner Lewis J. Valentine assured La Guardia he was keeping a sharp lookout for potential political saboteurs and that the activities of relevant consulates had been placed under close surveillance. Power plants, water-pumping stations and floodgates were given extra police protection under the War Emergency Program, which was drawn up by top-ranking officers. The Board of Transport reported that the subway system was equipped to accommodate large numbers of people in an emergency and that most stations were well adapted for use as bomb shelters.[5]

La Guardia's concern for safeguarding New York against enemy attack would have brought a melancholy smile to the faces of those refugees hazarding the choppy Atlantic waters, to say nothing of German U-boats lurking beneath the waves, in that autumn of 1939. In a spirit of generosity it might be conceded that the US administration, in refusing to relax the immigration quota, had failed to realise that people clamouring to reach New York Harbor were not merely fleeing persecution – they were escaping almost certain death at the hands of the Nazis. The numbers leaving Germany and Austria swelled from 36,000 in 1938 to 77,000 the following year. The majority of these emigrants were seeking what they believed to be a safe haven in neighbouring countries like Belgium, France and the Netherlands, all of which would shortly be overrun and occupied by the Germans. Some of the more fortunate, who made it to New York, were soon surprised to learn that their troubles were far from over. To paraphrase a saying, for many it was a leap from the frying pan into the freezer compartment.

There is a curious social phenomenon that tends to characterise ethnic communities of great multicultural cities: newly landed immigrants more often than not find that they are not welcomed by those who arrived in earlier waves of political or economic exile. The opposite often takes place when encountering visitors from the old country, who find they have little in common with their uprooted compatriots in the New World. Apart from a shared language and culinary tastes, these immigrants have acquired an identity that is quite often totally alien to visitors from their homeland. Jewish refugees arriving in New York in the 1930s were far fewer in number than those who had come before, but likewise their cultural identity was worlds apart from the Jews who preceded them, starting with the great surges of immigration of the mid-nineteenth century and beyond.

EAST SIDE, WEST SIDE

The pogroms that took place in Russia, Poland and other countries under Tsarist dominion began in 1881, following the assassination of Tsar Alexander II, a crime widely blamed on the Jews. The 33 years between that time and the outbreak of war in 1914 witnessed one of the greatest mass population movements in recorded history. Fully a quarter of the Jews living under the Romanovs fled overseas, and unlike almost all other immigrant groups that landed in the United States, the Jews overwhelmingly chose to set up home in New York City.[6] This wave of settlers was made to feel right at home in their new country, given the number of their co-religionists who had preceded them. In New York, they encountered many synagogues and mutual aid societies founded by immigrants, from the Sephardic Jews of Brazil who came to New Amsterdam in the mid-seventeenth century to the Lithuanian Jews who fled the famine of the 1860s.

Around half of the 2 million victims of the Russian pogroms went to the United States and a large number of them took up residence in the Lower East Side, alongside the existing Jewish community. It was a source of comfort to these people to join co-religionists who could trace their roots to the same home towns and who, almost without exception, spoke Yiddish as their daily language. The extent of this migration to New York was unprecedented, in that by 1920 the city had more than 5,000 Jewish organisations of every description, with at least a million members.

Although the Lower East Side has historically been regarded as a Jewish enclave, other ethnic groups had for decades made their home in this area located on the south-eastern side of Manhattan, close to the East River and Port of New York. In the 1930s, this was the city's most densely populated neighbourhood, with 163,000 inhabitants per square mile. More than 50 per cent of Lower East Side residents spoke a foreign language exclusively at home, yet despite the mass influx of European Jews in that decade, they accounted for less than 40 per cent of the population. Italians made up the second-largest ethnic minority population, living mostly east of the Bowery, between the Brooklyn and Manhattan bridges.[7]

This is a story of overlapping immigrant groups supplanting one another and each contributing to the character and visible face of the city. From the nineteenth century onwards, the neighbourhood has witnessed influxes of economic immigrants from Poland, Italy, Ireland and other European countries in which poverty was endemic. The sounds and sights of the streets, apart perhaps from dress (though this was not always the case), in the 1930s mirrored the potpourri of languages and ethnic types one would have encountered in the previous century.

Pushcarts lined the noisy cobbled roads and tenement entrances, shifting from one side of the street to the other, from sun to shade, according to the season. Even after the great wave of Jewish immigration, a large number of the pushcart vendors were Italian, hawking their peppers, plum tomatoes, romaine lettuce and aubergines to a clamour of Polish, Russian and Greek housewives. Other market traders specialised in household goods like women's rayon undergarments, spools of thread, buttons and socks. While girls helped their mothers with the shopping, boys tended the stalls alongside their fathers. The pushcarts added a lively bazaar atmosphere to the streets, though at the time few of the peddlers suspected that theirs was a dying trade. In 1938, in response to complaints by retailers of unfair price competition, the commissioner of markets slapped a near blanket ban on New York's 14,000 pushcarts, which were corralled into modern enclosed markets.[8]

As was the case with much of New York's commercial life in the 1930s, the pushcart trade of the Lower East Side was under ruthless Mafia control. However, this business was an almost inconsequential cog in the well-organised machine of the city's infamous Five Families. It was a system of corruption and graft on a community level, run by petty crooks, though equally damaging to traders struggling to eke out a living with their melons and bananas. More often than not, the cop on the beat was notoriously on the take, demanding bribes from traders in exchange for turning a blind eye to non-payment of the weekly licence fee to operate a pushcart. In some instances, traders were forced to pay up to $1,000 for a licence and, more importantly, the guarantee of a prime market spot to set out their wares.

The police stepped back from squabbles between pushcart vendors and shopkeepers when the latter demanded payment for the use of pavement space in front of their premises. This was the domain of the neighbourhood supremo, the so-called 'block president', a thug who acted as intermediary between the police, traders and shopkeepers. These fixers would not hesitate to deploy strong-arm tactics to resolve disputes over graft payments.

In the late 1930s this colourful medley of Lower East Siders was joined by the Jewish newcomers escaping the tyrannies of Germany and Austria. They were a breed apart from the predominantly poor, unsophisticated and deeply religious Jews who already lived in the neighbourhood. A large number of the refugees of the 1930s had abandoned a comfortable middle-class existence, for the most part in the more affluent neighbourhoods of Berlin and Vienna. They spoke German, not Yiddish, and considered themselves first and foremost citizens of the countries they had left behind.

The tenement dwellers refused to embrace these refugees, whom they looked upon as moneyed, faithless outsiders. Similarly, the new arrivals were only too happy to give the Lower East Side a miss. This was by no stretch of the imagination a desirable place to live. 'Cosy squalor' might be the most charitable description of a neighbourhood in which half the tenements lacked central heating and private toilets. Nearly 2,000 local shops languished vacant and boarded up. A report by the New York Regional Plan Association in 1931 described the Lower East Side as 'America's most considerable and incorrigible slum'. The social reformer Jacob Riis, on a visit to the Lower East Side, found a three-room dwelling occupied by 20 people. This family and their lodgers slept on piles of clothing, some in a cellar measuring four by six feet. By early 1930, 82 breadlines had been set up across New York City, serving more than 80,000 people daily. By the end of that year, the Lower East Side accounted for 50 of those breadlines, with some 50,000 people queuing for food every day.[9]

Many of those with the means to buy their way out migrated to Williamsburg in Brooklyn, which became the home of the city's ultra-Orthodox Hasidic sect. Following this mass exodus of the 1930s and exacerbated by deteriorating living conditions, the Lower East Side began to take on the appearance of an empty and abandoned neighbourhood.[10]

Washington Heights, which sits north of Harlem and runs for nearly 30 city blocks to 183rd Street, began to develop as a residential area after 1905, when the subway was extended to the neighbourhood, attracting large numbers of immigrants of Irish descent. They were followed by European Jews fleeing the rise of fascism in their home countries, as well as newly prosperous Jews from the Lower East Side seeking better living conditions uptown. The red-brick Washington Heights tenement buildings were occupied by refugees a notch or two below the top intellectual and social echelons, who established themselves in the some of the city's more genteel areas. The neighbourhood was named after Fort Washington, the camp of General George Washington and his troops during the American War of Independence. More than a century and a half later, Washington Heights had once again become the scene of open conflict.

NEIGHBOUR PROBLEMS

The newly landed refugees discovered that while they had escaped the clutches of the Gestapo, life in their new abode was far from harmonious and not without perils of its own. The Irish who had emigrated to New York three or four decades ahead of the Jewish refugees were already established in a tightly knit society in Washington Heights. They made no secret of their resentment, verging on undisguised hatred, of the generally better-educated Jews. America's entry into the Second World War in 1941 brought an end to the activities of pro-Nazi demagogues like the Catholic priest Charles Coughlin and the leader of the right-wing Christian Mobilizers Joseph McWilliams. But the late 1930s were racked with violent clashes between anti-Semitic Irish gangs and their Jewish neighbours, who soon learned to give as good as they got: 'There were areas where the Jews and Irish lived in close but inharmonious relationship. These were the most explosive neighbourhoods and during these turbulent years became the main battlefields in which ethnic conflicts became street brawls between warring tribes.'[11] One sensationalist Jewish journal went so far as to conjure up memories of the escape from death at home, by suggesting that 'pogroms might be in the making'. The battle lines were drawn to the east and west of Broadway, which intersects Washington Heights on a north–south axis. In keeping with New York's ghetto society of the day, the Irish inhabited the streets closest to the Harlem River to the east, while most of the Jews occupied the western side, bordered by the Hudson River.

The period between the era of large-scale Jewish immigration and America's declaration of war against Hitler in December 1941 saw almost constant confrontations between these ethnic groups. This almost invariably turned into attacks on synagogues and Jewish youths in the street, which in turn led to retaliation by Jewish vigilante defence units. Jewish community leaders denounced the Irish-dominated police force for failing to halt the violence, and few would deny that there was more than a grain of truth in this accusation. Hence confrontation became a regular feature of neighbour-hood life in the late 1930s and well into the war years. An uneasy truce was achieved between the Irish and Jews only when the Catholic Church stepped in to condemn the violence, which by this time had spread to the same two ethnic communities in the South Bronx.

New York is frequently held up as a symbol of the American 'melting pot', a city in which people of diverse ethnic backgrounds come together to rejoice in the American dream, itself a concept vaguely defined by sound bites like 'haven of liberty' and 'land of opportunity'. One aspect of New York life often given as an example of this cultural blending is the vast number of ethnic restaurants lining the streets of Manhattan. As Cecil Beaton remarked:

> No foreigner exiled in New York need remain at home for his national atmosphere. He is certain to find, somewhere on Manhattan, a restaurant to transport him to the gastronomical delights of home, whether he be from Canton or Bucharest, Stockholm or Marseilles.[12]

This observation by a European visitor to New York in the 1930s in reality points to a state of affairs quite different to that of the oft-cited melting pot.

No Cantonese launderette owner in Mott Street would have dreamed of travelling uptown for a Chinese dinner; nor would a Puerto Rican grocer have ventured beyond the confines of East Harlem for a Caribbean meal. It might be that the term 'stew pot' offers a more accurate description, signifying as it does a hotchpotch of ingredients, coexisting in close proximity, frequently knocking into one another, but never fusing into a homogeneous whole. This was recognised by Cecil Beaton, the traveller who extolled the profusion of cuisine to be had in Manhattan's restaurants. Beaton also recognised within New York a network of other foreign cities, inhabited by immigrants who may not have learned the language but who have nevertheless become impregnated by the national character: 'the races of Manhattan group themselves as in Europe [...] the Spaniards are the neighbours of the French, the Germans of the Austrians, and [...] the Greeks are situated behind the Italians.'[13]

Since the Depression years, September in Little Italy's Mulberry Street has been the scene of bouncy music and rows of Neapolitan food stalls, set up to celebrate the feast of San Gennaro. Mulberry is intersected by Canal, south of which a multitude of dragons, fireworks and steaming woks take over the neighbourhood during the Chinese New Year celebration. The asphalt divide separating the two communities is less than 30 yards across, yet in the 1930s it could have equalled the distance between Naples and Shanghai, for all the intermingling that went on between Chinese and Italian residents.

Likewise, the black people who began moving into Brooklyn's Bedford–Stuyvesant in 1932, taking advantage of the opening of the A Line subway linking this enclave to Harlem, would have nothing to do with the Hasidic Jews of nearby Williamsburg. The feeling, it might be added, was mutual. For that matter, there was a good deal of enmity between those who belonged to the Hasidic sect and the modern Orthodox Jews who later settled in the neighbourhood.

A classic New York 'stew pot' scenario of the era was Palm Street in south-west Harlem, not far from Central Park. This large apartment-block development underwent a demographic transformation from Jewish to Hispanic in the late 1920s, and in the 1930s it saw a shift from a predominantly Spanish-speaking population to an African American one. Puerto Rican migration to New York was unrestricted, since they were residents of an American territory and therefore held US citizenship. The Caribbean islanders began moving from East Harlem to the Palm Street area and they were soon followed by black people who had mostly migrated from the south. The influx of low-income tenants triggered a drop in rental values and resulted in an exodus of middle-class Jewish families from what they perceived as a deteriorating neighbourhood. Poor Cubans and immigrants from Central and South America were also drawn to Palm Street, where they were met with hostility by members of the black community, almost none of whom could afford to follow the Jewish residents departing for greener pastures. Moreover, the American-born black people held the Spanish-speaking immigrants in cultural contempt, considering them to be foreign intruders.

The boundaries were shifting in an uncomfortable direction for the ethnic groups caught up in these demographic movements. East Harlem had for many years been Italian Harlem, an area settled by immigrants moving uptown from Little Italy, many of whom would work as builders in the northwards-shifting real estate boom. By the 1930s, there were more than 100,000 Italians living in East Harlem's crowded and run-down buildings. West Harlem, on the other hand, in the wake of a property market crash that hit that side of the district, became the preserve of poor African Americans. Then with the arrival of Puerto Ricans, East Harlem increasingly became Spanish Harlem. The borders of the various domains were delineated by the people who lived within them. Italians recognised that west of Lexington Avenue was not their world, while young black people and Puerto Ricans took care to give the Italian neighbourhood a wide berth.

James Bryce, who served as Britain's ambassador to Washington in the early twentieth century, in spite of his patrician background took an interest in the lives of common folk. On one occasion he went on a tour of New York's densely peopled tenement districts. He observed 'how largely New York is a European city, but a European city of no particular country'.[14] In the 1930s, as is the case today, about a third of New York's population was foreign-born, a demographic fact evidenced by the city's more than 100 daily and weekly foreign-language newspapers. In the years of the Great Depression, it would have been ingenuous to expect harmonious relations to prevail among the Irish, Italian, black and Hispanic communities, all of whom fought to cling to the lowest rungs of the prosperity ladder. It was a scramble for whatever could provide a means of sustenance for one's family. In the broader sense, life in the city's ethnic communities took on the quality of a battle against outsiders engaged in an identical struggle for survival.

There was among the ethnic minorities a shared resentment of the Jews, who were the first of the twentieth-century immigrants to acquire a comparatively enviable social and economic status. At the time of the First World War there were more than a million Jews in New York, most of them living in squalid and overcrowded Lower East Side tenements. Within a few years, many had moved into the garment trade, frequently setting up their own businesses, which deservedly became known as 'sweatshops', for the deplorable working conditions suffered by the cheap labour they employed. Prosperity brought the growth of close-knit community schools, social clubs, relief organisations, trade unions and retail shops in non-Jewish neighbour-hoods. This became a source of antagonism towards a better-educated and well-connected group of immigrants. Hostility was also directed against the Jews by pro-Nazi organisations, which whipped up anti-Semitic rallies, marches and not-infrequent acts of violence. These groups, as we have seen, were disbanded on America's entry into the war, at which point they ceased to pose a problem for law and order.

A measure of shared affluence cures many a social ill. The Second World War provided an antidote to ethnic conflict in New York. Beginning in September 1939, thousands of jobs began to open up in the shipbuilding and repair industries of the Brooklyn Navy Yard and other war industries, first to supply Britain and other US allies, and later to equip the millions of American troops departing from New York Harbor.

The ghettos may have resembled a no-man's-land, but they also served an important social purpose, which was to reinforce a sense of cultural pride. People found their own voice within the confines of these neighbourhoods, each ethnic group in its own way, and this helped to ease tensions.

By 1930, Puerto Ricans in New York numbered between 53,000 and 150,000, depending on whose statistics one chooses to accept. The gradual economic recovery threw up opportunities for the Hispanics to move from domestic service and other low-skilled work to jobs in city departments. Some were employed in the postal service, while others opened small businesses in the Spanish-speaking neighbourhoods, known as the barrios, which acted as social gathering as well as shopping venues, thus helping to safeguard their way of life. Language is the determining feature of ethnic identity. The ability to communicate with others is a powerful cultural tool, one that sustains and reinforces a group's like-mindedness. It was this shared language that helped the Puerto Rican immigrants to adapt to an alien culture. Five Spanish-language magazines and several daily newspapers acted as an adhesive to keep the community together, along with dozens of support organisations, professional societies and social clubs.

There were at least 200,000 Irish living in New York before the outbreak of the Second World War. They held fiercely to their identity after the Irish Civil War of the early 1920s, when many supporters of the republican opposition emigrated to New York. In 1932 the New York Irish established an annual music and dance festival, which spread to communities across the United States. They developed other outlets for traditional culture, even in Harlem. There were Irish dance halls and stadiums for sports such as soccer and hurling. More significantly, Irish Americans became a potent force in local politics, to the extent that the Democratic machines of the Bronx and Brooklyn remained under Irish control throughout the decade and beyond. One of the greatest Irish immigrant success stories of the 1930s was the rise to power of William O'Dwyer, who sailed for New York in 1910 after abandoning his training for the priesthood. O'Dwyer moved up the professional ladder in dramatic style, from construction worker to tough NYPD cop to Brooklyn district attorney, finally becoming New York City's one hundredth mayor in 1939. His prosecution of the organised crime syndicate Murder, Inc. made him a national celebrity.

The saga of America's black community in the Depression days was fraught with difficulties. The immigrants from the south were burdened with an unemployment rate of around 50 per cent, double that of the white population. Black middle-class community leaders were on the scene to help people assert their identities, men like financier James 'Soldier Boy' Semler and dancer Bill 'Bojangles' Robinson, who in 1931 co-founded the New York Black Yankees baseball team. The black community also set up their own political organisations. Two of the most important were the Democrats of Bedford–Stuyvesant and the Citizens' League for Fair Play, both of which worked through pressure groups to promote jobs and educational opportunities for black people.

The Italians saw themselves as the least threatened of all New York immigrants. Small wonder, as the various Italian neighbourhoods added up to more than a million people, or 17 per cent of the city's population, some tracing their New York origins back centuries. It was, after all, the Florentine navigator Giovanni da Verrazzano who was the first to sail into New York Harbor in 1524. From the late 1930s onwards, working-class families saw a steady improvement in their standard of living. Educational levels were low compared with those of the Jewish community, but a great number of Italians had moved into skilled and semi-skilled occupations. They were prevalent in businesses such as building materials, while Italian barbers, bakers and tailors abounded from Little Italy to Harlem. The Italians were as militant as any when it came to seeing off interlopers on their territory. But at the same time they were wholly at ease with their identity, and it did no harm having in office a mayor with the surname of La Guardia.

Determining tribal boundaries, revitalising popular traditions and the steady revival of the job market in the late 1930s combined to diffuse friction among New York's established as well as its newly landed immigrants. Theirs was a different identity to the one left behind in the Old Country, for some easier to embrace than for others. The snowy-bearded James Bryce was on the right track when he exclaimed that New York was 'a European city of no particular country'. But this was the view of an outsider; moreover, it was one voiced from the perspective of a British aristocrat who would have struggled to grasp the complexities of coexistence in the ghettos. For the immigrants, nostalgic memories of Europe might have served as a cushion in the difficult period of adjustment to their new life in an alien culture. But had any been asked if they would sooner be living in a tyrannical Germany or Italy, a violently racist Deep South, or an impoverished Puerto Rico or Ireland, there is no doubt the answer would have been a resounding no.

The reader will not have failed to be moved by the photo in the plate section depicting a group of Jewish children crowded around the railing of their boat as it steams into New York Harbor. Before them across the bay stands the Statue of Liberty, and, three and a half miles to the north, the red-brick and limestone Ellis Island immigrant processing centre. As the deckhand threw out the mooring line, the children would have caught their first glimpse of the Manhattan skyline, the towers of Battery Park and Wall Street, and the landscape rising majestically in the distance to the skyscrapers of midtown Manhattan. The children's backs are turned to the camera, and we can only envisage the looks of joy and wonder on their faces, as we see them waving to the symbol of their deliverance from horrors that defy the imagination. Manhattan's skyscrapers, those defining features of Gotham, commandeered by Hollywood, whose fantasy factory transformed a great ape atop the Empire State Building into a worldwide household image, brick and steel towers celebrated by novelists, poets and artists, were surely a vision of enchantment for that boatload of children disembarking in a new world, out of harm's reach.

The crusading Fiorello La Guardia furiously smashing up slot machines with his sledgehammer; John D. Rockefeller Jr driving the last rivet into what was to become the Eastern Airlines Building; the thousands of homeless huddled around the fire in their makeshift Hoovervilles; a cacophony of competing tongues resounding through the pushcart-congested streets of the Lower East Side; Benny Goodman leading his big band at Carnegie Hall and Duke Ellington tickling the ivories to enraptured audiences at the Cotton Club; ermine-wrapped ladies sipping cocktails at the Waldorf; a chorus line of Rockettes kicking their shapely legs into the air at Radio City – these are the icons of New York City in the 1930s.

The skyscrapers, however, have to be the showstoppers: those colossal, in-your-face spires that prevail in breathtaking silence over the uproar of Gotham's streets many hundreds of feet below. The vision of the Chrysler Building and the Empire State Building endures in the mind's eye, towering above the lights of Manhattan, which glitter like a spray of crystal beads. Those who call Gotham home and those who have the good fortune to visit the city stand in awe of this spectacle, for nowhere in the world will you see anything like it. New York, New York, it's a helluva town.

NOTES

FOREWORD

1   *The WPA Guide to New York City* (New York: Random House, 1939), p. 167.
2   Le Corbusier [Charles-Édouard Jeanneret-Gris], *When the Cathedrals Were White*, trans. Francis E. Hyslop Jr (New York: McGraw-Hill, 1947), p. 77.
3   Vladimir Mayakovsky, *The Bedbug and Selected Poetry*, trans. Max Hayward and George Reavey (Cleveland, OH: World Publishing Company, 1960), pp. 172–81.

INTRODUCTION

1   Joseph O'Neill, *Netherland* (London: Fourth Estate, 2008), p. 81. O'Neill is here referring to the Manhattan of the early twenty-first century rather than that of the 1930s, but it is not difficult to imagine this description applying to the city in earlier decades.
2   John Gunther, *Inside U.S.A.* (London: Hamish Hamilton, 1947), p. 549.
3   'Gotham' was first used as a nickname for New York City by Washington Irving in his satirical journal *Salmagundi*, with reference to the town of Gotham in Nottinghamshire, England, whose early inhabitants acquired a reputation for doing ridiculous things, such as trying to drown an eel.
4   Birdland was named after the alto saxophone virtuoso Charlie Parker, familiarly known to his fans and fellow musicians as 'Bird'. Parker was the dynamic personality who served as the inspiration for Birdland and its after-hours gigs. The club's fortunes declined in the 1960s, when it finally shut, only to reinvent itself in 1986 uptown in Broadway, on the corner of 105th Street. In the first ten years of its reincarnation more than 2,000 emerging artists performed at the club. On many occasions, artists who were the icons of the original club in 52nd Street visited the new Harlem venue.

CHAPTER 1: BROTHER, CAN YOU SPARE A DIME?

1 Among other Native American terms that lay claim to being the origin of the name 'Manhattan' we have *manahatouh* (source of timber for wood), *mannahata* (island of many hills) or simply *menatay* (island).

2 The map depicting the New York area that is most nearly contemporary with Hudson's voyage is a manuscript chart held in the archives at Simancas, a town in northern Spain. It portrays the east coast of North America from Newfoundland to Chesapeake Bay. It was sent to Philip III of Spain in March 1611 by the Spanish ambassador in London, and was a copy of one made by an English surveyor who had returned from a voyage to North America three months previously. This in turn was most likely a copy of one drawn by Hudson, as we know that Hudson's papers were seized in England and never reached Holland.

3 The name 'Waldorf-Astoria' was spelled with a hyphen from the time of the hotel's reopening in its new location in 1931 to 1949, when it became 'Waldorf=Astoria'. The double hyphen was intended to represent 'Peacock Alley', the hallway that had joined the two original buildings, the Waldorf and the Astoria, which stood on the site that became the Empire State Building. In 2009 the hyphen was abandoned, and the hotel is now known as 'Waldorf Astoria New York'. For the sake of consistency, however, I have used a single hyphen throughout, even where, as here, the reference is to the present day.

4 M. L. Booth, *History of the City of New York from Its Earliest Settlement* (1859), quoted in William L. Stone, *History of New York City* (New York: Virtue & Yorston, 1872), p. 12.

5 Wall Street's name refers to a large stockade built as a protection from Native Americans, after a massacre in 1653 in which 120 European settlers were killed. This stockade extended across the lower part of Manhattan, from the East River to the Hudson.

6 Booth, quoted in Stone, *History of New York City*, p. 12.

7 Ibid.

8 Ibid.

9 The war that followed in 1665 was the second in a series of four conflicts fought between England and the Dutch Republic. The first confrontation (1652–4) arose over trade disputes and was fought entirely at sea, ending in a victory for the English Navy. The second (1665–7) was again sparked by trade, with England determined to assert its supremacy in world commerce. The next war, between 1672 and 1674, was part of the broader Franco-Dutch War (1672–8), from which England withdrew under demands laid down by Parliament. The final conflict (1780–4) set two modern powers, Great Britain and the Dutch Republic, on a collision course against the backdrop of the American War of Independence. However, as in the past the underlying *casus belli* was trade. The war ended in 1784 with a Dutch defeat, confirming Great Britain as mistress of the seas and the world's dominant commercial power.

10 Quoted in Edwin G. Burrows and Mike Wallace, *Gotham: A History of New York City to 1898* (New York: Oxford University Press, 1999), p. 305.

11 There is no consensus about how New York acquired its nickname, the 'Empire State'. Some historians attribute it to George Washington, who remarked that the state's natural geographical features endowed it as 'the seat of empire'. It has also been linked to the state's large population and wealth.

12 Throughout the late 1800s, most immigrants arriving in New York entered at the Castle Garden depot near the southern tip of Manhattan. Then, in 1892, the federal government opened a new immigration-processing centre on Ellis Island in New York

Harbor. This 27-acre island, government property since 1808, had long been the site of an arsenal and a fort, but its most celebrated years were from 1892 to 1943, when it served as the country's chief point of entry for European immigrants. With the removal of immigration and naturalisation services to Manhattan, Ellis Island was used as a detention centre for immigrants with inaccuracies in their entry papers and for those awaiting deportation.

13 The Bronx takes its name from Jonas Bronck, a Swedish farmer turned sea captain, who sailed from Amsterdam to the New World with his family in 1641 and set up the first settlement for the Dutch West India Company in America. This was made possible by negotiating a peace treaty with the original inhabitants, the Weckquaesgeek, who had lived on the land for several thousand years before the arrival of the European colonists. Bronck described the lovely bit of real estate he had found to the north of Manhattan as 'a land covered with virgin forest and unlimited opportunities […] a veritable paradise [that] needs but the industrious hand of man to make it the finest and most beautiful region in all the world'. Quoted in Harry Tecumseh Cook, *The Borough of the Bronx, 1639–1913: Its Marvelous Development and Historical Surroundings* [self-published, New York, 1913], p. 10. In 2014 the Swedes paid tribute to his discovery by unveiling a monument in Bronck's hamlet in the municipality of Sävsjö, while a band struck up 'The Star-Spangled Banner'.

14 New York can be said to have played a part in stoking the flames of the Spanish–American War of 1898. The two press barons who controlled the city's most influential papers, Joseph Pulitzer and William Randolph Hearst, fought a bitter circulation war by publishing inflammatory and largely fabricated stories about the persecution of Cubans at the hands of their Spanish masters. The papers, Pulitzer's *New York Journal* and Hearst's *New York World*, contended that the only way for the Cubans to throw off their colonial yoke was through American intervention.

15 In spite of its reputation as a colourless borough, the Bronx has been the birthplace of a number of cultural luminaries. Consider, if you will, such high-profile personalities as Woody Allen, Lauren Bacall, Anne Bancroft, Ralph Lauren and Calvin Klein.

16 Bob Kane realised his boyhood dream in that Batman was a runaway success from his first appearance in *Detective Comics* (No. 27) in 1939. Within a year of the debut publication, Kane was working in a studio in the New York Times Building. In 2010, a pristine copy of this comic sold at auction in New York for a record-breaking $1.075 million. The bidder and seller remain anonymous.

17 Kenneth T. Jackson (ed.), *The Encyclopedia of New York* (New Haven, CT: Yale University Press, 1995), p. 151.

18 John Kenneth Galbraith, *The Great Crash 1929* (1955; London: Penguin, 2009), p. 97.

19 Quoted in the *New York Times*, 30 March 1930.

20 Galbraith, *Great Crash*, p. 133.

21 *New York Times*, 1 January 1930.

22 Quoted in Albert Parry, *Garrets and Pretenders: Bohemian Life in America from Poe to Kerouac* (Mineola, NY: Dover, 1960), p. 357.

23 Tin Pan Alley, originally located at the corner of Broadway and 14th Street, was a district famed for its composers and music publishers. The name may derive from the tinny sound of pianos used at the time by song pluggers. Songwriter Monroe Rosenfeld described the sound of 'umpteen different tunes being pounded out on tinny old pianos in all the different places like the banging of tin pans in an alleyway'. Quoted in Christopher Winn, *I Never Knew That about New York* (London: Ebury, 2013), p. 142. 'Tin Pan Alley

changed the way music was produced and marketed. In the 1920s, when sales of sheet music began to decline, the industry began producing recordings and promoting them on the radio. In the 1930s the advent of motion pictures with sound made possible the filming of musicals and helped bring songs to a wider public' – Jackson (ed.), *Encyclopedia of New York*, p. 1187.

24 The political organisation known as Tammany Hall, named after Tamanend, a leader of the Lenape tribe, was founded in New York in 1789, after the American War of Independence. It controlled city politics and helped mainly Irish immigrants to occupy positions of political power. Although its activities were at first mostly social and ceremonial, Tammany Hall gradually became the city's most powerful and corrupt political machine. It controlled Democratic Party nominations and political patronage in Manhattan for nearly a century. Tammany Hall ceased to exist in the 1960s.

25 Leslie Charteris, *The Saint in New York* (London: Hodder, 1935), p. 50.

26 Alyn Brodsky, *The Great Mayor* (New York: Truman Talley, 2003), p. 221.

27 Quoted ibid., p. 33.

CHAPTER 2: THE LITTLE FLOWER AND GOLIATH

1 La Guardia, quoted in the *New York Times*, 17 September 1937.

2 The concept of political 'fusion' goes back to the New York gubernatorial elections of 1854, in which the Whig candidate was supported by 11 other parties, including women's and black groups.

3 The Board of Estimate was formed in 1901 with the authority to set the city's budget. It was headed by the mayor, the president of the City Council, the comptroller and the presidents of the five boroughs. It was abolished in 1990 when the US Supreme Court ruled unconstitutional its system of giving equal representation to boroughs with wide disparities of population. This violated the constitutional requirement of 'one person, one vote'.

4 Construction of Gracie Mansion began in 1799, on a site overlooking the East River strait known as Hell Gate. The house was built for a Scottish immigrant, the shipping magnate Archibald Gracie, and among its many distinguished guests were the Marquis de Lafayette and Alexander Hamilton. It was acquired by the city in 1891. The mansion fell into disrepair in later years and between 1924 and 1936 was the original location of the Museum of the City of New York (now located on Fifth Avenue). Between 1936 and 1942, when La Guardia became its first mayoral occupant, it was a historical-house museum.

5 Albert Halper, *Union Square* (1933; New York: Belmont, 1962), p. 153.

6 New Yorkers are much given to renaming their landmarks after outstanding public figures. Hence the 59th Street Bridge, also known as the Queensboro Bridge, became the Ed Koch Queensboro Bridge in 2010. Koch, mayor of New York City from 1978 to 1989, is one of only four mayors – along with La Guardia, Robert F. Wagner Jr and Michael Bloomberg – to have served three terms, or 12 years. Koch was one of New York's most folksy leaders, fond of clambering onto a park bench to harangue his constituents with a hearty 'Hey, how'm I doin'?' Likewise, the Triborough Bridge became Robert F. Kennedy Bridge in 2008, in memory of the US senator assassinated in 1968. The FDR Drive itself was originally the East River Drive, designed by Robert Moses, New York's 'Master Builder'.

7 Alyn Brodsky, *The Great Mayor* (New York: Truman Talley, 2003), p. 254.

8 The term 'New Deal' was coined by Roosevelt upon accepting the 1932 Democratic presidential nomination. In his speech, expressed in the most forceful of terms, he said, 'I pledge myself to a new deal for the American people. This is more than a political campaign. It is a call to arms.'

9 David Playne and Gillian Playne, *The Timeline History of New York City* (London: Palgrave Macmillan, 2003), p. 22.

CHAPTER 3: TROUBLE IN THE STREETS

1 *New York Times*, 9 January 1931.

2 *New York Times*, 22 March 1934.

3 *New York Times*, 16 March 1934.

4 William L. Stone, *History of New York City* (New York: Virtue & Yorston, 1872), p. 85.

5 The Great Migration of the early part of the twentieth century was the first of several mass relocations from the southern United States to New York and other cities of the north. In the 1940s and early 1950s black people became a majority urban population in many cities for the first time in US history.

6 Jeffrey S. Gurock, *When Harlem Was Jewish, 1870–1930* (New York: Columbia University Press, 1979), p. 98.

7 Jonathan Gill, *Harlem* (New York: Grove, 2011), p. 283.

8 A 'five-and-ten' or 'five-and-dime' store was a retail outlet in the United States in the early to mid-twentieth century that sold a variety of cheap products. The best-known and arguably the most successful were those run by F. W. Woolworth Company, one of the original pioneers.

9 Quoted in the *New York Times*, 21 March 1935.

10 Quoted in the *New York Times*, 21 March 1935.

11 *New York Times*, 21 March 1935.

12 Quoted in the *New York Times*, 26 March 1935.

13 The term 'bootleg' goes back to the nineteenth century and smugglers' practice of concealing bottles in the legs of their high boots. Before that the bootleg was the place to secrete knives and pistols.

14 The elevated railway, or 'El' as it was popularly known, was first drawn by cable, then by steam engines. The lines were not electrified until 1902. The network was set up on a 999-year lease of the Metropolitan Elevated Railway Company's lines to the operator, the Manhattan Railroad Company. It was generally agreed that the lines would be torn down before expiry of the lease in 2878.

15 In fact, this was the second incarnation of the Waldorf-Astoria. The first hotel had been housed in two buildings, the Waldorf (opened in 1893) and the Astoria (opened in 1897), located on Fifth Avenue. The original hotel closed in 1929, when the site was sold to the developers of what would become the Empire State Building.

16 Herbert Asbury, *The Gangs of New York* (New York: Arrow, 2002), p. 307.

17 *New York Times*, 3 November 1937.

CHAPTER 4: 'I CAN'T FIGGER WHAT DIS CITY IS COMIN' TO'

1 Carl Sifakis, *The Mafia Encyclopedia* (New York: Checkmark, 1987), p. 20.

2 Luciano's droopy eye was the result of a knife wound he had received earlier that year, when attackers severed the muscles in his right cheek.

3 Johnny Torrio was one of the few bosses of his day to be spared a violent death. He collapsed of a heart attack in 1957, while waiting for a haircut in a Brooklyn barbershop.

4 Charles Dickens, *American Notes* (Oxford: Oxford University Press, 1957), p. 213.

5 Fred Bell, *Midnight Scenes in the Slums of New York* (London: W. Kent & Co., 1881), p. 81.

6 Ibid.

7 Herbert Asbury, *The Gangs of New York* (New York: Arrow, 2002), p. 337.

8 The author of the Prohibition legislation was Andrew John Volstead, a dour Minnesotan of Norwegian descent, who served as a congressman for 20 years. The Act defined an intoxicating beverage as one that contained more than 0.5 per cent of alcohol by volume. Prohibition became law over the veto of President Woodrow Wilson, a descendant of Scottish and Irish forebears, from whom he inherited an arguably more enlightened attitude towards drinking. The law provided federal agents with the power to investigate and prosecute violations of the amendment and defined the use of injunctions against lawbreakers. The Act was modified in 1933 to permit the sale of 3.2 per cent beer and wine, and it was subsequently repealed later that year.

9 Leslie Charteris, *The Saint in New York* (London: Hodder, 1935), p. 97.

10 Sifakis, *Mafia Encyclopedia*, p. 299.

11 In one extraordinary incident in 1926, a gang of mafiosi got their hands on a light aircraft to stage a bombing raid on a farmhouse near Chicago where a rival gang was operating a still: 'It was the first and only time real bombs were dropped from a plane in the United States in an effort to destroy human life and property' – Sifakis, *Mafia Encyclopedia*, p. 45.

12 C. Alexander Hortis, *The Mob and the City* (New York: Prometheus, 2014), p. 96.

13 Magaddino had no lack of enemies and was the target of some quite determined assassination attempts. Rival gangsters once tossed a bomb at him, killing his sister instead, and later a hit man hurled a hand grenade through his kitchen window. He survived these and other attacks in his 50-year criminal career, to die of a heart attack at the age of 82.

14 Thomas E. Dewey was famed as a fearless and incorruptible prosecutor who did not hesitate to use every means at his disposal, including controversial techniques like exorbitant bail and phone tapping, to get his man. His obsession with results earned him national-hero status, so that the public took more of an interest in results than means. It was widely known, for instance, that Lucky Luciano's conviction was obtained through fraudulent confessions. Dewey's political downfall came in 1948, when he lost the US presidential election to Harry S. Truman, having been defeated four years previously by Franklin D. Roosevelt. Dewey was the only Republican to be nominated for president twice and lose both times.

15 A year after Luciano's sentencing Warner Bros. premiered a film, *Marked Woman* (1937), starring Bette Davis and Humphrey Bogart. The plot was loosely based on Dewey's anti-crime crusade and his conviction of Luciano.

16 Dannemora has played host to a number of notorious killers. Alumni include Julio González, perpetrator of the arson attack on the Happy Land social club in the Bronx that killed 87 people in 1990, serial rapist and murderer Robert F. Garrow, convicted in 1973, and the notorious 'Brooklyn Strangler' Vincent Johnson, who murdered five women in 1999–2000. Living conditions in the prison would seem to be as inhospitable today as they were in the 1930s. In 2015 two convicted murderers were so desperate to break out they tunnelled through the sewer system.

17 Sifakis, *Mafia Encyclopedia*, p. 149.

18 Valentine was reputed to be one of America's three best-known law enforcers, along with the FBI's J. Edgar Hoover and the comic-strip detective Dick Tracy. His talents for organising the police force were almost legendary, and, in 1946, after Valentine stood down as New York police commissioner, General Douglas MacArthur summoned him to occupied Japan to reorganise and modernise the country's police departments.

19 Quoted in the *New York Daily News*, 29 March 1999.

20 Quoted in the *New York Times*, 27 January 1935.

21 Quoted in the *New York Times*, 7 February 1934.

22 Quoted in the *New York Times*, 9 October 1936.

23 Sifakis, *Mafia Encyclopedia*, p. 103.

24 This estimate was given by a member of a commission chaired by Paul Blanshard, the respected head of the Department of Investigation and Accounts, set up in 1934 to investigate the rackets. The figure has been disputed, but it is beyond question that the numbers game represented a huge income, filched from those New Yorkers who could least afford to squander their money on gambling.

25 It is said that he was so badly shaken by the murder that he was unable to drive the getaway car and was shoved into the rear seat while one of the killers took the wheel.

26 Franklin D. Roosevelt's original 'Brain Trust' was a group of close advisers assembled in 1932 and composed of ten economists, politicians and lawmakers. It included such distinguished figures as Harold L. Ickes, who was Washington's longest-serving secretary of the interior, associate Supreme Court justice Louis Brandeis and Harry Lloyds Hopkins, one of the chief architects of the New Deal.

27 The PWA, as its title implied, was a public works construction agency, responsible for building dams, bridges, hospitals and schools. Its rival agency was the Works Progress Administration (WPA), headed by Harry Hopkins, which focused on smaller projects and hired jobless, unskilled workers.

28 The song's opening lyrics give an idea of the play's fervour for the city:

> The more I travel across the gravel,
> The more I sail the sea,
> The more I feel convinced of the fact
> New York's the town for me.

29 *New York Times*, 22 November 1934.

30 Edward Robb Ellis, *The Epic of New York City* (New York: Old Town, 1966), p. 532.

CHAPTER 5: ALL THAT JAZZ

1 Quoted in the *New York Times*, 30 July 1928.

2 Quoted in Harvey G. Cohen, *Duke Ellington's America* (Chicago, IL: University of Chicago Press, 2010), p. 54.

3 Nearly four decades later, in 1969, Ellington was back in the White House, invited by Richard Nixon to celebrate the president's seventieth birthday and receive the distinguished Presidential Medal of Freedom.

4 'Satchmo' is believed to be a contraction of 'Satchel Mouth', although the origins of this nickname are unclear. He was also called 'Pops', a term he used when he couldn't remember a person's name – something that happened frequently. This author can recall driving past Satchmo's house in Queens on a Sunday morning and seeing Armstrong in his front garden, playing his trumpet to a throng of neighbours and admirers.

5   Le Corbusier [Charles-Édouard Jeanneret-Gris], *When the Cathedrals Were White*, trans. Francis E. Hyslop Jr (New York: McGraw-Hill, 1947), p. 159.

6   Quoted in Lionel C. Bascom, *A Renaissance in Harlem* (New York: Avon, 1999), p. 64.

7   Ted Gioia, *The History of Jazz* (New York: Oxford University Press, 1997), p. 101.

8   *Metronome* liv (February 1938).

9   *New York Times*, 20 January 1938.

10 Jack Stine in conversation with the author.

11 *The WPA Guide to New York City* (New York: Random House, 1932), p. 167. 'The Great White Way' is a nickname for a stretch of Broadway in the midtown section of New York City, specifically the portion that encompasses the Theater District, between 42nd and 53rd streets. Nearly a mile of Broadway was illuminated in 1880 by Brush arc lamps, making it among the first electrically lighted streets in the United States. The headline 'Found on the Great White Way' appeared in the *New York Evening Telegram* in 1902. This journalistic sobriquet was inspired by the millions of lights on theatre marquees and billboard advertisements that illuminate the area, especially around Times Square.

12 William L. Stone, *History of New York City* (New York: Virtue & Yorston, 1872), p. 657.

13 *New York Times*, 12 March 1933.

14 Van Alexander, quoted in *Metronome* liv (February 1938).

15 The BBC began transmitting a high-definition television service from Alexandra Palace in London in 1936, three years before NBC. This service is regarded as the birthplace of modern television.

CHAPTER 6: GOTHAM GETS A FACELIFT

1   Moses was famed, and feared, for his ability to take arrogance to uncharted heights. When in 1954 he was sworn in for a second term as parks commissioner and city construction coordinator by Mayor Robert F. Wagner Jr, Moses stormed into Wagner's office after the ceremony demanding to know why he had been passed over for membership of the City Planning Commission. The obvious reason was the conflict of interest this would have created, since the function of the commission was to pass on the merits of projects proposed by the other two bodies. Moses was having none of it: he got the third job or he resigned all his posts. Wagner was not easily intimidated, but he found himself unable to resist the full fury of Robert Moses. He relented, at which point Moses left his office and returned moments later with a blank appointment form, which he filled in himself and put before Wagner to sign.

2   Robert A. Caro, *The Power Broker: Robert Moses and the Fall of New York* (New York: Knopf, 1974), p. 448.

3   Roosevelt and La Guardia quoted ibid., pp. 426–7.

4   Ibid., p. 432.

5   *New York Herald Tribune*, 24 January 1935.

6   *New York Times*, 4 January 1935.

7   *New York Times*, 5 July 1936.

8   A product of nineteenth-century engineering (it was completed in 1883), the Brooklyn Bridge was a moving sight for artists and poets of the 1930s, notably Harold Hart Crane, whose long poem *The Bridge* (1930) was inspired by the view from his Columbia Heights home. The last two verses in particular reflect the powerful image the bridge conveyed to the poet:

Under thy shadow by the piers I waited;
Only in darkness is thy shadow clear.
The City's fiery parcels all undone,
Already snow submerges an iron year...

O Sleepless as the river under thee,
Vaulting the sea, the prairies' dreaming sod,
Unto us lowliest sometime sweep, descend
And of the curveship lend a myth to God.

9   It is somewhat ironic that Robert Moses, the man who built hundreds of miles of roadways for New York's motorists, never learned to drive, yet he maintained a staff of chauffeurs on 24-hour call.

10 The Brooklyn Navy Yard was a key factor in ending unemployment in New York. After the United States entered the Second World War the naval facility, as the gateway for warships and military supplies sent to Europe, created thousands of jobs for dock workers. The Garment District also benefited from the war by providing uniforms for troops.

11 Caro, *Power Broker*, p. 5.

12 Quoted in the *New York Times*, 23 February 1933.

13 Quoted in the *New York Times*, 4 April 1936. Mussolini espoused some curious views on the rise of great metropolises, as epitomised by New York City. Il Duce advanced the theory that the phenomenon of mass migration to cities, in his words 'metropolitanism', was an evil, since the new urbanites fell prey to sterility. There came a point, according to him, at which cities were swollen to such a size that they perished and dragged the whole nation to ruin. Not surprisingly, the Italian dictator then warned of the 'yellow and black races' at the doors of New York and other US cities.

14 Mary Harriman Rumsey was the founder in 1901 of the Junior League for the Promotion of the Settlement Movement, a charitable organisation designed to encourage privileged young women to take part in voluntary work for the betterment of their communities, which has evolved into today's Junior League movement. Later in life, in June 1933, she became a key figure in the New Deal, when President Roosevelt appointed her chairman of the Consumers' Advisory Board of the National Recovery Administration. Her career was cut short, however, when she was killed in a horse-riding accident in November 1934.

15 *New York Herald Tribune*, 6 June 1939.

16 *Harper's Monthly*, 1856, quoted in Ric Burns, James Sanders and Lisa Ades, *New York: An Illustrated History* (New York: Knopf, 1999), p. 71.

17 William Karlin, 'New York slum clearance and the law', *Political Science Quarterly* lii/2 (June 1937), p. 241.

18 *New York Times*, 24 November 1938.

19 The post-1930s years of the La Guardia administration stand out less in terms of major achievements than his earlier days of battling the mob and creating public works programmes. Nevertheless, there were some outstanding moments. One of the mayor's most memorable gestures came during a newspaper strike in 1945, when he went on the radio to read Sunday comic strips like *Little Orphan Annie* and *Dick Tracy* to the city's children. The readings can be viewed at https://www.youtube.com/watch?v=xH9tCcrrcak.

20 *New York Times*, 21 September 1947.

CHAPTER 7: THE THING ABOUT SKYSCRAPERS

1   Queensbridge Houses, located in Long Island City and named for the nearby Queensboro Bridge, opened to residents in 1939. In order to cut costs, lifts originally stopped only on every other floor. The unique Y shape of the buildings was intended to provide light and fresh air to tenants regardless of the location of their apartments. The complex spans 29 six-storey buildings and today houses nearly 7,000 people.

2   Alfred Charles Bossom, *Building to the Skies* (London: The Studio, 1934), p. 9.

3   Le Corbusier [Charles-Édouard Jeanneret-Gris], *When the Cathedrals Were White*, trans. Francis E. Hyslop Jr (New York: McGraw-Hill, 1947), p. 11.

4   Sarah Bradford Landau and Carl W. Condit, *Rise of the New York Skyscraper* (New Haven, CT: Yale University Press, 1996), p. 396.

5   In December 1941, the Mitchel Air Force base east of New York scrambled several fighter squadrons to intercept approaching German aircraft. The report turned out to be a false alarm, but the fear of an attack was real enough to motivate the authorities to produce more than a million metal ID tags for New York schoolchildren and conduct drills in how to deal with a gas attack.

6   Alyn Brodsky, *The Great Mayor* (New York: Truman Talley, 2003), p. 386.

7   *New York Times*, 5 January 1930. In 1907, alarmed at the approach of factories, leading merchants and residents formed the Fifth Avenue Association, whose aim was to protect what was to become New York's prosperous and fashionable shopping street from the 'wrong' sort of development.

8   The demolition of French's Hotel was an occasion of great personal satisfaction for Pulitzer. During the Civil War, he had been denied entry to the hotel after turning up in a tattered Union Army cavalry-officer uniform.

9   David Garrard Lowe, *Art Deco New York* (New York: Watson-Guptill, 2004), pp. 115–16.

10   Though none of his works was as dazzling as New York's Flatiron Building, many would argue that the 'father of skyscrapers' was the Chicago architect Louis Henry Sullivan, who designed among others Chicago's Auditorium Building (1887–9) and Buffalo's Prudential Building (originally the Guaranty Building) (1894–5). Sullivan exercised a key influence on modern architectural design and was mentor to Frank Lloyd Wright. He served as the model for the fictional character of Henry Cameron in Ayn Rand's 1943 novel *The Fountainhead*.

11   Accelerated winds near skyscrapers are caused by a downdraught effect. This happens where the air hits a building and, with nowhere else to go, is pushed up, down and around the sides. The air forced downwards increases wind speed at street level. In 1983, New York engineering consultant Lev Zetlin called for laws to counteract the effects of buildings on street wind. A *New York Times* story of 8 December 1983 on the persistent problem quoted Zetlin's views: 'The inertia of our profession is to stay just to the building you're designing. There should be a city ordinance to make sure that, when somebody designs a tall building, tests are done to prevent severe winds on the street.' Alas, no such laws were ever enacted.

12   The earliest example of a building erected in New York to celebrate a businessman's achievements was the Pulitzer Building (1890). This was followed by the Singer Tower (1908), the Bush Tower (1918), the Lefcourt Building (1930), the Chrysler Building (1930) and Trump Tower (1983).

13   Quoted in the *New York Times*, 5 January 1926.

14   In the early twentieth century New York was the centre of the American garment industry. The city was producing more than half of the nation's clothing and creating thousands

of jobs for newly arriving immigrants, the majority of them Jews from Germany. These designers, tailors and seamstresses brought with them significant skills acquired in the garment trade, one of the few occupations open to Jews in nineteenth-century Europe.

CHAPTER 8: SEVENTY-SEVENTH FLOOR, PLEASE

1 Forty Wall Street was the world's tallest building for less than two months in 1930. Formerly the Bank of Manhattan Trust Building, it is currently known as the Trump Building, or more commonly as 40 Wall Street. Seventy Pine Street, formerly known as the American International Building, 60 Wall Tower and originally as the Cities Service Building, was the last skyscraper to be built in Lower Manhattan during the Depression. The building has been described as an 'extravagantly Expressionist' endeavour that, strangely for a group that sought to break with the past, 'held up the unified artistry of the Gothic cathedral as an ideal' – Eric P. Nash, *Manhattan Skyscrapers* (New York: Princeton Architectural Press, 1999), p. 87.

2 *New York Times*, 4 October 1928.

3 Robert A. M. Stern, *New York 1930* (New York: Rizzoli, 1987), p. 606.

4 Reynolds suffered a run of bad luck at that time. Shortly after giving up his senate seat, he was accidentally shot by New York City mayor John Purroy Mitchel outside the latter's home in Riverside Drive. Mitchel's automatic pistol fell from its holster as they alighted from his official car and discharged a cartridge, which hit Reynolds in the thigh and finger. He was rushed to St Luke's Hospital, where he was treated for superficial gunshot wounds.

5 Walter P. Chrysler, *Life of an American Workman* (New York: Curtis Publishing, 1937), p. 102.

6 Ibid., p. 172.

7 The Bank of New York, founded in 1784 by former secretary of the treasury Alexander Hamilton, was the city's oldest bank.

8 Vincent Curcio, *Chrysler* (Oxford: Oxford University Press, 2000), p. 424.

9 Madeleine Ruthven, 'Chrysler Building', *Poetry* (May 1937), p. 77.

10 Chrysler, *Life of an American Workman*, p. 36.

11 Curcio, *Chrysler*, p. 639.

12 *New Yorker*, 12 July 1930.

CHAPTER 9: ANYTHING YOU CAN DO

1 James Nevius and Michelle Nevius, *Inside the Apple* (New York: Free Press, 2009), p. 239.

2 The Empire State Building takes its name from New York State's unofficial nickname, which appears on automobile number plates. The state has had many nicknames, but this is the one that has endured, though there is little consensus among historians on its origin.

3 IND (Independent) and BMT (Brooklyn–Manhattan Transit Corporation) were two subway lines, which today form the B Division of the New York City subway system.

4 Pennsylvania Station was technologically advanced for its day, being the first in the United States to accommodate the use of electric traction, but it had a relatively short lifespan of 54 years. The austere building itself was fronted by colossal Tuscan columns, while the interior consisted of a concourse of glass and wrought iron and a monumental waiting room. The vast main hall was a copy of the tepidarium of a Roman bath. The station facilitated traffic for commuters on the Long Island Railway and also offered regular connections

to New England. It was demolished in 1965 amid a great outcry by conservationists. Its replacement was opened in 1968, as part of a complex far less pleasing to the eye, which also houses offices and Madison Square Garden.

5 Thomas Kelly, *Empire Rising* (New York: Picador, 2005), p. 8.
6 *New York Times*, 27 July 1930.
7 Andrew Eken of Starrett Brothers & Eken, quoted in Charles River Editors, *The Race to the Top of New York City's Skyline* (e-book, Cambridge, MA: Charles River Editors, 2015), p. 56.
8 Paul Starrett, *Changing the Skyline* (New York: Whittlesey House, 1938), pp. 288–92.
9 Raskob had reserved the top five floors for the Empire State, Inc. syndicate, while special lifts led to the observation tower on the eighty-sixth storey. The remaining 16 storeys make up the tower, with the pinnacle representing the final 205 feet.
10 Starrett, *Changing the Skyline*, p. 314.
11 *New York Times*, 21 August 1934.
12 The Manhattan Life Insurance Building was a 348-foot tower in Broadway, built in 1894. It was New York's first skyscraper to pass 330 feet in height.
13 As a tribute to the film's enduring relationship with the Empire State Building, in 2004 the tower lights were dimmed for 15 minutes to mark the death of actress Fay Wray.
14 Quoted in Robert M. Fogelson, *Downtown: Its Rise and Fall, 1880–1950* (New Haven, CT: Yale University Press, 2001), p. 24.
15 Ayn Rand, *The Fountainhead* (New York: Bobbs-Merrill, 1943), p. 353.

CHAPTER 10: YOU'RE THE TOP

1 As told to the author by Deidre Dinnigan, the Waldorf-Astoria archivist.
2 *New York Times*, 15 March 1893.
3 Cecil Beaton, *Portrait of New York* (London: B. T. Batsford, 1938), p. 19. Beaton cites the self-service automat – a kind of restaurant in which customers help themselves from vending machines – as a symbol of New Yorkers' infatuation with eating out: 'The Automat represents a high point in civilisation. Here, *en masse*, yet in pleasant conditions, people can eat well at surprisingly low cost. Around the marble walls are rows of dishes, each an appetising still-life framed in chromium' – ibid., p. 44.
4 Ward Morehouse III, *The Waldorf-Astoria* (New York: M. Evans, 1991), p. 258.
5 Marie Christine Boyer, *Manhattan Manners* (New York: Rizzoli, 1985), p. 226.
6 Peacock Alley gained such a wide-reaching celebrity status that it inspired two Hollywood films, each with the same title. The actress and dancer Mae Murray starred in the 1922 silent version of *Peacock Alley* as well as the 1930 romantic musical remake.
7 Lucius Boomer could have laid his anxieties to rest. In 1933 Charles Pierre Casalasco's Pierre fell victim to the Depression and filed for bankruptcy. Since then, the hotel's ownership has changed hands several times, with John Paul Getty, Trusthouse Forte and Four Seasons among its proprietors. The Pierre was taken over in 2005 by Taj Hotels, the current managers.
8 Barack Obama is the first US president not to stay at the Waldorf-Astoria on his visits to New York. The view of US intelligence services is that the sale of the hotel to a Chinese holding company in 2014 has raised the risk of electronic spying to an unacceptable level.
9 Quoted in the *New York Times*, 14 March 1934.
10 Morehouse III, *Waldorf-Astoria*, p. 258.

CHAPTER 11: THEY ALL LAUGHED AT ROCKEFELLER CENTER

1 The Sixth Avenue El was the second elevated railway to be built in New York City, after the Ninth Avenue El, and the first to be removed. It ran on a north–south axis, roughly from Battery Place to 58th Street, and was torn down in 1938.

2 Ivy Ledbetter Lee is considered the founder of America's modern public-relations industry. When he died of a brain tumour in 1934 at the age of 57, his funeral service at Manhattan's Madison Avenue Presbyterian Church was attended by many of his clients. These included Rockefeller, along with the top executives of the American Tobacco Company, New York Central Lines, RCA and the International Sugar Corporation, among others. Lee was eulogised at the service as a man of 'delight and friendly ways', public-relations qualities to the core.

3 Address by John D. Rockefeller Jr at the opening of the Rockefeller Center gymnasium, December 1936. Quoted in Raymond B. Fosdick, *John D. Rockefeller Jr: A Portrait* (New York: Harper, 1956), p. 263.

4 The Rockettes were founded in St Louis, Missouri, in 1925, inspired by the Ziegfeld Follies. They were brought to New York by the theatrical impresario Samuel 'Roxy' Rothafel to perform at his Roxy Theatre in Times Square, and later followed him to Radio City Music Hall.

5 RCA was set up shortly after the First World War by the US military. The idea was to create a company with sufficient clout to secure America a commanding position in the global telecommunications business, until that time dominated by Great Britain.

6 It speaks volumes of America's retreat into cultural as well as political isolationism that Herbert Hoover, who in 1925 was serving as secretary of commerce, refused to send a delegation to the exhibition, explaining that the country had nothing modern to display.

7 The term 'art deco' – a shortened form of the term 'Arts Décoratifs' in the 1925 Paris exhibition's title – was coined in the late 1960s by the British art historian Bevis Hillier. Before that time it was called 'art moderne' or the 'vertical style'.

8 Glen Leiner, 'Radio City Music Hall', *The Modernist* [special edition of the magazine of the Art Deco Society of New York] (2000), p. 21. Edward Durell Stone was an architect who created the main lobby and the grand ballroom of the second Waldorf-Astoria. He was also the design architect for MoMA.

9 Le Corbusier [Charles-Édouard Jeanneret-Gris], *When the Cathedrals Were White*, trans. Francis E. Hyslop Jr (New York: McGraw-Hill, 1947), p. 33.

10 Today the tree is usually a Norwegian spruce between 70 and 100 feet in height, topped by a 550-pound star.

11 Leiner, 'Radio City Music Hall', p. 22.

12 Le Corbusier, *When the Cathedrals Were White*, p. 33.

13 *New York World-Telegram*, 24 April 1933.

14 The US Passport Office was located in the International Building, while Congress passed an Act allowing goods sent from foreign countries to go through customs and be stored in the basement.

15 William Stephenson, who was celebrated as an audacious spymaster in a biography, *A Man Called Intrepid* by William Stevenson (no relation), ran British Intelligence out of room 3663. This became the base of operations for the future head of the Central Intelligence Agency (CIA), Allen Dulles. 'Another of Stephenson's colleagues was the British naval intelligence officer known as Agent 17F, later to become famous as the novelist Ian Fleming. In the first James Bond novel, *Casino Royale*, Fleming has James Bond earn his

"licence to kill" with the rifle assassination of a Japanese cipher expert operating out of the RCA Building' – Daniel Okrent, *Great Fortune: The Epic of Rockefeller Center* (New York: Viking, 2003), p. 411.

16 *New York Times*, 1 January 1939.

CHAPTER 12: VILLAGE LIFE

1 Terry A. Cooney, *The Rise of the New York Intellectuals* (Madison, WI: University of Wisconsin Press, 1986), p. 19.

2 The *New Republic* was founded in 1914 by Herbert Croly and Walter Weyl, both leaders of America's intellectual progressive movement, along with the political commentator Walter Lippmann. The magazine was financed by heiress Dorothy Payne Whitney and her husband Willard Straight. It continues to be published today as a respected journal of liberal thought and the arts.

3 *New York Times*, 13 May 1933.

4 Cary D. Wintz (ed.), *Remembering the Harlem Renaissance* (New York: Garland, 1996), p. 208.

5 Langston Hughes, 'Harlem literati in the Twenties', *Saturday Review*, 22 June 1940.

6 *New York Times*, 18 December 1906.

7 Carnegie's mansion in 91st Street now houses the Cooper Hewitt, Smithsonian Design Museum, the only museum in the United States devoted exclusively to historical and contemporary design.

8 *Life*, 27 December 1937.

9 Sam Hunter (ed.), *The Museum of Modern Art* (London: Thames & Hudson, 1984), p. 19.

10 *New York Times*, 8 August 1939.

11 Robert Greenberger and Matthew K. Manning, *The Batman Vault* (Philadelphia, PA: Running Press, 2009), p. 8.

CHAPTER 13: HUDDLED MASSES YEARNING TO BREATHE FREE

1 Theodor Friedrichs, *Berlin–Shanghai–New York*, trans. Frederick Rolf (Nashville, TN: Cold Tree Press, 2007), p. 81.

2 American Jewish Committee, 'The situation of the Jews in Germany 1933–1939' [the first part of the manuscript 'The Jews in Nazi Germany', produced by the American Jewish Committee, New York, 1939], p. 7. Available at http://ajcarchives.org/ajcarchive/DigitalArchive.aspx (accessed 28 April 2016).

3 The number of Jews in Germany declined from an estimated 525,000 at the time of Hitler's takeover in January 1933 to 185,000 when war broke out in Europe in September 1939.

4 Quoted in Anthony Heilbut, *Exiled in Paradise* (Boston, MA: Beacon, 1984), p. 213.

5 New York's penchant for disaster preparedness reached its quixotic zenith in the Cold War hysteria of the 1950s. A handful of rusting black and yellow metal signs can still be seen attached to some apartment blocks in the outer boroughs. They are usually placed over basement entrances and bear the legend 'Fallout Shelter', above which is given the maximum number of people allowed inside in the event of an attack. One cannot help but wonder what would have happened during a nuclear firestorm when the 201st person came knocking on the door of a shelter designed to accommodate 200 people.

6 Many of the Irish went to Boston, while Germans and Scandinavians tended to set up home in the north-western states. A large number of Poles, Slovaks and Slovenes

settled in Pennsylvania, where work was to be found in the thriving coal-mining industry.

7   Suzanne Wasserman, 'The good old days of poverty: the battle over the fate of New York city's Lower East Side during the Depression' [PhD thesis, New York University, 1990], p. 15.

8   La Guardia was a committed foe of the pushcarts. In 1938 the mayor received a letter from a representative of the peddlers, complaining about alleged 'high-handed practices by the police'. La Guardia instructed his deputy mayor to make it clear to the pushcart spokesman that 'we have got to get rid of these peddlers'.

9   Wasserman, 'The good old days of poverty', pp. 47–8.

10 Ibid., p. 98.

11 Ronald H. Bayor, *Neighbors in Conflict* (Baltimore, MD: Johns Hopkins University Press, 1978), p. 150.

12 Cecil Beaton, *Portrait of New York* (London: B. T. Batsford, 1938), p. 44.

13 Ibid., p. 94.

14 James Bryce, *The American Commonwealth* (1888; Indianapolis, IN: Liberty Fund, 1995), vol. 2, p. 96.

BIBLIOGRAPHY

Abbott, Berenice, *New York in the Thirties* (New York: Dover, 1939).

Adams, D. K., *Franklin D. Roosevelt and the New Deal* (London: Historical Association, 1979).

Arnold, Rebecca, *The American Look* (London: I.B.Tauris, 2009).

Asbury, Herbert, *The Gangs of New York* (New York: Arrow, 2002).

Bailey, Colin, B., *Building the Frick Collection* (London: Scala, 2006).

Bailyn, Bernard, and Donald Fleming (eds), *The Intellectual Migration* (Cambridge, MA: Harvard University Press, 1969).

Balfour, Alan, *Rockefeller Center: Architecture as Art* (New York: McGraw-Hill, 1978).

Ballon, Hilary, and Kenneth T. Jackson (eds), *Robert Moses and the Modern City* (New York: Norton, 2007).

Bascom, Lionel C., *A Renaissance in Harlem* (New York: Avon, 1999).

Bastin, Bruce, *Never Sell a Copyright* (London: Storyville, 1990).

Bayer, Patricia, *Art Deco Architecture* (London: Thames & Hudson, 1992).

Bayor, Ronald H., *Neighbors in Conflict* (Baltimore, MD: Johns Hopkins University Press, 1978).

Beaton, Cecil, *Portrait of New York* (London: B. T. Batsford, 1938).

Behr, Edward, *Prohibition* (London: BBC Books, 1997).

Bell, Fred, *Midnight Scenes in the Slums of New York* (London: W. Kent & Co., 1881).

Benton, Mike, *Superhero Comics of the Golden Age* (Dallas, TX: Taylor, 1992).

Berrol, Selma, *The Empire City* (Westport, CT: Praeger, 1997).

Bingham, Jane, *Popular Culture: 1920–1939* (London: Raintree, 2013).

Bletter, Rosemarie Haag, and Cervin Robinson (eds), *Skyscraper Style* (New York: Oxford University Press, 1975).

Block, Alan, *East Side–West Side* (Cardiff: University College Cardiff Press, 1980).

Bloom, Alexander, *Prodigal Sons* (New York: Oxford University Press, 1986).

Bossom, Alfred Charles, *Building to the Skies* (London: The Studio, 1934).

Boyer, Marie Christine, *Manhattan Manners* (New York: Rizzoli, 1985).

Breitman, Richard, and Allan J. Lichtman, *FDR and the Jews* (Cambridge, MA: Harvard University Press, 2013).

Brodsky, Alyn, *The Great Mayor* (New York: Truman Talley, 2003).

Brown, Lois, *Encyclopedia of the Harlem Literary Renaissance* (New York: Facts on File, 2006).

Bryce, James, *The American Commonwealth*, 2 vols (1888; Indianapolis, IN: Liberty Fund, 1995).

Bryson, Bill, *One Summer: America 1927* (London: Black Swan, 2013).

Burns, Ric, James Sanders and Lisa Ades, *New York: An Illustrated History* (New York: Knopf, 1999).

Burrows, Edwin G., and Mike Wallace, *Gotham: A History of New York City to 1898* (New York: Oxford University Press, 1999).

Caro, Robert A., *The Power Broker: Robert Moses and the Fall of New York* (New York: Knopf, 1974).

Charles River Editors, *The Chrysler Building* (e-book, Cambridge, MA: Charles River Editors, 2015).

———— *The Race to the Top of New York City's Skyline* (e-book, Cambridge, MA: Charles River Editors, 2015).

Charteris, Leslie, *The Saint in New York* (London: Hodder, 1935).

Charters, Samuel B., and Leonard Kunstadt, *Jazz: A History of the New York Scene* (New York: Doubleday, 1962).

Chepesiuk, Ron, *American Gangster* (Preston: Milo, 2007).

Christin, Pierre, and Olivier Balez, *Robert Moses: The Master Builder of New York City* (London: Nobrow, 2014).

Chrysler, Walter P., *Life of an American Workman* (New York: Curtis Publishing, 1937).

Clark, William C., and J. L. Kingston, *The Skyscraper: A Study in the Economic Height of Modern Office Buildings* (Chicago, IL: American Institute of Steel Construction, 1930).

Cohen, Harvey G., *Duke Ellington's America* (Chicago, IL: University of Chicago Press, 2010).

Condit, Carl W., *The Rise of the Skyscraper* (Chicago, IL: University of Chicago Press, 1952).

Cook, Harry Tecumseh, *The Borough of the Bronx, 1639–1913: Its Marvelous Development and Historical Surroundings* [self-published, New York, 1913].

Cooney, Terry A., *The Rise of the New York Intellectuals* (Madison, WI: University of Wisconsin Press, 1986).

Cuneo, Ernest, *Life with Fiorello* (New York: Macmillan, 1955).

Curcio, Vincent, *Chrysler* (Oxford: Oxford University Press, 2000).

Denning, Michael, *The Cultural Front* (London: Verso, 1996).

Dickens, Charles, *American Notes* (Oxford: Oxford University Press, 1957).

Dickstein, Morris, *Dancing in the Dark* (New York: Norton, 2009).

Ellis, Edward Robb, *The Epic of New York City* (New York: Old Town, 1966).

Escritt, Stephen, and Hillier Bevis, *Art Deco Style* (London: Phaidon, 1997).

Farrell, Frank, *The Greatest of Them All* (New York: K. S. Giniger, 1982).

Fecher, Charles A. (ed.), *The Diary of H. L. Mencken* (New York: Knopf, 1989).

Feingold, Henry L., *A Time for Searching* (Baltimore, MD: John Hopkins University Press, 1995).

Ferriss, Hugo, *The Metropolis of Tomorrow* (New York: Ives Washburn, 1929).

Flowers, Benjamin, *Skyscraper* (Philadelphia, PA: University of Pennsylvania Press, 2009).

Fogelson, Robert M., *Downtown: Its Rise and Fall, 1880–1950* (New Haven, CT: Yale University Press, 2001).

Fosdick, Raymond B., *John D. Rockefeller Jr: A Portrait* (New York: Harper, 1956).

Friedrichs, Theodor, *Berlin–Shanghai–New York*, trans. Frederick Rolf (Nashville, TN: Cold Tree Press, 2007).

Galbraith, John Kenneth, *The Great Crash 1929* (1955; London: Penguin, 2009).

Gill, Jonathan, *Harlem* (New York: Grove, 2011).

Gioia, Ted, *The History of Jazz* (New York: Oxford University Press, 1997).

Glancy, Dorothy J., 'Preserving Rockefeller Center', *Urban Lawyer* xxiv/3 (January 1992), pp. 423–77. Available at http://digitalcommons.law.scu.edu/cgi/viewcontent.cgi?article=1320&context=facpubs (accessed 20 April 2016).

Greenberger, Robert, and Matthew K. Manning, *The Batman Vault* (Philadelphia, PA: Running Press, 2009).

Greif, Martin, *Depression Modern* (New York: Universe, 1975).

Groth, Michael, *The Road to New York: The Emigration of Berlin Journalists, 1933–1945* (New York: K. G. Saur, 1988).

Gunther, John, *Inside U.S.A.* (London: Hamish Hamilton, 1947).

Gurock, Jeffrey S., *When Harlem Was Jewish, 1870–1930* (New York: Columbia University Press, 1979).

———— *Jews in Gotham* (New York: New York University Press, 2012).

Halper, Albert, *Union Square* (1933; New York: Belmont, 1962).

Hammett, Jerilou, and Kingsley Hammett, *The Suburbanization of New York* (New York: Princeton Architectural Press, 2007).

Heilbut, Anthony, *Exiled in Paradise* (Boston, MA: Beacon, 1984).

Herner de Larrea, Irene, *Diego Rivera: Paradise Lost at Rockefeller Center* (Mexico City: Edicupes, 1987).

Hodges, Gao, and Graham Russell, *Taxi! A Social History of the New York City Cabdriver* (Baltimore, MD: John Hopkins University Press, 2007).

Holland, James, *The War in the West* (London: Bantam, 2015).

Hoover, Herbert, *The Memoirs of Herbert Hoover: The Great Depression, 1929–1941* (London: Hollis & Carter, 1953).

Hortis, C. Alexander, *The Mob and the City* (New York: Prometheus, 2014).

Hungerford, Edward, *The Story of the Waldorf Astoria* (New York: G. P. Putnam's Sons, 1925).

Hunter, Sam (ed.), *The Museum of Modern Art* (London: Thames & Hudson, 1984).

Hutchinson, George (ed.), *The Cambridge Companion to the Harlem Renaissance* (Cambridge: Cambridge University Press, 2007).

Irving, Mark (ed.), *1001 Buildings You Must See Before You Die* (London: Cassell, 2007).

Jackson, Kenneth T. (ed.), *The Encyclopedia of New York* (New Haven, CT: Yale University Press, 1995).

Jay, Martin, *Permanent Exiles* (New York: Columbia University Press, 1985).

Jones, Gerard, *Men of Tomorrow* (New York: Arrow, 2006).

Kammen, Michael, *Colonial New York: A History* (New York: Scribner, 1975).

Karatzas, Daniel, *Jackson Heights* [self-published, New York, 1990].

Karlin, William, 'New York slum clearance and the law', *Political Science Quarterly* lii/2 (June 1937), pp. 241–58.

Karp, Walter, *The Center* (New York: American Heritage, 1982).

Kelly, Thomas, *Empire Rising* (New York: Picador, 2005).

Kiernan, R. H., *President Roosevelt* (London: George G. Harrap, 1948).

Krinsky, Carol Herselle, *Rockefeller Center* (New York: Oxford University Press, 1978).

Kroessler, Jeffrey A., *New York, Year by Year* (New York: New York University Press, 2002).

Krout, John A., and Allan Nevins (eds), *The Greater City* (New York: Columbia University Press, 1948).

Landau, Sarah Bradford, and Carl W. Condit, *Rise of the New York Skyscraper* (New Haven, CT: Yale University Press, 1996).

Lankevich, George J., *American Metropolis* (New York: New York University Press, 1998).

Le Corbusier [Charles-Édouard Jeanneret-Gris], *When the Cathedrals Were White*, trans. Francis E. Hyslop Jr (New York: McGraw-Hill, 1947).

Leiner, Glen, 'Radio City Music Hall', *The Modernist* [special edition of the magazine of the Art Deco Society of New York] (2000).

Lovelace, Delos W., *King Kong* (New York: Grosset & Dunlap, 1932).

Lowe, David Garrard, *Art Deco New York* (New York: Watson-Guptill, 2004).

Lowenstein, Steven M., *Frankfurt on the Hudson* (Detroit, MI: Wayne State University Press, 1989).

McCarthy, James Remington, *Peacock Alley* (New York: Harper, 1931).

McDarrah, Fred W., *Greenwich Village* (New York: Corinth, 1963).

Maeder, Jay (ed.), *Big Town, Big Time* (New York: Daily News Books, 1998).

Mann, Arthur, *La Guardia* (Philadelphia, PA: Lippincott, 1959).

Mayakovsky, Vladimir, *The Bedbug and Selected Poetry*, trans. Max Hayward and George Reavey (Cleveland, OH: World Publishing Company, 1960).

Mendelsohn, Joyce, *The Lower East Side* (New York: Columbia University Press, 2009).

Messler, Norbert, *The Art Deco Skyscraper in New York* (Frankfurt: Peter Lang, 1983).

Miller, Donald L., *Supreme City: How Jazz Age Manhattan Gave Birth to Modern America* (New York: Simon & Schuster, 2014).

Moore, Lucy, *Anything Goes* (London: Atlantic, 2008).

Morehouse, Ward, III, *The Waldorf-Astoria* (New York: M. Evans, 1991).

Morrone, Francis, *The Architecture Guidebook to New York City* (Layton, UT: Gibbs Smith, 1994).

Moudry, Roberta (ed.), *The American Skyscraper* (New York: Cambridge University Press, 2005).

Mushabac, Jane, and Angela Wigan, *A Short and Remarkable History of New York City* (New York: Fordham University Press, 1999).

Nash, Eric P., *Manhattan Skyscrapers* (New York: Princeton Architectural Press, 1999).

Nevius, James, and Michelle Nevius, *Inside the Apple* (New York: Free Press, 2009).

New-York Historical Society, Empire State Building file (ref. F 128.75 .E5 C45 197z).

Okrent, Daniel, *Great Fortune: The Epic of Rockefeller Center* (New York: Viking, 2003).

O'Neill, Dennis (ed.), *Batman Unauthorized* (Dallas, TX: BenBella, 2008).

O'Neill, Joseph, *Netherland* (London: Fourth Estate, 2008).

Ormiston, Rosalind, and Michael Robinson, *Art Deco* (London: Flame Tree, 2013).

Parker, Selwyn, *The Great Crash* (London: Piatkus, 2008).

Parry, Albert, *Garrets and Pretenders: Bohemian Life in America from Poe to Kerouac* (Mineola, NY: Dover, 1960).

Pietras, David, *A Look inside the Five Mafia Families of New York City* [self-published, New York, 2013].

Playne, David, and Gillian Playne, *The Timeline History of New York City* (London: Palgrave Macmillan, 2003).

Raab, Selwyn, *Five Families* (London: Robson, 2006).

Rand, Ayn, *The Fountainhead* (New York: Bobbs-Merrill, 1943).

Roberts, Andrew, *The Storm of War* (London: Allen Lane, 2009).

Robins, W. Anthony, *New York Art Deco: A Guide to Gotham's Jazz Age Architecture* (Albany, NY: State University of New York Press, 2016).

Rock, Howard B., *Haven of Liberty* (New York: New York University Press, 2012).

Rodgers, Cleveland, *Robert Moses: Builder for Democracy* (New York: Henry Holt, 1952).

Roussel, Christine, *The Art of Rockefeller Center* (New York: Norton, 2006).

Rutkoff, Peter M., and William B. Scott, *New School* (New York: Free Press, 1986).

Sanderson, Peter, *The Marvel Comics Guide to New York City* (New York: Simon & Schuster, 2007).

Shaw, Arnold, *52nd Street: The Street of Jazz* (New York: Da Capo, 1971).

Shlaes, Amity, *The Forgotten Man* (London: Jonathan Cape, 2007).

Shulman, Harry Manuel, *Slums of New York* (New York: A. & C. Boni, 1938).

Sifakis, Carl, *The Mafia Encyclopedia* (New York: Checkmark, 1987).

Starrett, Paul, *Changing the Skyline* (New York: Whittlesey House, 1938).

Stern, Robert A. M., *New York 1930* (New York: Rizzoli, 1987).

Stewart, Rex, *Jazz Masters of the Thirties* (New York: Macmillan, 1972).

Stone, William L., *History of New York City* (New York: Virtue & Yorston, 1872).

Sutton, Horace, *Confessions of a Grand Hotel* (New York: Henry Holt, 1951).

Tauranac, John, *The Empire State Building* (Ithaca, NY: Cornell University Press, 2014).

Taylor, William R., *In Pursuit of Gotham* (New York: Oxford University Press, 1992).

Tirro, Frank, *Jazz* (New York: Norton, 1993).

Towles, Amor, *Rules of Civility* (London: Hodder, 2012).

Vail, Ken, *Jazz Milestones* (Chessington: Castle Communications, 1993).

Valentine, David T., *History of the City of New York* (New York: G. P. Putnam, 1853).

Van Leeuwen, Thomas, *The Skyward Trend of Thought* (Cambridge, MA: MIT Press, 1988).

Wasserman, Suzanne, 'The good old days of poverty: the battle over the fate of New York city's Lower East Side during the Depression' [PhD thesis, New York University, 1990].

White, Elwyn Brooks, *Here Is New York* (New York: Little Bookroom, 1999).

Williams, Mason B., *City of Ambition* (New York: Norton, 2013).

Willis, Carol (ed.), *Building the Empire State* (New York: Norton, 1998).

Winn, Christopher, *I Never Knew That about New York* (London: Ebury, 2013).

Wintz, Cary D. (ed.), *Remembering the Harlem Renaissance* (New York: Garland, 1996).

Wolman, Ruth E., *Crossing Over* (New York: Twayne, 1996).

The WPA Guide to New York City (New York: Random House, 1939).

Wyman, David S., *Paper Walls* (Amherst, MA: University of Massachusetts Press, 1968).

Zaczek, Iain, *Art Deco* (Bath: Parragon, 2001).

Zunz, Olivier, and David Ward (eds), *The Landscape of Modernity* (Baltimore, MD: Johns Hopkins University Press, 1992).

INDEX

References to notes are indicated by n.

CHEVROLET
amels
PLANTERS
PEANUTS
CAPITOL
THE PAUSE THAT REFRESHES
Coca-Cola